D1631013

PENGUIN BOOKS

ARABELLA BOXER'S BOOK OF ENGLISH FOOD

'This is a book of an ephemeral milieu of great hosts and hostesses. The elegant and percipient introductory essays and the sample menus alone are worth the price of the book' – Glynn Christian in the *Sunday Telegraph*

'A captivating exploration and celebration of the flowering of English cooking in the 1920s and '30s' – Philippa Davenport in the *Financial Times*

'That rare thing, a cookery book with an argument: *viz*, that English cookery was once both good and independent of the cuisines of her neighbours . . . a rollicking good read' – Paul Levy in the *Observer*

'A book which celebrates a gastronomy which we would be unwise to forget. It's a rediscovery of British food remembered from before the War' – Derek Cooper

'I recommend it, not only for its excellent food but also for the superb introductions and details of social history in the great houses with their shimmering hostesses' – Jennifer Paterson in the *Evening Standard*

ABOUT THE AUTHOR

Arabella Boxer is half Scottish, half American. She was born in 1934 and lived for the first ten years of her life in Scotland, until the family moved to London. She was educated in the UK, Paris and Rome. She is the author of a number of cookery books, including *First Slice Your Cookbook*, *Arabella Boxer's Garden Cookbook*, *Mediterranean Cookbook*, *The Sunday Times Complete Cookbook* and *A Visual Feast* (with Tessa Traeger).

Arabella Boxer was Food Writer for *Vogue* from 1966 to 1968 and from 1975 to 1991, and has also contributed series of food articles to the *Sunday Times Magazine* and the *Telegraph Magazine*. She was awarded the Glenfiddich Cookery Writer of the Year Award in 1975 and 1978 and a Glenfiddich Special Award in 1992. She was also winner of the 1991 André Simon Award and the 1992 Michael Smith Macallan Award for fine writing about British food. A founder member of the Guild of Food Writers, she lives in London. She was married for twenty-four years to Mark Boxer, cartoonist and journalist. She has two children and two grandchildren.

ARABELLA BOXER'S BOOK OF ENGLISH FOOD

A REDISCOVERY OF BRITISH FOOD
FROM BEFORE THE WAR

PENGUIN BOOKS

PENGUIN BOOKS

Published by the Penguin Group
Penguin Books Ltd, 27 Wrights Lane, London W8 5TZ, England
Penguin Books USA Inc., 375 Hudson Street, New York, New York 10014, USA
Penguin Books Australia Ltd, Ringwood, Victoria, Australia
Penguin Books Canada Ltd, 10 Alcorn Avenue, Toronto, Ontario, Canada M4V 3B2
Penguin Books (NZ) Ltd, 182–190 Wairau Road, Auckland 10, New Zealand

Penguin Books Ltd, Registered Offices: Harmondsworth, Middlesex, England

First published by Hodder and Stoughton 1991
Published in Penguin Books 1993
10 9 8 7 6 5 4 3 2 1

Copyright © Arabella Boxer, 1991
Illustrations copyright © Jessica Gwynne, 1991
All rights reserved

The moral right of the author has been asserted

Printed in England by Clays Ltd, St Ives plc

For my mother and sisters,
and in memory of my father

Contents

Acknowledgements

I should like to thank all the authors and publishers who have given me permission to quote from their books, and all the friends and acquaintances who have looked out recipes, lent me books, and generally given support and encouragement. In particular, I am deeply grateful to the following:

The Hon. Charles Allsopp, for the recipe from *Minnie Lady Hindlip's Cookery Book*; Hilary Arnold; Mrs Jonathan Blackburn; Georgina Boosey; Kate Boxer; Susan Campbell; Hugh Cecil; Paul Channon MP; Chatto & Windus, for recipes from *Party Food and Drink* by Rosemary Hume; Mrs Dorothy Child; Glynn Christian; Condé Nast Publications Ltd, for recipes from *Vogue*, and *Vogue's Cookery Book*; Constable Publishers, for recipes from *Eat At Pleasure Drink By Measure* by Olof Wijk; *Country Life*, for recipes from *Lightning Cookery* by Countess Morphy; Lillie Davies; J. M. Dent & Sons Ltd, for recipes from *Come Into the Garden, Cook* by Constance Spry, and *The Constance Spry Cookery Book* by Constance Spry and Rosemary Hume, and *Good Cookery* by W. G. R. Francillon; André Deutsch Ltd for a recipe from *Personal Choice* by Ambrose Heath; Polly Devlin; the Duchess of Devonshire; Katie Forshall; James Fox; Hamish Hamilton Ltd, for recipes from *The Complete Hostess* by Quaglino; Lady Harrod; Harrods Ltd, for recipes from *A Year's Dinners* by May Little; Colin Haycraft, of Duckworth, for recipes from *When The Cook Is Away* by Catherine Ives, and *Be Your Own Chef* by Lucie Marion; Lady Dorothy Heber-Percy; William Heinemann Ltd, for recipes from *What Shall We Have Today?*, and *What Shall We Have To Drink?* by X. Marcel Boulestin, reprinted by permission of the Peter Fraser and Dunlop Group Ltd; Adrian Higham, for recipes from *Vegetable Cultivation and Cookery* by Eleanour Sinclair Rohde; Lady Anne Hill; Houghton Mifflin Company, for recipes from *June Platt's Plain and Fancy Cookbook*; Mrs Nancy Lancaster; Mrs Elizabeth Lewthwaite; Loelia Lady Lindsay of Dowhill, for recipes from *Lady Sysonby's Cook Book*; Jane Longman; David McKenna CBE, for recipes from *Kitchen Essays* by Lady Jekyll; The Macdonald Group, for recipes from *Food In England* by Dorothy Hartley; Lady John Manners; Paul Manousso; Methuen

ACKNOWLEDGEMENTS

& Co., for recipes from *The Perfect Hostess* by Rose Henniker
Heaton; Michael Joseph Ltd, for recipes from *The Alice B. Toklas
Cook Book*, and *Wheeler's Cookery Book* by Macdonald Hastings
and Carole Walsh; Joyce Molyneux; Nigel Nicolson; The None-
such Press, for recipes from *Lovely Food* by Ruth Lowinsky; Tom
Parr; Frances Partridge; Jennifer Paterson, for a recipe from *Feast
Days*; Max Reinhardt; Mrs Maud Shimwell; Mrs Michael Stanley,
for recipes from *English Country House Cooking*; Mrs Oliver Steel;
Lord Stuart of Findhorn; Sir Tatton Sykes; the *Vogue* Library;
Lucy Ward; Francis Wyndham.

Preface

The excellence of British food can be appreciated by studying it in the microcosm that existed between the two world wars. As illustration, I have used the cookery books of the period, those published between 1920 and 1940. It should be remembered, however, that these books were written for the most part by the mistresses of households, who, almost without exception, did not know how to cook, although they were often skilled in training cooks and having good food at their table. None the less, the recipes of those days were sketchy by modern standards. Oven temperatures were seldom mentioned, and quantities were variable, to say the least. By dint of trial and error, I have managed to make most of them work to my satisfaction; the others I have regretfully discarded. I have added my own list of ingredients, for these were seldom listed separately, if at all, and put my own modifications in italics, within square brackets. In a few cases I have had to rewrite the recipe in my own words, for the sake of clarity. I have altered a few minor things, like the amount of sugar, which almost always seems excessive by today's standards. Instead of the flavourings that were then in vogue, but are hard to find today, like Anchovy Essence and Mushroom Ketchup, I have often chosen to substitute Tabasco, or lemon juice, which perform a similar function, and in a cleaner way I prefer. Besides the recipes drawn from books, there are others from my own family records, or given by friends and acquaintances. Some I have devised myself, drawing on contemporary sources.

Many of the old dishes work well today, but used in a different context. The kedgeree that used to be a feature of country house breakfasts now turns up as a main course at luncheon, or a light evening meal. A hot savoury like toasted cheese works well as a TV snack, or supper dish, while the fried goujons of sole that would formerly have been offered as a first course at dinner now constitutes a main dish for either meal. Most of the vegetable dishes in this book make admirable first courses, while the savoury sandwiches listed under picnics make good evening snacks, before or after the cinema, or while watching TV.

The English pattern of eating was by no means as hidebound as people pretend. The customary roast on Sunday, followed by a series of dishes of hashed and reheated meat on successive days, was widespread, but only at a certain level of affluence. Below that level, the weekly budget would not rise to a joint, while above that level, in the large country houses for instance, the remains of the joint would have been sent up to the nursery, or served in the servants' hall. In really big houses like Chatsworth, a whole carcase of beef or lamb would be consumed at one time: the prime joints in the dining-room, and the lesser parts in the nursery, schoolroom, housekeeper's room, or servants' hall.

There has been a lot of talk, usually tinged with nostalgia, about 'nursery food'. In effect, it was probably less good than people like to recall, for bad relations often existed between nursery and kitchen. In her memoirs, *Astride the Wall*, Ursula Wyndham's memories of nursery food add a sour note: 'Greasy mutton, overcooked vegetables wallowing in the water they had been cooked in, burnt rice puddings . . . This prison fare was the unsupervised production of the kitchen maid, whose more import-ant task was to assist the cook in preparing many courses for the dining room twice a day.'

INTRODUCTION

Introduction

In the years between the two world wars English food underwent a brief flowering that seems to have gone almost unremarked at the time, and later passed into oblivion. The pomposity of the Edwardian meals that dominated the early years of the century was a thing of the past; meals became shorter and more informal, and the dishes themselves more light-hearted. Meals were rarely more than three courses, except for a formal dinner, and a more relaxed attitude became the norm.

I find it regrettable that this trend was cut short by the outbreak of the Second World War in 1939. Such things take time to reach all levels of society, and this one had hardly had time to spread beyond the sophisticated world in London and the south before war was declared, and the country was plunged into austerity. Food rationing dragged on for fifteen years, and when Elizabeth David's first book, *A Book of Mediterranean Food*, was published in 1950, it found a public starved of interesting food – for monotony, not hunger, was the curse of our wartime diet – and of foreign travel. The reading public embraced this vision of a Mediterranean world wholeheartedly, and with an enthusiasm that has never abated. Restaurants with names like Le Matelot sprang up, with strings of garlic and fishing nets incorporated in their decor, and our own English food was forgotten. This misplaced passion still continues; today it is north Italian food that dominates the scene, with its robust dishes of sausage and polenta, Parmesan and olive oil. All this is intrinsically good, and enjoyable in the extreme when eaten in Tuscany, or in a good restaurant, but it does seem slightly ridiculous that pesto should have become a national dish.

The English are a strange mixture of complacency and insecurity, for they genuinely don't seem to value their own culinary inheritance. Foreigners know better, and I learnt many years ago that the way to please visiting French, Italians, Americans or Swiss is to present them with a meal composed entirely of classic British delicacies. Some oysters or smoked eel to start with, then some lightly roasted game with all the traditional accompaniments, or a sirloin of Scotch beef, or a saddle of Welsh mountain lamb. A salad of mixed green leaves to follow, and don't be misled into thinking that mâche, rugola and pourpier have always been foreign imports, for all three were commonly grown in England in medieval times under their English names: lamb's lettuce (or corn salad), rocket and purslane. With the salad, two or three unusual English cheeses: a Single Gloucester, a Cornish Yarg, and a Little Devon made with ewes' milk; with them, some Miller's Damsel wheaten wafers made on the Isle of Wight, unsalted English farm butter, and hearts of celery. Then, in summer, a fruit fool made with raspberries or blackcurrants, served partly frozen, with a thinly iced lemon cake. In winter, a marmalade tart, served warm, with Devonshire cream.

Few people today seem aware that a discreet revolution in food took place in the 1920s and 30s. As Constance Spry wrote in 1942, looking back: 'The decade before the war seems to have had uncomplicated elegance as its keynote. The criterion of good food was subtlety of flavour and contrast, combined with that perfection of simplicity which is the hardest thing to achieve. That intelligent aim in food towards fewer courses and more discernment in their choice was in no sense dictated by austerity. On the contrary, it indicated a high level of epicurean taste.'

By the 1950s, this clearness of vision had been lost by all but very few. As Ruth Lowinsky, herself the author of three excellent pre-war cookery books, wrote: 'A palate is dwindling into a thing of the past.' And this is why, presumably, having lost touch with their own traditions as the English are wont to do, they went overboard for Mediterranean food.

English food of the 1920s and 30s is curiously hard to define, partly because it is understated. It lies at the other end of the spectrum from robust peasant cuisines for it is basically bland in flavour, although the accompanying sauces and garnishes are often sharp, sour, or spicy. Since a contrast in flavour was often the aim, the individual foods were almost always cooked and served separately, so that they met for the first time on the plate. This is in direct opposition to the French traditions, whereby different foods are encouraged to merge in the cooking process, and where sauces are an intrinsic part of the dish. The English food of the period demanded skill in execution, and elegance in presentation. It was above all careful cooking, requiring first-rate ingredients, precise timing, and stylish presentation. When practised without due care, it could be the worst food in the world, as many will remember to their cost.

Even when it was well done, the food of the time had its weaknesses, judged by today's standards. For their criteria were different from ours; there was not the same wish for variety, for a start. Every middle-class family had a cook, albeit a modest one, whereas people living at a comparable level today do the cooking themselves. Most families had the same dish for lunch every Sunday, either a roast chicken, or joint of beef or mutton, and the same series of dishes to follow. Even the very best cooks had a more limited range than good cooks do today. The professional cook who went out to cater for dinner parties, arriving with her sauces already made lest a prying kitchen maid should learn her secrets, did not offer a very wide range, whereas most cooks in private service prided themselves on their specialities, which favoured guests of the household seemed happy to eat time after time. Mrs Woodman, the redoubtable cook to the Mildmays for fifty years, had an asparagus ice for which she was famous. When the Queen Mother, then the Queen, was staying at Flete she asked for the recipe, but Mrs Woodman stoutly refused to part with it. 'Yer husband asked me for that,' she said, 'but I wouldn't give it to him.'

There were two significant outside influences on our food during this period; both affected a small section of society, yet had lasting effects. The first came from the United States, for a number of American women had married Englishmen and come to live over here. Some, like Nancy Astor and Emerald Cunard, had married before the First World War; others, like Lady Astor's niece Nancy Tree, now Lancaster, married during the inter-war years. Many of these young women were talented exponents of the minor arts: interior decoration, entertaining and dressing. Almost without exception, they seemed to have a social ease and a lack of shyness that many Englishmen found irresistible. Their high spirits, wit and sense of fun put many of their English contemporaries in the shade. A prime example was Wallis Simpson, a clever and manipulative woman who knew just how to amuse the Prince of Wales and his friends by providing the sort of relaxed and frivolous ambiance he craved, in striking contrast to the stuffy family circle at Sandringham and Windsor. Wallis Simpson was a perfectionist who prided herself on always being immaculately turned out, and having exquisite food.

Although the dishes Mrs Simpson served at her table were hardly typical, being a highly sophisticated version, American food was not widely divergent from our own, in that both shared common roots. Many of the early settlers who went out to America in the 1620s and subsequent years must have taken their receipts with them, and in some ways their food had stayed closer to its past than our own. Dishes like pumpkin pie and cheesecake are clear descendants from Stuart times, while some American recipes for mincemeat still include minced beefsteak, as ours once did. Words like broil, skillet, grind and scallion have stayed the same, while the US pint still holds 16 fluid ounces, as ours did until 1878.

The second influence came from France, in the endearing personality of Marcel Boulestin. Boulestin arrived in London as a penniless young man in 1906, having escaped from the clutches of Willy, Colette's first husband, for whom he had worked as a general dogsbody. In London he worked first as a journalist, then as a decorator. When war broke out in 1914, he enlisted in the French army, where he made friends with the painter and illustrator Jean-Emile Laboureur. Once the war was over, Boulestin returned to London where he tried to re-establish himself as a decorator, but without success. Several of his former clients, like Syrie Maugham, had become professional decorators themselves; others were beginning to feel the effects of the coming recession.

In 1923, Boulestin published his first cookery book, with illustrations by Laboureur. This small book, *Simple French Cooking for English Homes*, was an instant success, and was to be the first of many. The same year, Boulestin wrote cookery articles for the *Manchester Guardian*, the *Daily Express*, the *Morning Post*, the *Spectator* and *Vogue*. (He wrote regularly for *Vogue* until the end of 1928.) In 1925 he opened his first restaurant on the corner of Panton Street and Leicester Square; a few years later it moved to Southampton Street, where it has stayed ever since. Also in 1925, he started a cookery school where society ladies went, taking their cooks with them; in 1937 he became the first ever person to demonstrate cookery on television.

In 1933, André Simon and A. J. A. Symons founded the Wine & Food Society. André Simon, its President, a Frenchman married to an Englishwoman, was chief agent for Pommery Champagne in England. An anglophile, he delighted in helping to spread the appreciation of food and wine. The Society published a quarterly journal and its influence was considerable.

At a certain level, there had always been a French influence on food and drink in this country. Some of the best cooks, like the Duke of Devonshire's, had trained under French chefs. (Mrs Tanner, cook at Chatsworth in the 1920s and 30s, had been sent by her former employer, Lord Savile, to learn under Escoffier while he was chef at the Hotel Cecil in London and in the South of

France. She in turn trained her daughter Maud, who succeeded her as cook to the Devonshires.) It was the practice to have menu cards on the table in the evening, for weekend parties in the big country houses, and dinner parties in London, and these were always written in French. French wine, especially claret, was the most highly prized, while French brandy, Cognac, Armagnac, and other digestifs, also sweet liqueurs like crème de menthe, were extremely popular. Yet Marcel Boulestin was the first person to introduce the English to the cuisine bourgeoise. He was the ideal exponent of French family cooking, being at the same time sophisticated and down to earth. The dishes he taught his pupils and wrote about were far removed from those of the haute cuisine as served in his restaurant. They were simple, homely dishes, well within the capabilities of a modest cook. Thanks to him, unpretentious dishes like canard aux navets and veau braisé aux carottes began to find their way into the homes of the English middle class.

In 1934, Boulestin's place as food writer for *Vogue* was taken by June Platt, a cosmopolitan American who had lived for some years in France. Her food was an appealing blend of French and American which fitted in well with the mood of the time. This new style of food caught on with the fashionable set, a narrow circle of people who could afford to travel, and who were as much at home in New York or Paris, as in London. They lived for the most part in London, in houses or flats, or in medium-sized country houses, or divided their time between the two. These were not the aristocracy, whose life style seemed to remain in a semi-permanent status quo, about twenty-five years behind the times, where only the smallest changes were allowed to ruffle the surface. (At Flete, the Mildmays' house near Plymouth, years after electricity had been installed, the footmen still continued to carry the lamps in each evening, and remove them next morning, just as they had done with oil lamps which needed to be cleaned and refilled.)

Many of the great landowners, rich as they were, had been forced to retrench after the close of the First World War, as a result of increased taxation and the growing agricultural depression which preceded the recession. Almost without exception, they chose to do this by selling off their London properties, rather than diminish the size, or the style, of their country estates, or impoverish their collections of furniture and paintings. Most of the great private houses in London were sold to property developers and demolished between the wars, while others were destroyed by bombs during the blitz. Devonshire House was sold for one million pounds in 1919, and pulled down in 1924. This great house was built by William Kent in the eighteenth century; it stood in Piccadilly, opposite the Ritz, taking up a whole block, with a vast garden stretching away behind it. Hotels like Grosvenor House and the Dorchester, and blocks of flats like Brook House – in its turn destroyed by bombs – were erected on the sites of the great family houses, often bearing the same name. By the start of the Second World War only a few remained, like Apsley House, Spencer House and Londonderry House.

In the vast country houses like Blenheim, Chatsworth and Eaton Hall, there had been little change since Edwardian times. Like cumbersome ocean liners which continue to move days after their engines have been switched off, these huge establishments ploughed on majestically. As Lord Lambton remarked, recalling his youth at Lambton Castle and Fenton: 'The meals consisted of five courses, where they used to be six or seven.'

Few people thought of modernising their kitchens until after the Second World War. It took the butler at Chatsworth six minutes to walk from the kitchen to the dining-room. Most of the cooking was still done on Aga-style solid-fuel ranges; a thermostatically controlled gas oven was introduced in 1923, but there was no gas supply in the country. Electric thermostatically controlled ovens appeared on the market in 1933; Mrs Tanner, the cook at Chatsworth, persuaded the Duke of Devonshire to install one near the dining-room, so that she could serve soufflés. But her plan failed, for it took the butler too long to walk around the huge table, and the soufflé collapsed before it could be served. It was not here, in the houses of the mega-rich, that the move towards a new simplicity began, but in the more modest homes of a younger, more fashionable set.

The food in our own home was a good example of Scottish country house food. We lived in a fairly remote part of north-east Scotland, with little social life apart from shooting parties. My father was a purist about food, and liked only the very plainest things. He had a horror of cream and rich sauces, which literally made him ill. My mother is American, but unlike many of her compatriots who came to live in Britain in the 1920s, she had little interest in food at that time, although she learnt to cook after the Second World War, and thoroughly enjoyed it. We lived for the most part on prime ingredients, very simply cooked. We had our own farm, large kitchen garden with greenhouses, salmon river and grouse moor, so that we were almost self-supporting. Each

Sunday we had roast beef: a sirloin with the fillet – then called the undercut – still attached. My father was an expert carver, and gave each person a thickish slice of the undercut, with one or two thinner slices of the sirloin. For the next two or three days we ate cold roast beef, rather rare; this was our favourite food. I don't remember ever having it hashed up or reheated in any form. Salmon was always poached; when hot, it came with a sauce made from its cooking liquor, reduced. We ate a lot of salads, for my father loved cold food. He insisted on making the salad dressing himself; bottles of olive oil and vinegar, salt, pepper, sugar and Worcestershire Sauce were laid out on a side-table. My father was terribly fussy about his food; the only comments I remember hearing were criticisms.

Each winter, before the war, my parents would spend two months travelling to warm places like Mexico or South Africa, or sailing with friends. My father had had tuberculosis as a young man, and had been advised to winter abroad. Then my sisters and I would have food that seemed even duller than when our parents were at home. For good as our food was, in its way, it was not the sort to appeal to a child. It never occurred to me then that food could be fun, or in any way enjoyable.

In the 1930s my parents had a small house in St James's Place, and each summer my mother would travel south to enjoy herself. My father would join her for a little while, then he would go back to Scotland with a sigh of relief. For although he loved travelling, he disliked London and social life equally. In the early thirties, before I was born, my sisters would also go to London, but they had to stay with Nanny in the Stafford Hotel next door, for the house was too small to hold them all. In London the two little girls found themselves thrown into another world without warning, with terrifying ordeals like Lady Astor's fancy-dress parties, and dancing classes with the little princesses. Our Scottish nanny took it all in her stride, and remained unimpressed. When one of the smart nannies at the dancing class enquired whether we were going away for our summer holidays, Nanny replied dourly: 'We're away the noo.' My eldest sister was less phlegmatic. When faced with a crowded London street for the first time, she burst into tears, wailing: 'All these people, and nobody knows us.'

This privileged way of life changed abruptly – and for good, in our case – with the outbreak of war in 1939. Our house in Scotland was turned into a hospital for wounded soldiers and the family moved into one end of it. Our cook, Mrs Jones, found herself cooking for about a hundred people, including patients and nursing staff. It is to her credit, and to the nature of our somewhat austere diet, that our food changed hardly at all, and my father was delighted to feel justified in banning cream outright from our table. (Mrs Jones was later awarded the OBE.)

After only eighteen years, the country found itself once again in the grip of food rationing. But this time the Government was prepared, and ration books were already printed, awaiting distribution. Much had been learnt during the First World War, when food rationing had only been imposed halfway through, in 1916. By 1920 it was already coming to an end, unlike the aftermath of the Second World War when rationing dragged on for almost ten years. The study of our national diet brought about by the First World War was to prove of immense value, not only in combating the war to come, but also in the depression in the early thirties. By 1931 the nation's health was causing grave concern, especially in poor mining districts like Yorkshire and Lancashire. The Ministry of Health set up an Advisory Committee on Nutrition, which issued a series of pronouncements, urging the British to eat more fruit and raw vegetables, cheese and milk, and oily fish. As usual, their advice was largely ignored for, as George Orwell points out in *The Road to Wigan Pier*, it is only the rich who want to eat healthy food and breakfast on orange juice and Ryvita. The poor, living on the breadline in a permanent state of lassitude and depression, needed the quick lift they got from food like sliced white bread and jam, sweet tea, and fish and chips.

The Second World War saw a great improvement in the nation's health. Rations were issued to rich and poor alike, and a loaf of eight-five per cent extraction was made compulsory. Although greyish in colour and unappealing, this was far more nourishing than the seventy-two per cent extraction 'white' loaf, so much loved by the undernourished. To quote Orwell again: 'English working people everywhere refuse brown bread; it is virtually impossible to buy wholemeal bread in a working class district.' (This was written in 1931; once war had broken out, they had no choice.)

For the well-off, and especially for the young, the end of the First World War was followed by a period of euphoria. Everyone wanted to enjoy themselves and to live, at least for a time, purely hedonistic lives. As Loelia Lindsay recalls in her memoirs: 'Wounded soldiers in their blue suits and red ties disappeared from the square gardens and hospital wards became ballrooms again.

London was dancing mad – the aftermath of the short-leave-from-France frenzy. It seemed we couldn't have enough of it.'

The same mood, influenced by the United States, brought in its wake such things as gramophones, dinner jackets, cocktails, cigarettes, sports cars, nightclubs, and jazz. Cocktail parties became fashionable, and buffet dinners replaced the formal dinners of the past. Meals were held later than ever before, reaching extremes in certain households. Staying at Fort Belvedere, country home of the Prince of Wales, in 1930, Diana Cooper wrote to Conrad Russell: 'Everything is a few hours later than other places. (Perhaps it's American time.) A splendid tea arrived at 6.30. Dinner was at 10. Emerald (Cunard) arrived at 8.30 for cocktails.'

Fort Belvedere was an exaggerated case, but even in traditional country houses the meals were served later than in other places, and this still goes on today. Breakfast at nine, or nine thirty on Sundays, lunch at one thirty, tea at five, and dinner at eight thirty was, and still is, considered normal.

There was a general resolve among the younger generation never to return to the stuffy formality of pre-war days, or seven-course meals, and batteries of servants. This coincided with a growing reluctance on the part of the working classes to spend their lives in domestic service, as many had been happy to do before the First World War. Most of the men who had served in the armed forces showed little inclination to go back into service; having tasted independence, they preferred to find jobs in factories. It became progressively harder to find male living-in staff for the big houses, and the balance of indoor servants became predominantly female. For young women, domestic service for a good employer still offered a fairly enjoyable life, with chances of improvement, and the possibility of finding a husband among the male employees. Lady Anne Hill remembers the servants in her parents' house in Suffolk in the 1920s: 'They were tremendously overworked and underpaid, but they had great fun. I knew the maids frightfully well – I used to play whist with them. I remember roars of laughter.'

The number of living-in servants seems unbelievable today. In a sense, it became a vicious circle, for the more numerous they were, the more junior servants were needed to wait on them. At Chatsworth in 1930 there were thirty-nine living-in servants, with about twenty more coming in each day. At times like Christmas when all the family came to stay they must have been kept busy, for this meant six rival nurseries installed, with six resident nannies and nursery maids, for the old Duke had twenty grandchildren at that time. While the nursery maids were responsible for making breakfast and tea, both the main meals had to be carried up to the various nurseries by the footmen.

Chatsworth was exceptional, even among country houses, but in more modest establishments the number of staff was still considerable. In 1928, Sir Roderick Jones and his wife, the writer Enid Bagnold, were living in London and Rottingdean. The Joneses were not especially rich, although Sir Roderick must have been earning a good salary as head of Reuters, yet they employed thirteen indoor servants and five outdoor ones, including a chauffeur, two grooms and two gardeners. All were ruled by Cutmore, the butler/valet, who supervised the weekly move from London to Sussex. The cook and most of the servants were sent ahead by train, with a taxi to meet them, while the Joneses and their children, Cutmore and the silver canteen, were conveyed in two cars. Milk and papers were stopped in one house and started in the other. For longer periods, caretakers were installed in the empty house.

All things considered, life below stairs must have been more fun in the really big houses. Flete had about fifty bedrooms, and a living-in staff of eighteen. A Devon lady who had been second kitchen maid there from 1936–8 spoke to me nostalgically of the life, which involved travelling round the three great Mildmay houses at different times of year, leaving a skeleton staff behind in each one. The maids had alternate evenings off, unless there were people staying, and alternate Sundays, with two weeks' holiday a year. This gave them lots of time to visit their families, and a bus was sometimes laid on to take them to the local hops. She left regretfully after two years, 'to better herself'. She had to do this, she explained, as there was no future for advancement if you stayed in the same house all the time, especially one like Flete, where the housekeeper, cook, butler and valet all stayed for fifty years.

In less old-fashioned houses, the decreasing number of servants was offset by the advances in domestic technology. Central heating began to replace the endless series of coal fires, while refrigerators simplified the preparation and storage of food. Gas and electric cookers gradually ousted the old black ranges, which had to be cleaned every day. By 1939 there were nine million gas cookers throughout the UK, and one and a half million electric cookers. Both, by this time, boasted thermostatically controlled ovens.

Entertaining in the country houses did not change much, except that visits became shorter. Apart from Christmas and the summer holidays, guests came for weekends which were called 'Saturday to Monday', and for shooting parties. These usually lasted for three days in the middle of the week, which meant that no serious 'shot' could hold down a job and still be free to accept invitations to shoot.

One of the hardest things for us to envisage nowadays is the sheer scale. At their first dinner party after their marriage in 1930, the Duke and Duchess of Westminster entertained seventy-two guests to dinner. They were all seated at one table, covered with a single damask cloth. This was at Eaton Hall, in Cheshire, where they could put up forty weekend guests. In London, at her house in Charles Street, Mrs Ronnie Greville had fifty-six guests to dinner in November 1928. They had an eight-course dinner, and Ambrose's band played throughout. In the same year, in the process of enlarging and redecorating their house at Rottingdean, Sir Roderick and Lady Jones commissioned Alan Walton, the fashionable decorator of the day, to marble two dining-tables for them, to seat twenty-eight guests. Lady Astor was another hostess who liked to entertain on a massive scale, although not always successfully, according to Harold Nicolson's diaries. In 1930, he wrote: 'Down to Cliveden. A dark autumnal day. Thirty-two people in the house. Cold and draughty. Little groups of people wishing they were alone: a lack of organisation: a desultory drivel. The party is in itself good enough. (Duff and Diana Cooper, Tom and Cimmie Mosley, Harold and Dorothy Macmillan, Bob Boothby, etc.) But it does not hang together. After dinner, in order to enliven the party, Lady Astor dons a Victorian hat and a pair of false teeth. It does not enliven the party.'

Behaviour was different in those days, when to be entertaining was considered a social duty. As Cynthia Asquith remarked, in her memoirs: 'We were brought up to believe that silence was never golden.' In his book of Anne Fleming's letters, Mark Amory described social life at Stanway in the 1920s: 'The atmosphere to be created was gaiety this side of boisterousness, of wit but not self-conscious exhibitionism. Serious topics were treated lightly, light matters given serious consideration, solemnity banned. Politicians might be present but they would not discourse on politics. Conversation should be general but sparkling.' At the table, guests would start to eat as soon as they had been served; only the governess waited until everyone had helped themselves. Women rarely drank spirits, or even much wine; barley water was always much in evidence. In many houses, as at Flete and Eaton Hall, drinks were never served before dinner, while at Cliveden, alcohol at any time was banned outright.

The standard of cooking varied from house to house, just as it always has. In many, the food must have been tedious in the extreme, with menus that rarely changed except in detail, based on a series of culinary clichés. In others, it was exceptional, as described by one writer in 1929: 'Clean, tasty English cooking – the fruits of a thousand years of civilisation.'

Food writing was in its infancy during the inter-war years, but the ratio of interest per volume was probably higher than it has ever been since. Some of the best cookery books of the day, interesting for the light they throw on social life as well as food, were written by society ladies, like Dorothy Allhusen, Minnie Lady Hindlip, Lady Sysonby and Nancy Shaw. Some of these books, like Lady Jekyll's *Kitchen Essays* and Alice Martineau's *Caviare to Candy*, were based on articles previously published in *The Times* and the *Yorkshire Post*. Others, like *Lady Sysonby's Cook Book*, were published for fun, for charity, or to make pin money. Few of the recipes work exactly, for it must be remembered that none of the authors actually knew how to cook. Yet they were clever women, adept at training inexperienced cooks, and having good food at their tables. The art of writing recipes had not yet been developed, however, and their instructions are often sketchy in the extreme.

There were other, more specialised writers: herbalists like Mrs Leyel, who wrote *The Gentle Art of Cookery* with Miss Olga Hartley in 1925, then went on to found The Society of Herbalists, known today as The Herb Society, and the Culpeper shops. After the Second World War she wrote the *Culpeper Herbals*, a series of six remarkable books which contain a wealth of fascinating information on a wide range of obscure plants, and which include some recipes. Another herbalist/author was Eleanour Sinclair Rohde, who wrote a number of books about herbs, herb gardens and vegetables in the 1930s. While lady gardeners were not exactly a novelty, their role was changing, in that a few exceptional women like Gertrude Jekyll, horticultural adviser to Sir Edwin Lutyens, and sister-in-law of Lady Jekyll, now chose to do some of the actual work in the garden themselves, albeit aided by eleven gardeners in Miss Jekyll's case, whereas formerly they would merely have expressed their wishes to the gardener. Miss Jekyll was a most interesting character, an artist craftsman, whose painting and metalwork gave way to horticulture as her eyesight deteriorated. Amateur gardeners of both sexes still concentrated for the most part on flowers, shrubs and trees, leaving the kitchen garden in the capable hands of the head gardener. The first serious attempt to combine gardening and cooking did not come until just outside the period of this book, when Constance Spry published her first book, *Come Into the Garden, Cook* in 1942.

Another unusual author was Florence White, who came from a family of Sussex inn-keepers, and who founded the English Folk Cookery Association in 1928. Miss White was no insular xenophobe, having travelled widely in France and the USA, but she devoted most of her life to collecting and preserving old English country recipes, which she published in 1932 as *Good Things in England*.

Books like these, devoted to British food, ceased for the most part on the outbreak of war in 1939. (The great exception was Dorothy Hartley's classic, *Food in England*, which was not published till 1954.) Most of the books published during the war years focused on rationing, while those that came after were almost all aimed at the post-war passion for foreign food.

Since the war, food writers have largely chosen to ignore English food of the 1920s and 30s. Our two greatest food writers, Elizabeth David and Jane Grigson, shared a preference for French food and made no bones about it. Both wrote one or two books about English food in the end, but it came low on their list of priorities. Jane Grigson admitted this, in *The Observer Guide to British Cookery*: 'It was Guy Mouilleron, when he was at the Café Royal, who told me not to be quite so ashamed of our cooking, that there were some good ideas and good recipes that he had taken up and adapted with great success. More recently, Anton Mosimann ticked me off for my poor opinion of bread and butter pudding, and converted me.' Once again we find the foreigner displaying a surer appreciation of our food than we do ourselves.

Few of my contemporaries seem to be aware of the good food that existed, at least in certain circles, before the war. When asked the subject of this book, I was met with general incredulity. 'Good food before the war – was there any?' was a typical response. 'Rather a non-starter, surely?' was another. 'Bangers and mash? Toad-in-the-hole?' enquired a third, while another, getting his timespan confused, ventured: 'Woolton Pie?'

Yet every now and then a random hint surfaces, suggesting that here and there, in unexpected corners, this sort of cooking still goes on, hidden from public scrutiny, just as it always has been. Reading (in *Tatler*) recently an account of staying with the Duke of Beaufort at Badminton, I was struck by a reference to the food: 'Three large cooks toil permanently in the kitchen, with a brief to produce top quality English dishes. You do not find elaborate cuisine at Badminton, which the Beauforts regard as "restaurant food" which you would have "during the week in London". In the country they eat fish pie with white sauce, hard-boiled eggs in cheese sauce, rather a lot of lamb and pheasant, and chops in aspic with minted peas arranged concentrically around the plate.'

The Hostesses

‖‖

Although there had been notable hostesses in earlier times, they had mostly operated within specific fields, like Trollope's Lady Glencora and her political soirées in the Palliser novels. In the twenties a new sort of entertaining became fashionable; one might call it entertaining for entertaining's sake. No longer did its proponents seek power, either for themselves or their protégés. Entertaining had become an end in itself.

Few of the hostesses were beauties, or even specially good-looking. Beauties had other things to do. The talents that made a good hostess were the very ones that a clever woman could cultivate, as a compensation for lack of beauty. What was needed was wit, originality, a light touch, boundless energy and a lot of money. A streak of frivolity and driving ambition also helped. Armed with most of these, a worldly and intelligent woman could create an amusing life for herself and her friends, while the beauties sat back and led a passive existence, receiving compliments, invitations and proposals of marriage from all sides.

In London, Paris and New York, standards of entertaining grew higher and higher. People in society were restless, spoilt, easily bored. The leading hostesses of the day were smart in the American sense, adept at creating an elegant and stylish ambiance, with interesting men and amusing, pretty women, sparkling conversation and delicious food.

The two most successful hostesses between the wars were

indubitably Lady Cunard and Lady Colefax. Neither wrote a cookery book, but both were reputed to have excellent food. Yet food was only one of the important assets a hostess needed to have up her sleeve; the talent to amuse, or to entertain, certainly ranked higher, and this both ladies possessed in abundance. Both were intelligent and cultivated women, although both were sometimes portrayed as silly geese by their acquaintances, for both had their own camps, with their champions as well as their detractors. Lady Cunard's field of activities was primarily musical, for the love of her life was the conductor Sir Thomas Beecham. Lady Colefax had a passion for royalty, and high society, but she also loved and prized intellectuals, and numbered Virginia Woolf among her friends. (Which did not stop Virginia Woolf being extremely malicious about her on occasion.)

Lady Cunard was American, born Maud Burke. In 1895 she married Sir Bache Cunard, of the shipping fortune, and came to live in England. Sir Bache was twenty years older than Lady Cunard, and by 1911 she had fallen in love with Thomas Beecham, and left Sir Bache. She installed herself and her daughter Nancy, later to become a symbol of the twenties, in a large house in Grosvenor Square, and concentrated her energies on entertaining, for which she had a genius. Like most of the great hostesses, Lady Cunard had little time for domestic – or family – life. In later years, when Nancy was looking for a house, her mother remarked: 'Only the banal need a home.' Relations between mother and daughter grew steadily worse. Nancy felt she had been neglected by her mother as a child, and never forgave her. Once as an adult, Nancy startled other guests during after-dinner games in a country house when she met the query, 'Who would you most like to see come into the room?' with the chilling reply: 'Lady Cunard, dead.'

Yet Emerald Cunard (she changed her name from Maud in 1926, at the age of fifty-four), was dearly loved by friends of all ages. Loelia Lindsay, writing in her memoirs *Grace and Favour*, writes: 'Beloved Emerald Cunard. From my gawky schoolgirl days onwards she was always kind and fun-providing, and of all the people I have known well, I am most grateful for having had Emerald as a friend.'

Osbert Sitwell paid tribute to her qualities as a hostess: 'Her airy and rather impersonal alertness, her wit, made her drawing room unlike any other. Lady Cunard loves to be amused, but she tires so quickly of dullness that she has her own method of dealing with it. She can goad the conversation like a bull, and she a matador, and compel it to show a fiery temper.' Sitwell also praises her dedication: 'It was largely her support, and the way she marshalled her forces, that enabled the wonderful seasons of opera and ballet to materialise. Her will power was sufficient, her passion for music fervent enough, to make opera almost compulsory for those who wished to be fashionable.'

As we have already noted, the great hostesses were rarely, if ever, beauties, and Lady Cunard was no exception. Loelia Lindsay describes her appearance: 'She has yellow, fluffy hair, a sharp little beaked nose, eyes swimming in mascara, and she has been unkindly described as "a canary of prey".' Siegfried Sassoon, never the most charitable of men, refers to 'that bobbed and bedizened blonde with startled and unspeculative eyes in a clown-painted face'.

During the latter part of her life, Lady Cunard showed great courage in facing adversity from two directions. Persecuted by her daughter Nancy's vindictive campaign in print, and deserted by Sir Thomas Beecham for a younger woman, she sailed back from New York in the middle of the war to find her house in Grosvenor Square had been destroyed by bombs. She sold off her possessions, moved into the Dorchester, and proceeded to entertain with all her old verve until her death in 1948.

Lady Colefax was inevitably in competition with Lady Cunard. They each had their own circles, which overlapped here and there, and their own admirers, but were rarely to be found in each other's houses. One of Lady Colefax's camp was Harold Nicolson, who commented in his diary: 'I think Sibyl Colefax is a clever old bean who ought to concentrate on intellectuals and not social guests.' Like Lady Cunard, Lady Colefax was married to a much older man, the barrister Sir Arthur Colefax. They lived in Argyll House in the King's Road (opposite the Fire Station today), which is a hostess's dream, with its romantic façade, wrought-iron gates, stone-flagged courtyard and lovely garden. But Lady Colefax was another redoubtable character who showed courage in adversity, for in 1930 they lost all their capital in the New York stock market crash. The same year Sir Arthur became deaf, and was forced to retire. Undaunted by this dramatic change in their fortunes, Sibyl Colefax set herself up as an interior decorator, doing much of the work herself. She made £2,000 in her first year, which was no mean sum for those days, while continuing to entertain in Argyll House. In 1934 she started her own firm, Sibyl Colefax, with premises in Bruton Street, and in 1938 she took on John Fowler, a Chelsea neighbour, as her partner. (In 1950, Sibyl Colefax was bought out by Nancy Lancaster, who, as Mrs Ronald Tree, and a niece of Lady Astor's, had been one of the most admired young American hostesses living in England between the wars. Colefax & Fowler continues today as one of the foremost London decorators.)

Sibyl Colefax continued to live, and entertain, at Argyll House until her husband's death in 1936, when she gave a series of 'last dinners' before quitting the house. Desmond MacCarthy describes one of these in his diaries: 'Sibyl had excelled even her own standards of lion hunting by assembling for dinner Harold Nicolson, Winston and Clementine Churchill, Duff and Diana Cooper, Somerset Maugham, Artur Rubinstein, and many others' (including Sir Philip Sasson and the Mountbattens).

In the immediate circle of the Prince of Wales and Mrs Simpson, Lady Cunard and Lady Colefax found themselves in direct rivalry, both deeply disapproved of by the rest of the royal family, who considered them a bad influence. Both were guests at a dinner party given by Mrs Simpson for the King in 1936. Luckily for us, that inveterate diner-out Harold Nicolson was there to record the scene: 'It is evident that Lady Cunard is incensed by the presence of Lady Colefax, and that Lady Colefax is furious that Lady Cunard should have been asked. Lady Oxford appears astonished to find either of them at what was to have been a quite intimate party.'

Another successful hostess-turned-decorator was Syrie Maugham, who lived next door to her rival Sibyl Colefax in the King's Road, and immediately opposite the other fashionable decorator John Fowler. The daughter of Dr Barnardo, Syrie had been married briefly – and unhappily – to Somerset Maugham. After the breakdown of her marriage she started working as a professional decorator. Of all the decorators of her day, she was one of the most brilliant, and the most innovative. As Ursula Wyndham recalls in her memoirs, *Astride the Wall*: 'Syrie Maugham was the first society decorator who started the fashion for the all-white drawing room, celadon green having been the previous "safe" colour, not likely to be mocked by sardonic friends.' In *Grace and Favour*, Loelia Lindsay describes all her contemporaries dragging old bits of furniture out of their attics and 'pickling' them, or painting them white, thereby making them look 'ultra smart'.

Syrie Maugham was also a gifted hostess, as was the American-born decorator Elsie de Wolfe. Unlike the others, Elsie de Wolfe was a successful decorator first, before going on to become a social figure. Like Ladies Colefax and Cunard, she married a rich English husband much older than herself: Sir Charles Mendl, the Paris representative of the News Department of the Foreign Office. The Mendls had two homes in France: an apartment in the Rue de Rivoli, and the exquisite Villa Trianon at Versailles. They entertained ceaselessly, both in France and in London during the season. Lady Mendl published a small cookery book under her maiden name, *Elsie de Wolfe's Recipes for Successful Dining*, filled with good recipes and outrageous comments: 'At Christmas time 1931, I had a table of gold (lamé), hoping that it might in some way draw us all back to the old gold standard . . .' Yet the recipes themselves are excellent, and grounded in common sense.

There were older hostesses like Mrs Ronnie Greville, survivors from the Edwardian era. Immensely rich in her own right, Mrs Greville was the daughter of an Edinburgh MP and Privy Councillor. She married Ronnie Greville, a well-connected but impecunious young man, and became one of the great hostesses prior to the First World War. She operated on two fronts: at 16 Charles Street, now the Guards' Club, and at Polesden Lacey, a large house with extensive gardens near Guildford, where King George VI and Queen Elizabeth spent part of their honeymoon. Mrs Greville was a clever woman, but without beauty, taste or charm. She knew how to surround herself with expert advisers, and in this way acquired a remarkable collection of objets d'art, notably English silver and Chinese porcelain.

Even today Polesden Lacey has an enchanting atmosphere, and it requires little effort of the imagination to picture oneself a guest in this delightful house, surrounded by beautiful objects and fashionable people. Mrs Greville's food was famous, simple but exquisite, and very formally served. The guest lists for her parties seem less inspired than her menus; one is left with an impression of minor royalties, foreign titles and politicians. Mrs Greville herself was reputed to be witty and good company.

Lady Astor was primarily a political hostess who entertained on a large scale at Cliveden and in London. Her parties were often amusing, although daunting. The great drawback for many was the ban on alcohol in any form, for Lady Astor was a rabid teetotaller. Another political hostess was Margot Asquith, later to become Lady Oxford. Born Margot Tennant, she was the second wife of Herbert Asquith, the Liberal Prime Minister who was later made Lord Oxford. Each weekend, according to *Edith Olivier's Journals*, Margot Asquith 'collected together fourteen people who had little in common, and who she hardly knew herself'.

Then there was the racing world: rich philistines for the most part, who were prepared to spend vast sums of money on their parties. Desmond MacCarthy describes one such event at the house of Mrs Rupert Beckett, in 1931: 'I enjoyed the glitter and splendour. It was a new "set" for me, rich, smart, racing people and I was amused. The enormously rich Lady Granard was there in ropes of pearls and her mild, exquisitely clean husband with a pearl the size of an electric button in his shirt.'

Also successful hostesses, but operating on a more modest scale, were some of the authors of contemporary cookery books. One of the most accomplished was Lady Jekyll, whose *Kitchen Essays* first appeared in *The Times* on Saturdays in 1921 and 1922. Agnes Jekyll was a remarkable woman; the youngest daughter of William Graham, a friend and patron of the pre-Raphaelites, she had been brought up in an intellectual and artistic environment, and became a notable hostess among the intelligentsia. She was at the same time an excellent organiser, and played an active part in many facets of public life. A pillar of the St John Ambulance Brigade, she was also a JP, a governor of Godalming Secondary School, of a hospital in the East End of London, and a borstal for girls.

Lady Jekyll's husband, Sir Herbert, was a sapper officer turned civil servant who had been, among other things, British Commissioner for the 1900 Paris Exhibition. He was also an amateur musician, a founder member of the Bach Choir, and a skilled wood-carver. The Jekylls lived at Munstead House in Surrey, next door to Sir Herbert's sister Gertrude, to whom he was devoted. This was the famed Miss Jekyll, the greatest horticulturist of her time, who worked closely for many years in partnership with Sir Edwin Lutyens.

Lutyens was also friendly with Sir Herbert and Lady Jekyll, and there is a good description of Munstead House in the biography of Lutyens by his daughter Mary: 'It was the apogee of opulent comfort and order without grandeur, smelling of pot-pourri, furniture polish and wood smoke. As well as the perfect food there were always the latest books laid out on a long stool in front of the fireplace. There seemed to be dozens of servants, yet the atmosphere was informal, homely; one felt at ease; it was almost impossible to be shy when staying there.'

Another remarkable cookery book was published in 1925, when its author was in her late seventies. This was *Minnie Lady Hindlip's*

Cookery Book. According to her great-grandson Charles Allsopp, Lady Hindlip 'was by all accounts a remarkable lady, no beauty but very amusing and a wonderful hostess. When she was asked why she liked going to children's parties she replied: "My dear, I ask who the little children are and then I think who they really are!"'

Also published in the twenties was *A Book of Scents and Dishes* by Dorothy Allhusen. Mrs Allhusen's country house, as described by Jessica Mitford in *Hons and Rebels*, evidently belonged in the same tradition as the Jekylls': 'Cousin Dorothy's house was deliciously comfortable and pleasant. Unlike most English country houses, the rooms were always glowingly warm. You got the feeling that the fires burned in the fireplace continuously all winter. Being a childless house, it had a quiet, timeless, clean quality often missing in the houses of other aunts and cousins. There were many old-fashioned touches: oranges stuffed with cloves in the chests of drawers, early morning tea in your bedroom, and savoury at the end of dinner – hot stuffed mushrooms or chicken livers wrapped in bacon.' It was while staying in this delightful house that Jessica Mitford first met her cousin Esmond Romilly, then on sick leave from fighting with the International Brigade in the Spanish Civil War. Over the weekend they fell in love and made plans to elope. A week later they left secretly for Spain, and another of the Mitford legends began to unfold.

Most admired of all the cookery books published in the 1930s was probably *Lady Sysonby's Cook Book*. This is an unusually interesting book with illustrations by Oliver Messel and an introduction by Osbert Sitwell. Ria Sysonby, whose daughter Loelia married the Duke of Westminster (and, later, Sir Martin Lindsay of Dowhill), was married to a courtier. Fritz Ponsonby, later Lord Sysonby, was Private Secretary first to Queen Victoria, and then to Edward VII. The Sysonbys lived in a grace-and-favour apartment in St James's Palace, and in the country, near Guildford. Unlike most great hostesses, Lady Sysonby was a beauty, and much in demand. Although they were by no means rich, she was always beautifully dressed, and had excellent food. Her daughter Loelia tells me: 'Any cook seeking a new situation had only to mention that she had been employed by Lady Sysonby, and she was at once engaged.'

Another esteemed hostess who wrote cookery books was Ruth Lowinsky, whose first book, *Lovely Food*, is a collector's item. Published in 1931 by the Nonesuch Press, it is beautifully produced on hand-made paper, with elegant and idiosyncratic illustrations by her husband Thomas Lowinsky. Ruth Lowinsky was an heiress. Her father, Leopold Hirsch, was a cultivated banker of German descent who had made a great fortune in South Africa in gold and diamonds, in the 1870s. The Hirschs lived in a magnificent house in Kensington Palace Gardens and Ruth was a student at the Slade, where she met her husband-to-be. Thomas Lowinsky was an original and interesting painter, also a discerning collector. His portraits of women are particularly striking, while his surrealist work is also much admired. In 1990 there was a retrospective exhibition of his work at the Tate Gallery.

Ruth gave up painting on her marriage, and turned her gifts to entertaining. Dumpy and undistinguished in appearance, she was immensely cultivated, sophisticated and amusing. The Lowinskys lived in Kensington Square with their four children. Each summer they were in the habit of taking a large country house; one year they rented Stanway from the Wemysses. (Since many aristocratic families owned several large country houses, it was considered quite normal to rent one or other out at certain times of year, when they did not want it themselves.)

Ruth Lowinsky published three cookery books in the 1930s, and a fourth, in the form of an anthology, after the war. Her recipes are original, but erratic. Since she did not learn to cook herself until the outbreak of war, she must have relied on information from her Austrian cook. I sometimes wonder what her friend Constance Spry must have made of the Lowinsky oeuvre in this respect, for Mrs Spry was the first cookery writer whose recipes actually worked. But it is for the spirit of her book that Ruth Lowinsky will be remembered. As she says in the introduction to *Lovely Food*: 'Remember that food must above all things be varied, surprising and original.'

Another influential publication was *The Week-End Book*, which was edited and published by Francis Meynell, the founder of the Nonesuch Press, and friend and publisher of Ruth Lowinsky. *The Week-End Book* was published annually, with revisions and additions, both in England and the USA, from 1924 until the 1950s. It is rather like a magazine in content, with sections on such disparate subjects as birds, architecture, music and after-dinner games. The cookery section deals with such things as lists for the weekend store cupboard, sandwich fillings, picnic food and dishes for the inexperienced cook. It proved immensely successful, and sold more than 50,000 copies in the first four years.

Mrs Simpson did not waste her time writing cookery books, for she had better things to do. Of all the hostesses of her day, she must rate as the most successful, in that her aim was clearly defined. She set out to please and entertain the Prince of Wales, and in this she succeeded beyond her wildest dreams. In social terms she was a brilliant figure, an instigator who enjoyed setting trends, and a perfectionist for whom no detail was too much trouble. She was always immaculately dressed, and proved herself well able to provide a stimulating ambiance, with witty repartee and first-rate food. In his diaries, Cecil Beaton describes going to sketch Mrs Simpson shortly before the abdication, in her rented house in Regent's Park. After the session was over, they were joined by the King and Wallis's Aunt Bessy for a quick drink before going on to dine with Emerald Cunard. Even at this informal occasion, a silver tray was handed round bearing no less than nine different sorts of canapés, eight of them hot, to accompany the cocktails.

Menus

IIII

Like all periods of transition and social upheaval, the two decades between the wars showed a wide variation in patterns of eating. These variations depended not only on the affluence of the households concerned, which would previously have been the main factor in deciding culinary habits, but also on the position of the family as regards fashionableness. In a household like the Mildmays, where Edwardian values were still upheld and old ways adhered to, meals were still formal and lengthy. Before a dinner party in their London house in Berkeley Square, for instance, the male guests were informed on arrival who they were to take in to dinner. The guests would assemble in the library and make desultory conversation, without drinks in any form, then they would line up in couples and troop in to dinner.

This would start with a choice of thick or thin soup, followed by a hot fish dish. Then came an entrée, either poultry or game, and a second meat dish. This might be followed by a separate vegetable course like the celebrated asparagus ice, then a pudding and a savoury. Finally the table was cleared of all extraneous dishes and the fruit plates would be handed round, each one bearing a small lace mat with a glass fingerbowl half filled with water, and a silver-gilt knife and fork. A series of fruit dishes would then be passed round, probably three or four or even five, each one bearing just one sort of fruit which had been sent up from the garden at Flete. These were followed by a silver cream jug and sugar bowl. Then came coffee, after which the ladies would withdraw, leaving the men to their port and brandy.

An unusual pattern is found in the menus of Mrs Ronnie Greville, at the dinners she held in Charles Street, or at Polesden Lacey. After three hot dishes – soup, fish, and poultry or game – a cold main dish was often served, possibly boeuf en gelée, or ham mousse, accompanied by a salad. This formula is repeated often, even in mid-winter.

At Faringdon, where Lord Berners was renowned for his food, the meals were rather idiosyncratic. Lord Berners loved rich food, and judging from descriptions of the meals, it would seem that his cook indulged him up to the hilt. Lobster was often served – as a first course – for Sunday lunch, followed by a chicken pie, or a roast fillet of beef. Friends speak fondly of a cold dish of Dover sole, poached fillets lying in a horseradish cream sauce with chives. Sliced chicken was served in aspic, with strips of red pepper set in the jelly. The vegetables were home-grown, very small, and beautifully cooked, and there was always home-made bread baked in a plait. The puddings were very popular with his guests: baked apples stuffed with chopped walnuts in a toffee sauce, summer pudding, strawberry shortcake, and pudding Louise, which is not unlike a Bakewell tart.

One group that broke with tradition in gastronomic matters, as in many others, was the Bloomsbury set. The writers and painters of the 1920s and 30s loved to eat and drink well, but lacked the funds – or the desire – to do it in the traditional ways. Having freed themselves from class distinctions, they ignored current patterns of behaviour in the kitchen and the dining-room, and chose to adopt a totally different way of eating, much closer to our own. They were almost without exception badly off, making do with a maid-of-all-work, who also did the cooking. These girls were such modest cooks, usually untrained and inexperienced, that their employers ended up doing some of the cooking themselves. Although Frances Partridge says she 'couldn't boil an egg or a potato when the second war began', some of them had begun to teach themselves. Virginia Woolf used to bake bread, which she enjoyed doing, and Carrington cooked frequently, often preparing food for weekend parties at Ham Spray. In a letter to Lytton Strachey she describes making 'brews of quince cheese [which] scent the whole house'; in another, dated April 1928, she describes making zabaglione: 'I made a Zambalione [sic] last night and just as it was finished Henry (Lamb) stepped backwards and knocked the bowl all over the carpet! But fortunately there were masses of eggs, so I quickly whisked up another one.'

The Bloomsbury set loved to travel, and they did this in a way that is familiar to many of us today, but was very unusual at that time. Whereas the rich and fashionable flitted about from Paris to New York to Cap Ferrat, staying in grand hotels, villas or yachts, the intelligentsia were more adventurous in that they were not afraid of discomfort, although their scope was of necessity more limited, and rarely stretched beyond France, Italy or Spain. Staying in inns, and eating very simply, they became familiar with the local cuisine and the vins du pays in a way that the rich never did, for the food in smart hotels had already become international, much as it is today. In another letter to Lytton Strachey, Carrington describes a meal in France, while travelling with Augustus and Dorelia John: 'Lunch was served outside under the planes. Hare pâté, grilled red mullet, a marvellous salad and delicious coffee, and Château des Papes Telegraphes, a whole bottle; our resolution for a cheese and salad lunch faded away!' (One of the things I love about Carrington's letters are her constant references to food and wine – especially wine; I remember one, which I can no longer find, which refers to having had a very good Nuit Sans [sic] Georges – spelling was not her strong point.)

Back home, meals in the Bloomsbury circle were simple, and very wholesome, most of the time, with the occasional splurge for a special occasion. Frances Partridge writes: 'Our Ham Spray food between the wars was simple and home-produced. We favoured an almost permanent ham, potted in one of the bathrooms, really wonderful brawn to a recipe by Boris Anrep, and ways of eating every piece of our own pig except the chitterlings, and a wonderful beestings pudding (this was a super-rich bread and butter pudding from a calving cow's first milk, plus sultanas). Home-grown local dishes were jugged hare and perdrix aux choux. We prided ourselves on growing all our own vegetables and fruit; raspberries were splendid, we had fine figs, grapes, peaches and nectarines, average apples and pears. Vegetables simply cooked, though salsify à la crème became a main dish. Seakale (simply boiled with butter), asparagus, celeriac, chicory forced in the woodshed for winter. Cabbages (I did have a splendid way of cooking them very slowly with cinnamon, brown sugar, bacon, sultanas, etc.). When we came to London our restaurant meals were most untypical, and a glorious treat – the Basque was a rarity – the Ivy a special favourite. Birthday dinner was often canard sous presse, and crêpes suzette, I don't know why.'

|||| *A dinner given by Chips Channon at Moir House, St James's Place, February 1925.*

'We began with blinis served with Swedish schnapps, to wash down the caviare. Then soup, followed by salmon, then an elaborate chicken. Then a sweet and a savoury. The candle light was reflected in my gold plate and the conversation was incessant. Eventually Cole Porter was sufficiently intoxicated to play the piano. He played for hours. I got to bed at 4.30 absolutely exhausted.'

|||| *A typical day in the life of Siegfried Sassoon, who in the mid-twenties decided to stay in bed all day and work at night. February 1924.*

'In bed all day. (As usual.) Haddock and baked apple at 5.30 p.m. Soup, omelette and stewed prunes at the Monico 10.45. It is now 4 a.m. and I've just had some tea and bolted three sponge cakes.'

|||| *Luncheon with Lady Cunard, May 1930.*

A poached egg in a baked potato
A lamb cutlet with six different vegetables
A silver bowl of tapioca beaten to a froth with cream, served cold, with strawberries

IIII   *A dinner at Buckingham Palace, March 1927.*

Consommé Messaline
Rosettes de Saumon de Balmoral, Régence
Cailles Epicurienne
Filets d'Agneau des Gourmets
Poulardes Rôties, Salade
Asperges, Sauce Mousseline
Soufflé Glacé Daphne
Paniers de Friandises
Kisch [sic] Lorraine
One of the guests, Lady Mildmay, commented: 'The dinner table was one solid mass of gold plate, and the flowers were too lovely, yellow daffodils, blue iris and very golden mimosa. Everyone said the dinner was the best they had ever eaten, but I do not really agree. There were six things in succession, all hot, and the peas were quite uneatable.'

IIII   *Marcel Boulestin's suggestion for a late supper, November 1928.*

'Nothing better, say at 3 o'clock in the morning, than a boiling hot soupe au choux and cold meat, with a very fresh, crisp salad. And you should drink with this one of those little pink or white wines from Anjou or Touraine, which have such a pleasant, sharp taste. (This is more suitable, though, for Chelsea than Bayswater – unless you happen to feel, for once, delightfully Bohemian.)'

IIII   *Dinner with Mrs Ronald Tree (Nancy Lancaster), in the 1920s.*

Fish Chowder
Poulets Rôtis au Cresson
Legumes, Salade
Mousse à l'Orange – Compote d'Oranges

|||| *Dinner (for the Japps) at Ham Spray, September 1925. From a letter to Lytton Strachey from Carrington.*

'The dinner was indescribably grand. Epoch making; grapefruit, then a chicken covered with fennel and tomato sauce, a risotto with almonds, onions, and pimentos, followed by sack cream, supported by Café Royal wine, perfectly warmed. (The cradle took Mrs Japp's breath away.)'

|||| *A buffet dinner at Lady Mendl's, at the Villa Trianon, Versailles, July 1932, as described in Vogue.*

'Some forty of us dined on the enclosed terrace by candle-light, with the illuminated garden for a background. Of course it was a buffet dinner, as every big dinner is now. Elsie Mendl's menu was hot soup, boeuf braisé with all kinds of vegetables, and ice cream and strawberries. Nothing could be simpler, and nothing better.'

|||| *Supper with Frances Partridge, November 1927.*

'We expected Dadie (Rylands) and Gerald (Brenan) at 41 about ten o'clock, and I had oysters for them, and cold partridges in aspic.'

|||| *A summer luncheon, suggested by Quaglino, 1935.*

Caviar de Sterlet, or Crab Cocktail
Goujons de Sole Frites, Sauce Dugléré
Noix de Veau en Aspic
Mousse de Jambon – Salade Niçoise
Fraises Monte Carlo – Biscuits à la Cuillère
Canapé Diane

‖‖ *Breakfast served at a ball, 1927, as described in* Vogue.

'At 2 a.m. tankards of pale and light draught bitters replace the champagne, and ordinary roasting tins full of delicious little chipolata sausages, still steaming in the medium in which they were cooked, oust the more elegant quail. Bacon and eggs are still popular, as are kippers.'

‖‖ *Dinner with Mrs Ronnie Greville at Polesden Lacey, Christmas 1931. (Note the cold main course.)*

Gnocchi à la Suisse
Faisans Braisés au Céleri
Viandes Froides – Salade
Bavarois Vanille – Compote de Mirabelles

‖‖ *A luncheon suggested by Marcel Boulestin, 1928.*

Oeufs à la Gelée
Pilaf aux Fruits de Mer
Pintade Farcie, Pommes Pailles & Salade Verte
Poires au Chocolat

‖‖ *An autumn luncheon, as suggested by Quaglino, 1935.*

Honey Dew Melon – Jambon de Bayonne
Ravioli au Jus de Veau
Grouse en Papillote, Pommes Soufflés
Aubergines Provençales
Compote de Fruits Frais – Gâteau au Chocolat

▌||| *Luncheon with Lady Mendl, 1930.*

Cream of Green Pea Soup
Crayfish Gloucester
Baked Chicken
Vanilla Ice with Hot Cherry Sauce

▌||| *A dinner at Ham Spray, May 1929, from a letter
                       to Lytton Strachey from Carrington.*

'We had a fine dinner with Moselle and Burgundy, cold salmon and
tartar sauce, followed by gammon and salad, followed by strawberries and kirsch, followed by brandies and coffee.'

▌||| *Dinner for Edward VIII, given by Chips
                       Channon at 5 Belgrave Square, June 1936.*

'Dinner was perfect, we began with blinis and caviare, then sole
muscat followed by boeuf provençal. It was served so speedily that
we had finished before eleven, and then the ladies left, curtseying
as they got up.'

▌||| *Luncheon with Madame (Helena) Rubinstein,
                       May 1933, as described in* Vogue.

'At lunch with Madame Rubinstein, you might begin with a clear
bouillon, then progress to a divine entrée of spinach purée rolled
up in little crêpes. Then a fish curry (made with lobster claws and
baby scallops), served with rice and chutney, followed by fresh
pineapple, or strawberries with kirsch. The coffee is black as the
ace of spades, in bright red cups.'

▌|||| *A dinner for four at Fort Belvedere, home of the*
Prince of Wales, in the 1930s.

'It began with oysters in unlimited quantity, followed by a mousse of ham and foie gras, and a salad, and ended with a dish of very hot cheese fritters.'

▌|||| *A dinner given by Mrs Ronnie Greville at*
Polesden Lacey, January 1932. (Note the cold
main course.)

Crème Crécy
Sole Frite, Sauce Diable
Soufflé de Jambon à la Parisienne
Boeuf à la Gelée – Salade
Poires à la Marquise
Barquettes de Caviar

▌|||| *Dinner at the Eiffel Tower, now the White*
Tower, in October 1929, from a letter to Julia
Strachey from Carrington.

'In the evening we had dinner with old Augustus (John) at the Eiffel Tour [sic]. Rather fun. Very late, at 9.30. Such a delicious meal. Snails. Wild duck and orange salad, and real iced raspberries with cream and two bottles of Burgundy.'

▌|||| *A dinner given for King George V and Queen*
Mary at Chatsworth, July 4th, 1933.

Crème Sarah Bernhardt
Barbue Grimaldi
Caneton à l'Anglaise, Poussins Rôtis, Légumes
Mousse de Jambon, Salade Waldorf
Soufflé Esterhazy, Fraises Romanoff
Chester Cakes

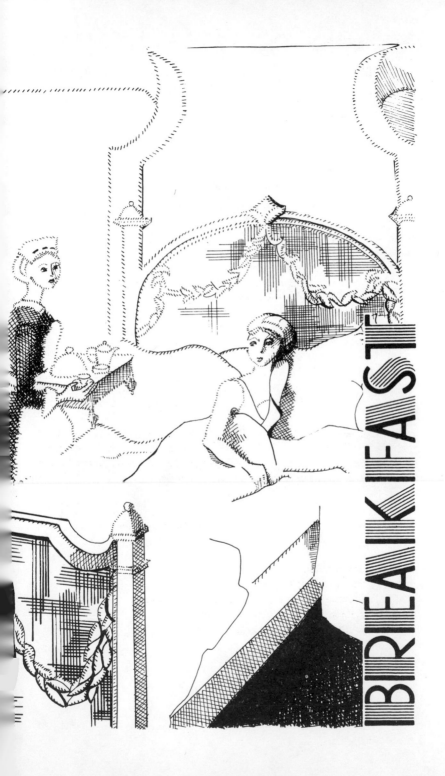

Breakfast

IIII
IIII

It was during this transitional period between the wars that the classic British breakfast took shape. In the large country houses the lavish breakfast of Edwardian days was still the norm. A row of silver dishes on hot plates offered a choice of fried, boiled or scrambled eggs, bacon, sausages, tomatoes, fried bread, devilled kidneys, and a fish dish: either smoked haddock, kippers or kedgeree. On the cold table stood a ham, a tongue, and cold game in season. When there was no game a cold fish dish like soused herrings might take its place. Coffee and tea were served, with copious amounts of toast, butter and marmalade.

In the south, things were already starting to change. According to social historian Arnold Palmer in his book *Moveable Feasts*, a radical change was taking place: 'By 1925 many women had decided to breakfast in bed, at 8.15 or thereabouts, on a glass of orange juice, a piece of toast melba, a cup of coffee unsugared and black, and cigarettes. Their husbands did little better, in fact they often shared the meal.' This was the American influence which was to spread throughout the twenties and thirties. Canadian Charles Ritchie, writing in his diaries in London just before the outbreak of the Second World War, was struck by 'the new, classless, Americanised English who have grapefruit for breakfast and prefer *The New Yorker* to *Punch*'.

By the end of the thirties, the most popular breakfast with all classes, except the super sophisticates of Charles Ritchie's world, and the poor who could not afford it, was bacon and eggs, toast and marmalade, and coffee or tea. Even among the very poor, fried bacon was considered the vital ingredient of a proper breakfast, more important even than the eggs. While coffee was the most fashionable drink in London and the south, tea was still the most widely drunk at all levels of society.

While fruit and fruit juices were starting to become popular on the breakfast table, American cereals had begun to appear in the shops, and were greeted with rapture. Even Lady Jekyll, normally the most sensible of women, writing in her weekly column in Saturday's *Times*, suggested serving 'a few spoonfuls of Puffed Wheat crisped hot in the oven and lying decoratively in small mother-o'-pearl shells', as an inexpensive alternative to salted almonds, for nibbling between courses at dinner parties.

For most people, the hallmark of the British breakfast is marmalade. This had been made in Britain for hundreds of years, with quince and other fruits. In the sixteenth and seventeenth centuries it was usually served sliced, as a dessert or sweetmeat, or as a digestive, or cure for colds. By the eighteenth century it was being made with Seville oranges, and in Scotland it began to be served at breakfast, as a preserve. Until then it had been pounded into a smooth paste; now it appeared in its familiar form, with little bits of peel within it. The first manufactured marmalade was Keiller's Dundee Marmalade, which started in 1797. Two other Scottish firms, Robertsons and Baxters, started selling their products in the 1860s, while the English firms of Coopers, Wilkins of Tiptree, and Elsenham began production between 1875 and 1890. Jellied marmalade also became popular. Robertson's Golden and Silver Shred were made in late Victorian times, and Rose's Lime Marmalade in the 1930s. There was a wide variety: before the First World War there were twenty-seven varieties of Tiptree marmalade on sale; today there are still ten different sorts.

By the eighteenth century Scottish breakfasts were famous, far superior to those in England. Writers like Dr Johnson, Boswell and Sir Walter Scott refer to a choice of tea, coffee or chocolate; hot porridge served with a mixture of cream and buttermilk; smoked reindeer ham, beef and mutton; smoked salmon and haddock, kippers and fresh herrings; bread, scones and thin cakes of oats and barley, eaten with fresh butter, blueberry jam, currant jelly and marmalade.

Our own breakfasts in Scotland before the last war were much like the traditional English country house breakfast, with a few differences. Whereas in most English houses porridge was only served occasionally, before hunting or shooting for instance, we ate it every day.

Scotsmen like my father ate their porridge standing up, and this seemed to me the most natural thing in the world, despite English mockery. They would help themselves to a dish of porridge from the hotplate, adding a pinch of salt and some cold milk, then instead of carrying it to the table, they would simply wander about the room as they ate it, reading the headlines of the newspapers, or gazing out of the window. In other words, they behaved just as we might with a glass of sherry, before sitting down to lunch.

My grandmother ate the same breakfast every day of her life:

porridge, a soused herring, and two oatcakes. Our cook made marvellous oatcakes: triangular, very thin and fragile in the extreme. She claimed to use no fat whatsoever, but I find this hard to believe. With them, we ate butter from the town, which my father perversely preferred to our own farm butter, and Tiptree Orange Marmalade, still in the glass jar it came in. Scones were baked fresh early each morning; these were the Scottish sort, baked on a griddle, thin, soft and triangular in shape. There was always toast as well, but there was never enough. My mother would ring and ask for more, but by the time it came it was too late, and no one wanted it. I remember this as a constant source of friction between my parents.

As well as the array of cooked breakfast dishes, and the cold table, there was an amazing electric contraption in which you boiled your own egg, so that you could have it exactly as you liked, freshly cooked. Even before the war, there was a modicum of self-help in our house which seems unusual in retrospect, at a time when most owners of large houses rang to have a log put on the fire. My father liked to boil his own egg, make the salad dressing, and make up his own packed lunch from the remains of the breakfast table, for a solitary day's shooting.

Porridge

▮|||

The porridge at our home in Scotland had a marvellous 'set' quality about it, almost like junket, that I have never been able to repeat; it was probably the result of long, slow cooking, then standing for a while on the hot plate. Nowadays I use a method of my own, a compromise between the old way and the speedy modern version made with Quaker Oats. I no longer eat it for breakfast, but when coming home late at night, tired and hungry, I find it comforting, sustaining and easy to digest.

½ pt [275 ml] water
½ tsp (or less) sea salt
1½ oz [45 g] medium oatmeal

Bring the water to the boil in a heavy pan. Add the salt, then sprinkle in the oatmeal, stirring constantly. Boil steadily for 5 minutes, stirring all the time, then transfer to a double boiler and cook gently for 15 minutes, stirring now and then. When the time is up, cover the pan, remove from the heat, and stand until ready to serve. Serves 1–2, with cold milk straight from the fridge.

AB

Kedgeree

▮|||

Originally a breakfast dish, this later became popular as a first course for luncheon, or as a supper dish. In these cases it can be made richer, with the addition of cream and extra butter, but for breakfast it is best made quite simply. It can well be made in advance and reheated.

1 lb [450 g] salmon
8 oz [225 g] long-grain rice
4 eggs, hard-boiled
2–3 oz [55–85 g] butter
sea salt and black pepper
¼ pt [150 ml] double cream (optional)
½ Tbs finely chopped parsley

If cooking the salmon specially (it is also a good way of using up remains of a large fish), put it in a saucepan and cover with cold lightly salted water. Bring slowly to the boil, then simmer gently for 3 minutes. Cover the pan, remove from the heat, and leave until it has completely cooled. Then drain the fish, discard skin and bones, and flake the flesh. Boil the rice as usual and drain well. Assemble in a buttered bowl standing over a large pan of simmering water. Fill with rice and fish in alternate layers, adding roughly chopped hard-boiled eggs, small bits of butter, and lots of sea salt and black pepper. (And cream, if used.) Cover with foil and leave to heat for about 25 minutes, mixing together gently now and then with a wooden spoon. Turn into a serving dish and sprinkle with a little chopped parsley. Serves 4, with a green salad, as a lunch or supper dish, or 5–6 for breakfast.

AB

Smoked Haddock with Poached Eggs

IIII

Composite breakfast dishes of this sort were not usually served in the big country houses, where the different foods were served separately, so that the guests could combine them, or not, as they pleased. But in the smaller houses this would be a popular breakfast dish, since the combination of smoked haddock and eggs has always been much liked. Nowadays it makes a good light dish for luncheon or supper.

2 smoked haddock
½ pt [275 ml] milk
4 freshly poached eggs
freshly ground black pepper

Cut each haddock in half and wash well. Put the pieces in a broad pan and pour over the milk. Add about the same amount of water, enough to barely cover the fish. Bring to the boil, cover the pan, and simmer gently for 12 minutes. Lift out the pieces of fish with a slotted spoon and drain in a colander, then lay them on a shallow dish. Place a poached egg carefully on each one and sprinkle with black pepper.

Alternatively, the fish can be taken off the bone and flaked, then piled on 4 rounds of hot (thinly) buttered toast. Sprinkle with black pepper, then lay an egg on top of each one. Serves 4.

AB

Mrs Anderson's Fish Cakes

▌|||

Another example of a traditional breakfast dish which makes an excellent light main course for lunch or supper. Mrs Anderson was cook to Kathleen, Duchess of Rutland, before and during the war. She specifies cod or haddock, but I have also used salmon, which was delicious. Her fish cakes are particularly good in that they use a thick béchamel instead of the more usual mashed potato, or breadcrumbs, and the result is very light and moist.

2 lb [900 g] cod or haddock fillet, or salmon
¾ pt [450 ml] milk, or ½ pt [275 ml] if using salmon
salt and black pepper
2 oz [55 g] butter
2 oz [55 g] flour
1 Tbs chopped parsley
2 eggs, beaten
dry white breadcrumbs
sunflower oil, for frying

Poach fish in lightly salted milk, unless using salmon, which should be cooked in plain water, also lightly salted. When the fish is done, drain it, reserving the milk. Strain it, reserving ½ pt [275 ml]. Melt the butter, add the flour, and cook for 1 minute, stirring. Add the ½ pt [275 ml] milk and bring to the boil, stirring till blended. Simmer gently for 3–4 minutes, adding salt and pepper to taste. Flake the fish, discarding skin and bone, and stir into the sauce, adding the chopped parsley. (Chop the larger flakes in half.) Chill the mixture for several hours, or overnight, then form into round cakes weighing about 3 oz [85 g] each. Shape them on a floured board, then dip first in beaten egg and then in breadcrumbs.

Mrs Anderson's fish cakes were shaped like round balls, but these have to be deep-fried. I prefer to flatten mine, and shallow-fry them in a ¾ inch [1.5 cm] layer of oil. Drain on kitchen paper before serving. Makes 10–12. If serving for lunch or supper, they can be accompanied by fried parsley (page 180), or a sauce. Iced tomato sauce (page 182), piquant sauce (page 177), sauce tartare (page 182), or egg and parsley sauce (page 178), all go well with them.

They also freeze well, after dipping in egg and breadcrumbs.

Lady John Manners

Another Fish Cake

▌|||

This is a simpler fish cake than the first, better for breakfast. It is less rich than Mrs Anderson's fish cakes, also firmer, therefore better for taking on picnics, or for eating cold, as a snack. The ratio of fish to potato can vary from 50/50 to 25/75, depending on what you have left over, but the higher the proportion of fish the better.

8 oz [225 g] cooked fish, free from skin and bone:
    cod, haddock, salmon
4 oz [120 g] freshly mashed potato
½ oz [15 g] butter, at room temperature
2 Tbs chopped parsley
salt and black pepper
1 egg, beaten
dry white breadcrumbs
frying oil

Mix the fish with the mashed potato, beating well with a wooden spoon. Beat in the butter, chopped parsley, and plenty of salt and black pepper. Chill for a few hours, if convenient. Then form into round cakes on a floured board. Dip them first in beaten egg, then in breadcrumbs. Heat a layer of oil about 1 inch [2.5 cm] deep in a frying pan, then fry the fish cakes until golden on both sides. Makes 4 large fish cakes. They freeze well, before frying.

Note: If using equal quantities of fish and potato, double the butter.

Adapted from *A Year's Dinners* by May Little

Herrings in Oatmeal

||||

This used to be a popular breakfast dish; now it makes a good lunch or supper dish. The herrings were usually fried, but I prefer to grill them. Herrings are not much eaten these days, which is a pity, for they are probably the best value for money, in terms of nutrition, to be found.

4 herrings, filleted and skinned
6 Tbs milk
approx. 4 oz [120 g] coarse oatmeal
1½ oz [45 g] butter

Rinse the herrings and pat them dry. Take out any stray bones, then dip each fillet first in milk and then in coarse oatmeal, patting it on well. Heat the grill, then lay the herrings on the rack, plump side uppermost. Dot them with butter and grill for 3 minutes, then turn and grill for another 3 minutes. Serve on hot plates. Serves 4. If to be eaten as a main course, they can be served with a mustard sauce, and some buttered leeks.

AB

Soused Herrings

||||

Although usually served as a first course at lunchtime, in my grandparents' house in Scotland these were a regular feature of the cold table at breakfast, together with a ham, tongue and cold game in season. Unlike rollmops which are salted and pickled, these are freshly cooked in a marinade, then eaten within a day or two of cooking. I use a mixture of white wine and vinegar for the marinade, but water can be substituted for the wine. (In this case, malt vinegar should be used.)

8 fl oz [250 ml] dry white wine
8 fl oz [250 ml] white wine vinegar
1 small onion, cut in rings
1 carrot, thinly sliced
3 stalks parsley
2 bay leaves

1 sprig thyme
½ Tbs sea salt
8 black peppercorns
3 cloves
6 herrings, filleted, without their roes

GARNISH
1 small carrot
½ small onion, cut in thin semi-circular slices
1 Tbs finely chopped parsley

Put the wine and vinegar in a pan with the sliced onion and carrot, herbs and seasonings. Bring slowly to the boil and simmer for 20 minutes, half covered. Leave to cool.

Later, have the herring fillets lying in a rectangular dish. Pour the cooled marinade over them, cover loosely with foil, and bake for 10 minutes at 350°F/180°C/gas 4. Remove from the oven and leave to cool. These may be served after cooling, or kept for 2–3 days in the refrigerator, in their marinade.

Before serving, prepare the garnish. Make grooves in the side of the carrot with a canelle knife and cut in thin slices. Put them in a small strainer, lower into a pan of boiling water, and cook for 2 minutes, then drain and rinse briefly under the cold tap. Divide the onion slices into single semi-circular rings. Lift the fillets out of the marinade and lay them on a flat dish. Moisten with a little of the marinade, and scatter the flower-shaped carrot slices, onion rings and chopped parsley over all. These are good served with thinly sliced rye bread and butter, or pumpernickel, and small glasses of neat vodka, but not at breakfast!

AB

Irish Potato Cakes

||||

Potato dishes of this sort were often served for breakfast, with fried bacon, eggs, tomatoes, etc. Nowadays they come in useful as part of a simple supper or lunch dish, good with ham and eggs, or grilled tomatoes and bacon. They are also good served with roast or grilled meat, as part of a more formal meal.

1 oz [30 g] butter
2 Tbs milk
¾ tsp salt
1½ lb [680 g] hot mashed potatoes (allow 2 lb [900 g]
    raw potatoes)
2 oz [55 g] flour
¾ tsp baking powder

Melt the butter in the milk and add it and the salt to the potatoes. Mix the flour and baking powder together. Add them. Knead lightly and roll out till the paste is about half an inch [1 cm] thick. Cut out into scone-shaped [*triangular*] pieces. [*Or, take egg-sized pieces and roll into a ball, then flatten.*] Bake on a greased and heated griddle, or cook in butter in a frying pan. [*Makes about 10–12; serves 5–6.*]

Vegetable Cookery by Elizabeth Lucas

0

A Breakfast Dish

▮|||

This recipe comes from a little book called Tempting Dishes for Small Incomes, which was published in 1872. Yet it is still relevant to the twenties and thirties, for more modest households that could not run to the lavish display of different dishes on offer in the great houses, often cooked mixed dishes of this sort for breakfast. Another, called chasse, included potatoes and grated cheese, as well as eggs, tomatoes and ham, but I prefer this simpler one. Nowadays when I can only face an oatcake at breakfast, I would make this for a light supper, with a green salad.

3 tomatoes, skinned and sliced, seeded and drained
1 oz [30 g] butter
3 oz [85 g] chopped ham, fat removed
salt and black pepper
2 eggs, lightly beaten
4 slices thick toast, buttered
1 Tbs chopped parsley

Take three tomatoes, slice them and put them in a stewpan with a little butter, a little finely chopped ham, pepper and salt, and let them cook for a few mintues; then add 2 raw eggs and stir all together for a few minutes till the eggs set, then serve on buttered toast with a little finely chopped parsley sprinkled over the top. [*Serve immediately. Serves 4 on toast, or 2 with a dish of boiled rice, and a green salad.*]

Tempting Dishes for Small Incomes by Mrs De Salis

Marmalade

▮|||

Although excellent marmalades were already being made commercially – Keiller's Dundee Marmalade was the first, in 1797 – many cooks preferred to make their own, just as they do today. This is an unusual recipe in that the fruit is boiled whole. The results are excellent: quite the best I know. Seville oranges are only in season for a few short weeks after Christmas, in January and February.

4 lb [1.8 kg] Seville oranges, washed
1 lemon, washed
3½ pt [2 litres] water
6 lb [3 kg] preserving sugar
1½ Tbs brandy

Put the whole oranges and lemon in a deep pan with the water.
Cover and cook gently for 2 hours, till very soft. Remove the
oranges and lemon, leaving the liquid in the pan. Cut the fruit in
half and scoop out the insides into a sieve placed over the pan they
cooked in. Sieve all the pulp back into the pan, then cut the rind
into strips, as thick or thin as you like, and add to the pan also.
Bring back to the boil, then remove from the heat and stir in the
sugar. (Preserving sugar gives a clearer jelly, but granulated sugar
will do perfectly well.) Stir until all the sugar has dissolved, then
put the pan back over the heat. Bring to the boil, then simmer,
uncovered, for 30–40 minutes, or until it sets when tested on a
saucer. Spoon into hot sterilised jars, dividing the strips of peel
evenly between the jars, and leave to cool overnight, covered with a
light cloth. Next day, cover with rounds of greaseproof paper
dipped in brandy, and screw down the lids tightly, or cover with
larger rounds of greaseproof paper secured with elastic bands.
Makes 10 lb [4.5 kg].

Sarah Stuart

Oatcakes

||||

*These were very popular at breakfast, especially
in Scotland. They are not easy to make, and
demand some practice. To be really good, they
should be very thin indeed, crisp and fragile:
impossible to butter without breaking.*

2 oz [55 g] coarse oatmeal
8 oz [225 g] medium oatmeal
¼ tsp bicarbonate of soda
½ oz [15 g] lard
¼ pt [150 ml] boiling water
approx. ½ oz [15 g] fine oatmeal

Mix coarse and medium oatmeal together with bicarbonate of soda.
Melt the lard and add it to the mixture. Mix it well, and pour on the

boiling water. Mix with enough fine oatmeal to give a fairly moist consistency. Divide into 3 or 4 pieces. Roll each one out very thinly, in a circle; cut each circle in quarters or 'farls'. Lay them on greased baking sheets and bake for 20 minutes, or until crisp and lightly coloured, at 325°F/170°C/gas 3, turning them over halfway through. Makes about 14.

Katie Colquhoun

FIRST COURSES

First Courses

||||
||||

Although by the 1920s meals had become shorter and simpler, they still conformed to a fairly rigid pattern. Certain dishes were considered suitable for one meal, but not for another. Egg dishes, for example, were often served for lunch, but never at dinner, while soup, which was the usual start to the evening meal, was never served in the middle of the day, except en gelée.

Soups came for the most part in two categories: thick and thin. At a formal dinner there was often a choice, and the footman would enquire which you preferred. Roughly speaking, the more elegant the occasion, the smoother, or clearer, the soup. A consommé was considered the ultimate test of a good cook, and the ideal start to an exquisite meal. It might be served quite plain, or with some small garnish floating in it: small vegetable dice, a few grains of rice, or minuscule soup pasta. In a less conventional household a more elaborate garnish might be served separately: round croutons piled high with whipped cream, or a bowl of saffron-flavoured rice, or even a jug of beetroot juice for adding, with cream, to a consommé made with duck and beef stock. This practice of handing round a number of elaborate garnishes separately, amused the English. Part of its appeal was that by enabling the guests to assemble their own dishes it pandered to their distrust of what they described as 'mucky food'. In practice it must have been quite tedious, in that the conversation was constantly being interrupted.

The place that soup held at the dinner table was taken by egg dishes at lunchtime. It amazes us today to realise just how many eggs people ate: in breakfast and lunch dishes, snacks and sandwiches, custards and mayonnaise, cakes and puddings, soufflés and ice cream. Many of the first-course dishes were based on hard-boiled eggs. Hot, they were sliced and served in sauces flavoured with boiled onions, or cheese, or curry. They were chopped and made into croquettes, often called egg cutlets, coated with more egg and breadcrumbs and deep-fried, then served with a spicy tomato sauce. Whole eggs were coated with a thick white sauce, then egg and breadcrumbs, before frying. Cold hard-boiled eggs were masked with mayonnaise, or with aspic, or with a curry-flavoured sauce, à l'Indienne. Poached eggs were concealed within a soufflé, or hidden inside a baked potato. Cold baked eggs were covered with a layer of mayonnaise, then with shelled shrimps.

In London, where hearty breakfasts were on the decline, popular breakfast dishes were often served as the first course for lunch: poached eggs on smoked haddock, kedgeree, and scrambled eggs with grilled mushrooms, or chipolatas. Soufflés were popular as first courses; these were usually made with fresh or smoked fish. Vegetable soufflés were more often served as a separate course after the main dish, while a cheese soufflé was treated as a savoury.

Vegetables did not feature much as first courses, apart from the obvious things like asparagus and artichokes, unless combined with another food like pastry, cheese or eggs. Plovers' eggs, and those of the black-backed gull which we used to gather from a nearby loch, were highly prized during their short season in late May and early June. They were served cold, as a first course at lunchtime: hard-boiled, unshelled, with celery salt and cayenne pepper, brown bread and butter.

Fish dishes were popular at both lunch and dinner. At lunchtime cold fish dishes, often uncooked, were served: smoked salmon or eel, dressed crab, or potted shrimps, while hot fish dishes were served at dinner. Whole whiting were fried in breadcrumbs and served with their tails in their mouths, while fried sprats and whitebait were also popular, especially with the men. One fish that has vanished without trace is the smelt, called éperlan in France. These were supposed to smell of cucumbers when very fresh, and were esteemed for their delicacy of flavour. They were served like whiting, simply fried, and my father loved them dearly.

Dover sole was prized for its versatility. Yet it too was often served simply, fried in breadcrumbs, either as whole fillets or cut in strips called goujons. It was garnished with fried parsley, or served with a contrasting sauce, usually cold, sometimes even semi-frozen, like a small sorbet. The fillets were served in literally hundreds of different ways: one of the best was Dugléré, a speciality of the Savoy. Another good dish that has been forgotten is a souchet of slips: a soup and fish dish combined. Baby soles were poached and served whole, each in a soup plate, with a delicately flavoured fish consommé spooned over them.

Consommé

IIII

This delicious consommé does not need clarifying but is best made over two days. It may be used as the basis for any of the consommés that follow, or for beef broth with cabbage toasts (see page 51), or it may be served as it stands. It can also be made in advance and frozen, although it loses something in the process. The original recipe calls for 12 pints [7.2 litres] of water, but few of us have pans that large. I use half that amount, filling up the pan from time to time with more cold water.

1 large chicken, preferably a boiling fowl
2½ lb [1.15 kg] shin of beef, cubed
2 large carrots, thickly sliced
2 onions, thickly sliced
2 leeks, thickly sliced
3 stalks parsley
3 sprigs thyme
1 large clove garlic, peeled
salt and black pepper
2 cloves

[*Start a day in advance.*] Wash a chicken carefully, put it in a large soup pot, add 2½ lb [1.15 kg] shin of beef and cover well with [6 *pt/3.6 litres*] cold water. Let stand for half an hour, then put on the fire and bring slowly to the boil. Remove the scum, add ½ a glass [*4 fl oz/120 ml*] of cold water and bring to the boil again. Repeat this process twice. Simmer very slowly for an hour, then add 2 large carrots, 2 white onions, 2 leeks, some parsley and thyme, 1 clove of garlic, salt and pepper, and 2 cloves. Let simmer for seven hours. Strain through a fine sieve and then through a wet cheesecloth. When cold [*after chilling overnight*], carefully remove grease. [*Makes 5–6 pt/2.75–3.6 litres, serves 12.*]

June Platt in *Vogue*

Beef Broth with Cabbage Toasts

IIII

A comforting soup for a supper party on a winter night.

1 green cabbage, tender leaves only
salt and pepper
8 bread rolls, 1 day old
2 oz [55 g] butter
4 oz [120 g] freshly grated Parmesan
4 pt [2.25 litres] beef stock, or consommé
1½ Tbs finely chopped parsley

Shred the tender part of a green cabbage very finely. Boil some water and add the washed, shredded cabbage and salt to taste. Cook for 5 minutes, then drain thoroughly. The cabbage should be tender and green, not soft and mushy.

Slice the rolls thinly and toast them to a delicate brown. Butter them well, pile a little cabbage neatly on each and sprinkle liberally with cheese. Put a tiny piece of butter on top of each one and set under the grill until the cheese and butter have melted together to a light brown. In the meantime, heat the beef broth to boiling point. Season to taste with salt and pepper. Pour it into a hot tureen and sprinkle with a little parsley. Place the tureen in front of the hostess and bring the cabbage toasts piping hot on a separate dish. The hostess then places 2 or 3 of the cabbage toasts in each soup plate and pours over them a ladleful of the hot bouillon. Serves 8. [*This dish really needs large old-fashioned soup plates, broad enough to hold 2 or 3 of the toasts. If you only have bowls, allow 1 toast per person, making them slightly more substantial.*]

June Platt in *Vogue*

Consommé à l'Estragon

||||

Lady Jekyll recommends this soup, with its 'clean and delicate flavour', for those who are trying to lose weight. Yet it is unusual and elegant enough for a dinner party. Like all the clear soups, it demands a good home-made stock, or, better still, a consommé (see page 51).

2½ pt [1.5 litres] chicken, veal or vegetable stock, or consommé
8 sprigs tarragon
2 egg whites
salt and black pepper

Make the required quantity of clear vegetable stock in the usual way, or use a chicken carcase or some veal, if convenient, with some ordinary stock. For garnish pick some 6d worth [*8 sprigs*] of tarragon, letting half simmer for 30 minutes in the consommé. About 10 minutes before dinner, whisk the whites of 2 eggs stiffly with salt and pepper, adding the rest of the tarragon leaves finely chopped [*about 1 tablespoon*]; take a heaped dessertspoon of the whipped whites and drop each to the required number [*six*] into a frying pan of boiling water to poach for 3 minutes [*turning them over halfway through*]; pour the boiling soup into a hot tureen [*or into cups*], drain each poached white, and let them float like snow islands on the top, serving one to each person. [*Serves 6.*]

    Kitchen Essays by Lady Jekyll

Consommé à l'Indienne

||||

A curry-flavoured consommé, usually served with some rice and/or chicken in it, was a popular dish, ideal for an after-the-theatre supper. This one is simply made, and very good. The garnishes may be served separately if preferred.

2 pt [1.2 litres] chicken stock, flavoured with carrot, leek and celery
2 medium onions, sliced
1 large Bramley apple, cored and sliced
1 Tbs dessicated coconut
½ Tbs curry powder
chicken or game bones (if available)

GARNISH
1 raw chicken breast
1½ oz [45 g] long-grain rice

One quart [1.2 litres] of good stock. Slice into it two onions, one large cooking apple, and add one tablespoonful of dessicated cocoanut, one dessertspoonful curry powder (or more if liked hot) and bones of roast chicken or game. Simmer one hour, strain, reboil; serve pieces of game or chicken and a little plain boiled rice. [*Poach the whole chicken breast in the soup during the last 15 minutes, then chop in neat dice. Boil the rice as usual and drain. Serve 1 Tbs chopped chicken and 1 Tbs rice in each bowl of soup. Serves 4.*]

    Lovely Food by Ruth Lowinsky

Garden Nectar

IIII

This beautiful ruby-coloured soup is an elegant variation of borscht. It can be served hot, chilled, or jellied. It looks best served in thin white china cups; sour cream may be served with it.

6 medium beetroots, coarsely chopped
4 carrots, coarsely chopped
2 stalks celery, coarsely chopped
2 lb [900 g] tomatoes, fresh or tinned, coarsely chopped
1 clove garlic, coarsely chopped
1 tsp chopped chives
1 medium onion, coarsely chopped
2 egg whites, lightly beaten
2 egg shells, crushed
1 tsp sugar
1 small bay leaf
3 cloves
5 black peppercorns
salt to taste

Scrub the beets and top them. Put them in a saucepan with the carrots and celery and cover with 3 pints [1.75 litres] water. Bring to the boil and cook till tender [*about 45 minutes*]. Strain off the liquid. In a separate pot put the tomatoes [*if fresh, add ¼ pt/150 ml water*], the garlic, the chives, the onion, the egg whites and shells, the sugar, a bay leaf, a few cloves and peppercorns, and salt to taste. Mash all together and cook over a slow fire for about ½ an hour, then strain through cheesecloth and add to the beet juice. [*Serves 8. If to be served cold, make a day in advance and chill overnight. If to be served en gelée, add ½ oz/15 g gelatine to every pint of liquid and chill overnight, then break up the jelly with a palette knife to serve in small cups or bowls. Sour cream may be served with the hot or chilled version, and lemon quarters with the jellied soup.*]

Vogue's Cookery Book edited by Hilda Powell

Celery Soup

IIII

Rarely seen nowadays except in a few good restaurants like Bibendum, celery soup was very popular before the war. It needs a generous sprinkling of chopped herbs to offset its pallor. It is always in season, and freezes well.

1 large bunch celery, inner stalks and leaves only, weighed after
    trimming, chopped (about 1 lb [450 g])
1½ oz [45 g] butter
1 lb [450 g] potatoes, peeled and chopped
2 pt [1.2 litres] light chicken stock
salt and black pepper
¼ pt [150 ml] single cream
1½ Tbs each finely chopped parsley and chives

Cook some finely cut hearts of celery in butter for 5 minutes, add same quantity of finely cut potatoes and braise [*covered*] for 10 minutes – cover well with stock and cook for 45 minutes – finish off with cream. [*Serves 6.*]

The Complete Hostess by Quaglino

Green Pea Soup

IIII

This exquisite soup is made from the recipe for jugged peas on page 124. At its best for a few short weeks in June and July, this strictly seasonal soup should on no account be overlooked.

approx. 12 oz [340 g] jugged peas, freshly cooked (see page 124)
1 pt [570 ml] light chicken stock
4 Tbs double cream

Discard the mint and put the jugged peas in the food processor with the chicken stock and cream, then process until blended. Taste for seasoning and adjust as required. Serve in small cups, white china for preference, hot or chilled. Serves 4.

AB

Bouillon de Poisson

||||

This is a good example of Marcel Boulestin's recipes: delicious, healthy and inexpensive, yet simple enough to fall within the ability of the most modest cook. It can be served as thick or thin as you like – in fact it is also good without being sieved at all – by passing through a coarse, medium or fine food mill, or through a sieve for a true bouillon. I don't bother with croutons, unless I have some rouille or grated Parmesan to top them with.

1–1½ lb [450 g–680 g] mixed white fish: cod, whiting, conger-eel, etc.
a few small crabs, when available
1½ Tbs olive oil
1 oz [30 g] butter
1 carrot, chopped
1 small onion, chopped
1 stalk celery, chopped
2 shallots, chopped
2 tomatoes, chopped
1 clove garlic, chopped
1 leek, chopped
1 sprig parsley
1 small bay leaf
1 sprig thyme
1 small sprig rosemary
sea salt and black pepper
½ tsp curry powder
6 fl oz [175 ml] dry white wine

Melt a small quantity of olive oil and butter mixed and fry in it one carrot, one onion, a piece of celery, two shallots, two tomatoes, one clove of garlic and one leek, all then cut in smallish pieces. Add a bouquet of parsley, bay leaf, thyme and rosemary, then add your fish also cut up in pieces, salt and pepper and a pinch of curry powder. Cook two minutes, then add a glass of dry white wine and [*1½ pt/825 ml*] boiling water, allowing for reduction. Bring to the boil and let it simmer for one hour, when it will be reduced by one-third.

Pass through a colander [*or food mill, or sieve*], pounding well the fish and vegetables against the sides, and serve the bouillon very hot, well spiced and with fried croutons. [*Makes 1½–2 pt/ 825 ml–1.2 litres, depending on the mill or sieve; serves 4–5.*]

What Shall We Have To Drink? by X. Marcel Boulestin

Goujons of Sole with Fried Parsley

▌▌▌▌

This was a favourite first course: small strips of sole, coated in egg and breadcrumbs, and deep-fried. They were often served with deep-fried parsley, crisp and emerald green, or with a fresh tomato sauce. The sauce was often cold, even semi-frozen. The piquant sauce on page 177 is a good example.

2 Dover sole, skinned and filleted
2 egg yolks
2 Tbs light olive oil
2 Tbs water
dry white breadcrumbs
frying oil

GARNISH
10 large sprigs parsley

Cut the fillets into strips diagonally, about ¾ inch [1.5 cm] wide. Beat the egg yolks with the olive oil and water. Dip the strips of fish in this, then in the crumbs. Heat the oil to about 360°F/180°C. Drop the goujons in, being careful not to crowd them, and cook for about 1½ minutes on each side, turning once. When they are golden brown and crisp, lift them out with a slotted spoon. Drain on kitchen paper, then transfer to a dish and keep warm. Allow the oil to come back to the desired temperature before putting in the next batch, then proceed as above. When all are done, lower the temperature of the oil slightly, to about 325°F/160°C, and drop in the sprigs of parsley, a few at a time. Cook them for about 30 seconds on each side, just long enough to become crisp and brittle, rather like the fried seaweed you get in Chinese restaurants. Drain on soft paper, then lay over and around the goujons. Serve immediately. Serves 4.

AB

Souchet of Slips

IIII

Lady Jekyll suggests this for supper before the theatre, since it combines soup and fish in one dish. It is quite delicious, and surprisingly exotic for an English dish, oddly reminiscent of Japanese food. (I tend to add a dash of soy sauce at the table, instead of the horseradish cream.) I make it whenever I can find slips in the market which is rare, alas. Dabs or other small flat fish can be used instead of sole, but do not have the same delicacy.

4 slips (baby soles), heads, tails and side fins removed, and
  skinned
some fish bones, preferably sole, plus the trimmings of the slips
  1 large onion, halved
  1 large carrot, halved
  1 large leek, halved
  2 stalks celery, halved
  5 sprigs parsley
  1 bay leaf
  ½ Tbs sea salt and 6 black peppercorns
  ¼ pt [150 ml] dry white wine

GARNISH
½ carrot, cut in thin strips, 1 inch x ¼ inch x ¼ inch [2.5 cm x
  5 mm x 5 mm]
½ leek, cut in thin strips, 1 inch x ¼ inch x ¼ inch [2.5 cm x 5 mm
  x 5 mm]
Horseradish cream (optional)

Make a fish stock with the fish bones and trimmings: put them in a large pan, adding the halved vegetables, herbs and seasonings. Pour on about 2½ pt [1.5 litres] water, adding a drop of white wine, or as much as you have handy. Bring slowly to the boil. Simmer gently for 30 minutes, then strain through a colander which you have lined with a cloth wrung out in hot water. Measure it; you will need just under 2 pt [1.2 litres] for four people. If you have more, reduce it by fast boiling, but do this after straining, not before. Then set aside.

Shortly before serving, bring a broad pan of salted water to the boil and reheat the fish stock in a separate pan. When the salted water boils, lower the heat and drop in the slips. Poach them gently for 5 minutes. While they are cooking, make the julienne garnish. When the fish stock reaches boiling point, drop in the strips of carrot and cook for 1 minute, then add the leeks and cook for another minute. When the slips have finished poaching, lift each one into a large soup plate, then ladle the fish consommé with its vegetable garnish over it. Serve at once, with the horseradish cream in a small dish, and brown bread and butter. Serves 4.

Adapted from *Kitchen Essays* by Lady Jekyll

Horseradish Cream

||||

¼ pt [150 ml] double cream, lightly whipped
1½ Tbs grated (fresh) horseradish, or Kochs Horseradish

Stir the grated horseradish into the lightly whipped cream, and serve in a small dish, with the souchet.

AB

Délices de Sole Murat

||||

An unusual combination of ingredients, this excellent dish is rarely, if ever, seen nowadays. Once popular as a first course, it is equally good today as a light main dish, needing no extra vegetable. It must be made with Dover sole, as lemon sole is not firm enough.

1 medium potato, peeled
2 artichokes
1 Dover sole, skinned and filleted
seasoned flour
1 oz [30 g] butter
2 tsp lemon juice
1½ Tbs finely chopped parsley

OPTIONAL GARNISH
2 tomatoes, thickly sliced
1½ Tbs olive oil

Boil the potato until tender; drain, then cut into ½ inch [1 cm] dice. Boil the artichokes, drain, then trim down to the bottoms and cut in cubes slightly smaller than the potato ones. Cut the fillets of sole into strips about 1½ inches [3.5 cm] by ½ inch [1 cm], roll them in seasoned flour, and fry in butter, adding a little lemon juice. Add the cubed potato and artichoke and cook all together for a few minutes, stirring gently. Serve on a round dish, sprinkled with chopped parsley. The dish may be garnished with a border of tomato slices which have been fried in olive oil. Serves 2.

Adapted from *Vogue's Cookery Book* edited by Hilda Powell

Filets de Sole Pochés

IIII

This utterly simple and exquisite dish should only be made with the very freshest of fish. It is very good served alone, after a surfeit of rich food, or as Boulestin suggests with melted butter or sauce mousseline (see page 180), or with sauce Dugléré (see page 178).

¼ pt [150 ml] dry white wine
sea salt and a few black peppercorns, roughly crushed
1 stalk parsley
1 bay leaf
1 mushroom, sliced
1 Dover sole, filleted, plus bones

A plain poached sole is not to be despised. It has flavour and delicacy, and is a very useful dish to serve as a contrast to 'rich' dishes. Put in a saucepan a glass [¼ pt/150 ml] of water, a glass [¼ pt/150 ml] of dry white wine, salt, coarsely broken peppercorns, parsley, bay leaf, one mushroom cut in slices and the bones of the sole. Bring to the boil and cook ten minutes, by which time the court bouillon is well flavoured. Put in the fillets of sole when boiling and let them poach for five to six minutes on a slow fire. When they are white and firm remove them, drain them well and serve at once with melted butter or sauce mousseline. [*Serves 1, but may be multiplied at will.*]

What Shall We Have Today? by X. Marcel Boulestin

Fillets of Sole with Horseradish Sauce

IIII

A favourite dish of Lord Berners, this came originally from the cold table at the Ritz. At Faringdon, it was served as a first course, at luncheon.

Make the poached fillets of sole on the previous page, using 2 large Dover sole for 4 people. After cooking, allow them to cool to room temperature, then lay them on a shallow dish and cover with the cold horseradish sauce on page 131. Chill for a couple of hours, then bring back to room temperature and sprinkle with 2 Tbs chopped chives before serving. Serves 4 as a first course, or 2 as a main dish. If serving as a main course, it may be accompanied by steamed or boiled new potatoes, served warm, and two salads: one of lettuce and one of sliced tomato.

Lady Harrod

Sole Dugléré

IIII

This was a speciality of the Savoy Hotel, served cold. It is still sometimes on their menu in the summer.

2 Dover sole, lemon sole, or plaice, skinned and filleted (8 fillets), with skin and bones

VEGETABLE TRIMMINGS
½ small onion, sliced
½ small carrot, sliced
ends of leek and celery
½ bay leaf
1 stalk parsley
salt and 6 black peppercorns
½ oz [15 g] butter
1 small onion, finely chopped
2 tomatoes, skinned, seeded and finely chopped
½ Tbs finely chopped parsley
freshly ground black pepper
4 Tbs dry white wine
½ Tbs flour
2 Tbs double cream

Put the fish bones, skins, etc. in a pan with the vegetable trimmings, bay leaf, parsley, salt and pepper. Just cover with water, bring to the boil, and simmer for 20 minutes. You only need 4 Tbs but keep the rest for another fish dish. Cut the fillets in half diagonally, so you have 16 pieces of fish. Melt the butter and cook the chopped onion until it softens and starts to colour, then add the chopped tomatoes and the parsley. Cook for 1 minute, adding salt and black pepper, then lay the fillets of fish on top of the tomatoes and spoon over them 4 Tbs fish stock and 4 Tbs dry white wine. Cover and simmer for 5–6 minutes, until they are cooked. Then transfer them to a shallow serving dish. Stir the flour into the cream and add to the pan, beating in well. Stir for 3 minutes over low heat, then pour over the fish and serve, either as a first course, or with boiled rice and a green salad as a light main dish. Serves 3 as a first course, or 2 as a main dish. To serve cold, cool the sauce quickly before pouring over the fish. (Stand it in a sink half full of cold water and stir to prevent a skin forming.) Serve at room temperature; do not chill.

AB

Fish Mayonnaise

IIII

This was usually served as a first course for a summer luncheon; today it would serve equally well as a main course. When crabs are not available, use twice the quantity of prawns. I sometimes lighten the mayonnaise by adding a little yoghurt, but this would not have been done then.

1¼ lb [570 g] haddock fillet (1 lb [450 g] after flaking)
12 oz [340 g] salmon steak, or tail end (8 oz [225 g] after flaking)
1 small crab, white meat only
8 oz [225 g] prawns
½ cucumber, peeled and diced

MAYONNAISE
2 egg yolks
½ pt [275 ml] light olive oil
5 Tbs yoghurt (optional)

salt and white pepper
lemon juice, to taste
6–8 feathery sprigs chervil, or 1½ Tbs chopped chives

62

For six you need enough home-made mayonnaise to coat 1 lb [450 g] fresh white poached fillet, ½ lb [225 g] flaked salmon, the flesh of one crab, a dozen large unshelled prawns for decoration, and a diced, well-drained cucumber. Mix all together carefully [*adding salt and pepper and lemon juice to taste*], arrange on a long white dish and garnish with snipped chives [*or sprigs of chervil. I keep back some of the cucumber dice and shelled prawns to scatter over the top, and lay the chervil, or chopped chives, over all. Serves 6 as a first course or 4 as a main dish*].

Eat At Pleasure Drink By Measure compiled by Olof Wijk

Smoked Salmon and Cream Cheese

||||

This is a useful way of using up a small amount of smoked salmon. It is good for canapés, or as part of a mixed hors d'oeuvre. I have made it less rich by using a low-fat cream cheese, and substituting yoghurt for half the cream.

8 oz [225 g] low-fat cream cheese
2 Tbs double cream
2 Tbs yoghurt
1 Tbs chopped chives or gherkins
6 slices pumpernickel
8 oz [225 g] smoked salmon
freshly ground black pepper
1 tsp lemon juice

Beat up some cream cheese with some double cream [*and yoghurt*] until it is fluffy and only just firm. Add chopped chives or finely chopped gherkins and spread it thickly on slices of pumpernickel [*cut in half for canapés*]. On the top of each slice, pile minced smoked salmon, sprinkle with a little black pepper and lemon juice. The mincing not only gives the smoked salmon a lightness and attractive appearance, but makes it go twice as far. [*Serves 6.*]

Eat At Pleasure Drink By Measure compiled by Olof Wijk

Salt Herrings

IIII

Pickled herrings were very popular, especially with the men. They exist in various forms – rollmops, soused herrings, etc. – and may be made with either fresh or salt herrings. These can be bought already prepared, in glass jars, but I prefer to make them myself.

4 herrings, split and boned
1 bay leaf, crumbled
1½ oz [45 g] coarse salt

Get the fishmonger to prepare the herrings for you. When you get them home, wash them well and pick out any bones that remain. Cut each one in half so that you have 8 fillets, trimming the edges neatly. Lay them in a rectangular dish and scatter the crumbled bay leaf over them. Put the salt in a heatproof jug and dissolve in a little very hot water. Then make up to ¾ pt [450 ml] with cold water and pour over the herrings. Place low down in the refrigerator for 24 hours, laying a small dish on the fish to keep them below the surface of the salt water. Next day, drain them and pat dry. They may be skinned or not, as desired. (The skins were left on for dishes of rollmops or Bismarck herrings.)

AB

Rollmops

IIII

Rollmops are uncooked herring fillets which have been salted, then left for a few days in a marinade. In the big houses these were usually laid out on the cold table at lunchtime, together with other cold dishes. In a more modest house, they would have been served as a first course, also at lunchtime. Bismarck herrings are made in exactly the same way, without being rolled up.

8 salt herring fillets, bought or home-made (see above)
½ medium onion, halved and thinly sliced
½ small pickled cucumber, or 1 dill pickle, cut in thin strips
3 bay leaves, crumbled
1 tsp mustard seed
8 black peppercorns

4 dried chillies
6 cloves
white wine (or malt) vinegar

If using bought salt herrings, soak them overnight in a mixture of milk and water to get rid of excess salt. If using home-made ones, simply rinse them and pat dry. Lay the fillets out flat, and put an onion slice and a strip of pickled cucumber on each one. Then roll them and pack tightly into a stoneware crock, or glass preserving jar, scattering the rest of the mixed seasoning over and among them. Using a mixture of vinegar and water, fill the crock (or jar) to the brim. If using wine vinegar, use ⅔ vinegar to ⅓ water; if using malt vinegar, use equal amounts of vinegar and water. Store in a cool larder, or at the bottom of the refrigerator, for at least 3 days, or up to 2 weeks. Serves 4.

AB

Cold Baked Eggs with Shrimps

This was a popular dish in the men's clubs, as a first course for lunch on a summer's day.

IIII

¼ oz [7 g] butter
4 large eggs
salt and black pepper
4 Tbs home-made mayonnaise
40 shrimps, peeled

Butter 4 ramekins (or oeuf en cocotte dishes) and break an egg into each one. Sprinkle with salt and pepper, stand them in a roasting tin half full of water, and bake for about 15 minutes at 325°F/170°C/gas 3, or until the whites are just set. Err on the shorter time, as the eggs will go on cooking slightly as they cool. Take them out of the roasting tin and leave to cool. Then spread 1 tablespoon mayonnaise over each one, and lay the shrimps over the top. Serve at room temperature; do not chill. Serves 4 as a first course.

AB

Shrimp Paste

||||

This lovely old-fashioned recipe should be made with small brown shrimps, although a simpler version can be made with prawns. It would have been served as a first course at lunch, or in sandwiches for picnics or tea. Today it serves equally well for dinner.

1 lb [450 g] brown shrimps, unshelled
1¼ lb [570 g] white fish fillet, i.e. haddock
sea salt and black pepper
ground mace
cayenne pepper
a dash of anchovy essence, or Tabasco
approx. 8 oz [225 g] butter

Shell the shrimps, and put heads and tails to boil in enough water to cover [*for 20 minutes*]. Drain, remove the heads and shells, and now cook the white fish in this shrimp water till soft. [*About 8 minutes, then drain.*] Let cool, and pound to a smooth paste [*or blend in a food processor*], with a careful seasoning of [*salt and pepper*], powdered mace, cayenne and one single spot of anchovy essence [*or a dash of Tabasco*]. Now measure, and add half as much butter. When smooth, stir in all the whole shrimps. Press into pots and flood with melted butter on top. The effect was a solid potful of shrimps, cemented together with a soft, delicately seasoned pink butter. It was a great delicacy and always served in fine white china. [*Makes about 1¼ lb/570 g; serves 6, with hot toast and lemon quarters. Once sealed with melted butter, the pots will keep for 2–3 weeks under refrigeration.*]

Food in England by Dorothy Hartley

Eggs Benedict

||||

This was an American dish which became very popular in England between the wars. It made an ideal dish for a late supper, eaten after the theatre, often in a nightclub. It was also popular with the sophisticated hostesses as a luncheon dish. Muffins were easily obtainable then; Elizabeth David (in English Bread and Yeast Cookery) *writes of hearing the muffin-man ringing his bell on Primrose Hill in the 1930s; apparently he made his rounds at weekends, mid-afternoon, just in time for tea. For many years they were almost impossible to buy, and quite a lot of work to make at home, but today they can be found in several of the big supermarkets. A recipe for making them can be found in* English Bread and Yeast Cookery.

4 muffins (bought, or 2 home-made muffins, split in half)
1 oz [30 g] butter
4 small slices ham, not too thin
4 eggs, freshly poached and drained
Hollandaise sauce (see page 180)

Toast the muffins under the grill, and butter the split (holey) side. Lay a slice of ham on each and trim to fit. Then lay a poached egg on the ham, and cover with a large spoonful of hollandaise sauce. Serve immediately. At whatever time of day this delicious dish is served, it needs no accompaniment, but may be followed by a green salad if desired. Serves 4.

AB

Egg Croquettes

IIII

Egg croquettes, sometimes called egg cutlets, were a popular first course for luncheon. They were usually served with a spicy tomato sauce, like the piquant sauce on page 177, or with fried parsley (see page 180). They are best made a day in advance and left overnight in the refrigerator to firm up.

3 hard-boiled eggs

PANADA
1 oz [30 g] butter
1 oz [30 g] flour
¼ pt [150 ml] milk

salt and black pepper
1 Tbs chopped parsley
1 egg, beaten
dry white breadcrumbs

FOR FRYING
1 oz [30 g] butter
1½ Tbs sunflower oil

Chop the hard-boiled eggs, make a panada [*thick white sauce*] with the butter, flour, and milk, add the eggs, season with salt and pepper, mix well [*adding the chopped parsley*], place on a wet plate [*and chill in the refrigerator overnight. Next day*], divide into equal portions, form into cork shapes, coat with egg and breadcrumbs, fry a golden brown in hot [*butter and oil*]. Serve on a hot dish, garnish with fried parsley. Enough to make eight croquettes. [*Serves 3.*]

A *Year's Dinners* by May Little

Oeufs Cendrillon

▌▌▌▌

This was a speciality of The Travellers' Club, and it comes courtesy of the late Robin McDouall, who was Secretary of The Travellers' Club for twenty-nine years. Before the war, this would have been served as a first course, but nowadays it seems more like a light main dish, or even a meal in its own right.

4 large floury potatoes

SAUCE MORNAY
½ pt [275 ml] milk
½ bay leaf
a pinch of mace
1 thick slice of onion
2 cloves
salt and black pepper
1 oz [30 g] butter
2 Tbs flour
2 oz [55 g] freshly grated Parmesan

POTATO PUREE
½ oz [15 g] butter
4 Tbs milk
salt and pepper

4 eggs

Bake the potatoes for 1¼ hours at 400°F/200°C/gas 6, until soft. While they are baking, make the sauce. Put the milk in a small pan with the bay leaf, mace, onion, cloves, and salt and pepper. Bring slowly to the boil, then remove from the heat and stand, covered, for 20 minutes. Then strain and reheat. In a clean pan, melt the butter, add the flour, and cook for 1 minute, stirring. Then add the reheated milk and bring back to the boil, stirring till smooth. Simmer for 3 minutes, adding salt and pepper to taste. Stir in the grated cheese, keeping back ½ oz [15 g]. Set aside.

When the potatoes are ready, cut a slice off the top of each and scoop out the flesh. Purée about ⅔ of it, adding a scrap of butter, a little hot milk, and salt and pepper to taste. Pile back into the skins, making generous hollows to hold the eggs. Keep warm while you poach the eggs. Drain them, then slip one into each potato. Spoon the sauce over them, sprinkle with the reserved Parmesan, and brown quickly under the grill. Serves 4.

Adapted from *Clubland Cooking* by Robin McDouall

Oeufs Mollets à l'Indienne

IIII

A dish of cold curried eggs: just the sort of thing you might be offered as the first course for a summer lunch. The eggs may be hard-boiled if preferred.

MAYONNAISE
1 egg yolk
salt and pepper
a little dry mustard
¼ pt [150 ml] oil
1 tsp white wine vinegar
1 tsp lemon juice
2 Tbs lightly whipped cream

4 large eggs
1 tsp curry powder
1 onion, finely chopped
1 Tbs oil
5 Tbs pulped tomatoes, fresh or preserved
5 Tbs dry white wine
sea salt and black pepper

2 tsp lemon juice
1½ Tbs sieved apricot jam
2 Tbs thick (or lightly whipped) cream
5 oz [140 g] rice, boiled and drained
paprika

First prepare the mayonnaise [*see page 181*], adding a little whipped cream. Place the eggs in boiling water and boil for 5 minutes from the time the water comes back to boiling point. Put immediately into cold water and leave 7–8 minutes, then peel carefully and slip into fresh cold water until wanted. Meanwhile, cook the curry and onion in the oil until soft, add the tomato pulp, wine, seasonings, and lemon; continue cooking for a few minutes and then strain. Add the curry sauce and apricot jam to the mayonnaise to taste, adding cream to mellow the flavour. Arrange the rice down the centre of a serving dish, dry the eggs and place on this. Spoon over the curry cream and garnish with a dusting of paprika. [*Serves 4.*]

The Constance Spry Cookery Book by Constance Spry and Rosemary Hume

Mimosa Eggs

IIII

Egg dishes were very popular, especially as first courses for luncheon parties. This is one of the best: light, pretty and quickly made.

6 large eggs
1½ oz [45 g] butter
3 Tbs flour
¾ pt [450 ml] milk, heated
3 Tbs freshly grated Parmesan
sea salt and black pepper

Hard-boil the number of eggs required. When done, put them under the cold water tap for a few minutes. Shell them, remove the yolks, slice the whites into thin slices, and put in a [*shallow*] fireproof dish. [*A white porcelain quiche dish works well.*] While the eggs are cooking, make a thick white sauce with the butter, flour and hot milk, working into a perfectly smooth cream with a wooden spoon, then add the grated cheese, and salt and pepper. Pour the sauce over the whites of egg, rub the yolks through a coarse sieve [or *Moulinex cheese grater*] over this and put in the oven for 3 minutes. [*At 375°F/190°C/gas 5. Or prepare in advance and reheat, loosely covered with foil, for 30 minutes at 325°F/170°C/gas 3. Sprinkle with a little finely chopped parsley before serving. Serves 4–5 as a first course, or 3 as a light main dish, with a green salad.*]

Lightning Cookery by Countess Morphy

Egg Mousse

▐▌▐

Most egg mousses – and there were many – were bland and slightly boring, but this one is superior, partly because the eggs are roughly chopped instead of being sieved, and partly because it is served with a sharp sauce of uncooked tomatoes. I have added some grated horseradish and substituted Tabasco for the anchovy essence.

6 hard-boiled eggs
1 Tbs gelatine
7 fl oz [200 ml] thick mayonnaise (home-made)
salt, pepper, cayenne
a dash of anchovy essence, or Tabasco
1–2 Tbs grated horseradish (optional)
2 Tbs lightly whipped cream

GARNISH (OPTIONAL)
½ bunch watercress, tender ends only

Chop the eggs coarsely and set aside. Dissolve the gelatine in 4 Tbs very hot water and while still hot add to the mayonnaise. Whisk well while cooling. Season highly, add the eggs [*horseradish, if used*], and lastly the whipped cream. Turn into a plain mould or soufflé dish. Leave to set. [*2–3 hours, or overnight, in the refrigerator.*]

Turn out and garnish. [*Or, serve in its dish, which precludes a garnish. Serve with the piquant sauce on page 177, in a sauceboat. Serves 3 as a first course, or 2 as a light main dish, with a green salad.*]

Party Food and Drink by Rosemary Hume

Oeufs Pochés Surprises

||||

A slightly more substantial version of oeufs en gelée, these need some oval metal moulds, or small china dishes, and some really good chicken stock. Given that, they are simple and inexpensive to make, yet elegant and appetising in appearance. They were a popular first course for summer luncheons, both in restaurants and at home. Today they may be served as a light main course, allowing two eggs per person.

1 pt [570 ml] chicken stock
2 large sprigs tarragon, plus 6 large leaves
6 eggs
½ oz [15 g] gelatine
6 large thin slices ham

GARNISH
a few sprigs watercress, or rocket, or small lettuce leaves

Put the chicken stock, strained and free from all fat, in a pan with the sprigs of tarragon, reserving 6 perfect leaves for the garnish. Bring slowly to the boil, then remove from the heat and stand for 30 minutes, covered. While it rests, poach the eggs and drain on a cloth. (Or, if you prefer, boil them for exactly 5 minutes, then drop into cold water and leave to cool before shelling.) When the stock has finished infusing, strain it and reheat 5 or 6 tablespoons. Dissolve the gelatine in this, then mix it with the rest of the stock. Pour enough to make a thin layer into each of 6 oval moulds, or dishes – the shape is important. Lay a tarragon leaf on each, then chill until the jelly has set. Trim 12 oval pieces of ham to fit the moulds, then lay one in each. Place a poached or soft-boiled egg in each mould, and cover with another piece of ham. Then pour over enough stock to cover, and chill for a few hours, or overnight. To serve, turn out on to a flat dish and garnish with sprigs of watercress, or rocket, or tiny lettuce leaves. Serves 6 as a first course, or 3–4 as a light main dish.

Adapted from *Lady Sysonby's Cook Book*

FIRST COURSES

A Summer First-Course Dish

▌|||

This is a delightfully simple dish, just the thing for a summer luncheon, or for an elegant picnic. I serve it in crisp lettuce leaves.

5 hard-boiled eggs, cooled and shelled
12 oz [340 g] shelled shrimps, or prawns

MAYONNAISE
1 egg yolk
¼ pt [150 ml] olive oil
1–2 tsp lemon juice
4 Tbs whipping cream

GARNISH
thinly sliced brown bread
unsalted butter
mustard and cress
small lettuce leaves, i.e. Little Gem

Take hard-boiled eggs, cut in small pieces, and same quantity of shelled shrimps [*or prawns*]. Mix up with a good cream mayonnaise sauce [*see page 181*]. Make very cold [*chill for 2–3 hours*] and serve with sandwiches of brown bread and mustard and cress. [*I usually pile the mixture into small lettuce leaves and lay on a platter. If small lettuces are not available, line small bowls with larger leaves and fill with the shellfish and eggs. Serves 3–4, as a first course.*]

Food for the Greedy *by Nancy Shaw*

Tomato Jelly Ring

▌|||

A chilled tomato jelly was originally an American dish which became popular in London about this time. Ideal as the first course for a summer luncheon, the ring can be filled with warm scrambled egg, as suggested here, or with a number of alternative fillings, based on shellfish, rice, avocados or cucumbers. The jelly is especially good when made with freshly squeezed tomatoes, but for this you need a vegetable juice extractor.

73

1 pt [570 ml] tomato juice, freshly made if possible
salt and pepper
celery salt to taste
paprika to taste
1 Tbs lemon juice
1 tsp sugar
1 tsp tomato ketchup, or ½ tsp Tabasco
½ oz [15 g] gelatine (1 packet)

A tomato jelly is a very nice garniture for a mixed salad, and it can also be used as the basis for a number of summer luncheon dishes. To make it, add seasonings of salt, pepper, celery salt, paprika, lemon juice, sugar, and tomato ketchup [*or Tabasco*] to a pint of tomato juice. [*Made at home for best results, in a juice extractor.*] Melt the gelatine in a little of the mixture made hot, pour into the rest of the juice, and stir well. Set in a ring mould. The centre can be filled with hot scrambled eggs, a combination of hot and cold that is surprisingly good. [*Serves 4.*]

Vogue's Cookery Book edited by Hilda Powell

Fillings for Tomato Jelly Ring

IIII   *I. Warm scrambled eggs*

4 large eggs
sea salt and black pepper
½ oz [15 g] butter
2 tsp chopped chives

GARNISH (OPTIONAL)
1 bunch thin asparagus, tips only

About 30 minutes before serving, cook the asparagus tips, if used. Beat the eggs lightly, adding sea salt and black pepper, and warm the butter in a shallow pan. Scramble the eggs as usual, then set aside for about 15 minutes before serving. Just before taking to the table, spoon the eggs into the centre of the ring and scatter the chopped chives over them. Arrange the asparagus tips around the ring and serve.

‖‖   *II. Sliced avocados in oil and lemon*

2 avocados
2 Tbs olive oil
1 Tbs lemon juice
sea salt and black pepper
½ bunch spring onions, bulbs only, sliced
2 Tbs chopped chives

Shortly before serving, prepare the avocados. After stoning and
peeling, cut them in quarters, then in small thick slices. Mix gently
with the oil and lemon juice, sea salt and black pepper. Stir in the
spring onions, then spoon into the centre of the ring. Scatter the
chopped chives over and serve soon after making.

AB

Macaroni Cheese

*This was a very popular luncheon dish, both in the
nursery and for simple meals in the dining-room.*

‖‖

8 oz [225 g] macaroni, cooked and drained

WHITE SAUCE
2 oz [55 g] butter
4 Tbs flour
1 pt [570 ml] full cream milk
salt and black pepper

4 oz [120 g] grated cheese: Cheddar, Gruyère, or Emmenthal
½ oz [15 g] butter

[*Cook half a pound of macaroni. Drain it well. Meanwhile prepare a
white sauce. The sauce must be kept to a consistency of thin cream.*]
Take a [*buttered*] fireproof dish. Pour in a thin coat of the sauce.
Sprinkle two [*heaped*] tablespoons of grated cheese. Then make a
bed with a third of the macaroni. Flatten it with a fork, pour some
of the sauce over it and sprinkle two [*heaped*] tablespoons of grated
cheese. Go on until all the macaroni is in. Pour over it what you
have kept of the sauce, which ought to be almost half of the whole
quantity. Sprinkle with two more [*heaped*] tablespoons of grated
cheese. Place here and there some small dabs of butter, and put

into a medium oven until the surface is a good golden colour [*40 minutes at 350°F/180°C/gas 4*], and the dish of macaroni is very hot and swollen. Serve in the dish. [*Serves 5–6, with a green salad.*]

Be Your Own Chef by Lucie Marion

Cauliflower Gratin

||||

A dish which seems to have graduated from the nursery to the dining-room, at least for simple meals like lunch or supper. It could be found equally well as a first course, before cold meat and salad, for instance, or as a light main dish.

2 small cauliflowers
salt
2½ oz [70 g] butter
3 Tbs flour
½ pt [275 ml] chicken stock
¼ pt [150 ml] single cream
pepper
1 oz [30 g] coarse breadcrumbs
½ oz [15 g] freshly grated Parmesan

OPTIONAL EXTRAS
4 oz [120 g] chopped ham
4 oz [120 g] rice

Cook the cauliflowers in lightly salted boiling water, either whole, or divided into florets. Drain well in a colander. If cooked whole, divide into fat sprigs after cooking, and cut the stalks into chunks. Lay them in a shallow dish which you have buttered well. To make the sauce, melt 2 oz [55 g] butter, add flour, and cook for 1 minute, stirring. Heat stock and cream together and pour on, stirring till blended. Simmer for 3 minutes, adding salt and pepper to taste. Pour the sauce over the cauliflower. Toss the breadcrumbs for a moment or two in ¼ oz [7 g] butter in a non-stick frying pan; stop as soon as they are light golden and crisp. Mix with the grated Parmesan and scatter over the surface of the dish. Reheat for 15 minutes at 350°F/180°C/gas 4, then brown quickly under the grill. Alternatively, make in advance and then cook for 30 minutes at the same temperature. Serves 4 as a first course, or 2–3 as a light main dish.

If serving as a main dish, you may like to add one (or both) of the following: some chopped ham, scattered over and among the sprigs of cauliflower, before pouring on the sauce; some long-grain rice, freshly boiled and well drained, laid in the bottom of the dish, underneath the cauliflower. In either of these cases, it will serve 4 as a main dish.

AB

Vermicelli Soufflé

IIII

This sort of dish was popular at the time as a luncheon dish, either as a substantial first course with some cold meat and salad to follow, or as a light main dish. I have had the recipe for many years but alas have forgotten the source.

4 oz [120 g] vermicelli
8 oz [225 g] tomatoes, skinned and chopped
2 oz [55 g] butter
2 Tbs flour
7 fl oz [200 ml] milk, heated
3 oz [85 g] grated Parmesan
salt and black pepper
3 egg yolks, beaten
4 egg whites
paprika

Cook the vermicelli in boiling salted water and drain well. Cook the tomatoes for a few moments in half the butter, then mix with the vermicelli. Put in the bottom of a buttered soufflé dish. Make a sauce with the remaining butter, flour, and heated milk. Stir in the grated cheese and season well with salt and black pepper. Add the beaten egg yolks off the heat. Beat the egg whites until stiff and fold in. Pour half the soufflé mixture over the vermicelli and mix lightly. Pour the rest on top and sprinkle with paprika. Cook for 25 minutes at 350°F/180°C/gas 4. Serve immediately. Serves 5–6 as a first course, or 4 as a main dish.

AB

MAIN COURSES

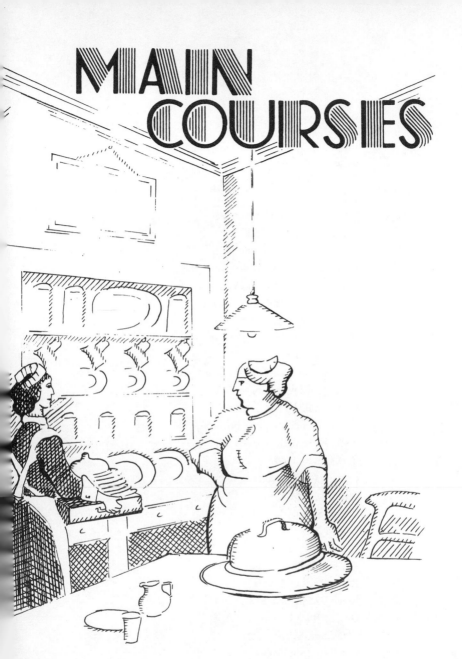

Main Courses

IIII
IIII

Main courses differed, depending on the environment and the time of day. In London, the main dish at lunchtime would probably be poultry, game, or fish, while in the country it was usually what was termed 'butcher's meat', or game. These would not have been roasts, but simple dishes like Irish stew or Lancashire hotpot, braised oxtail or beef olives: all the traditional meat dishes which were considered too heavy to serve in the evening.

For dinner, either in London or the country, meat or game was almost always served, usually plainly roasted. In the great Catholic houses, fish was always served on Fridays and fast days, but it was often very luxurious; lobster hardly seems a penance to our way of thinking.

Although the dishes themselves were simple, the manner of their serving had become more sophisticated, and this applied to the simplest dish as well as the grandest. A Lancashire hotpot was rarely cooked in its traditional lidded earthenware pot any more, except perhaps in Lancashire. Further south, meat and potatoes were layered in a broad shallow dish, thus presenting a neater appearance for serving at table, and facilitating the service. For a dinner party, a saddle of lamb was carved in the kitchen, the resulting cavity filled with a purée of turnips, and the strips of meat laid across it. Joints of meat were only carved at the table for family meals; for a dinner party they were always carved in the kitchen, and the slices of meat laid on a large dish, surrounded with piles of different vegetables.

Garnishes were carefully considered and rated of importance, but they differed widely from those of today. For garnishing was done with restraint, using materials intrinsic to the dish. Leeks and celery might be cut in julienne strips for laying over a dish of braised oxtail, while carrots and mushrooms were cut in flower shapes for garnishing a game casserole. A whole poached fish might be surrounded with a border of semi-circular slices of lemon alternating with sprigs of parsley; the effect was light, colourful and pleasing.

While most of the dishes are traditional, therefore familiar, one or two strike us as echoes of another age. The grilled rack of lamb, for instance, is a survival from Edwardian times that was still served in one or two houses. This was a twice-cooked dish, like the French range of dishes called Sainte-Ménéhould, where pigs' feet and breast of lamb are braised ahead of time, then coated with breadcrumbs and grilled, for serving with a piquant sauce. This sort of dish is calculated to appeal to the Englishman's palate: clean, crisp and dry, served with a separate, contrasting sauce or garnish. There is something rather delicious about well-cooked meat when it has been done intentionally, and braising is a better medium for this than roasting, since the meat stays moist and juicy.

Roast beef was always served medium rare, and the large joints then customary gave a nice range of doneness, stretching from the well-done outer crust to the pinkness in the centre. Mutton and lamb were always well-cooked, as were pork and veal. Game, on the other hand, was served very rare, and well-hung. When in prime condition, it was almost always roasted, except in the case of partridge, which was sometimes boiled, wrapped in a vine leaf, for serving cold, at breakfast or supper. When past their prime, game birds were slowly stewed in pies and casseroles, terrines and soups.

In old-fashioned houses, few fish dishes were served as a main course, except on fast days. The exceptions were those that incorporated pastry or potatoes, like fish pie, or rice, like fish curry. The same applied to salmon, and to boiled cod with egg or parsley sauce, which was often served for lunch on Friday. A whole Dover sole might be considered suitable as a main luncheon dish, but the endless dishes of sole fillets in sauce, or fried, were more often served as first courses. Inevitably, such things varied from house to house, according to personal tastes; Lord Berners, for instance, used to have lobster as a first course for Sunday lunch, often followed by chicken pie, and a cream pudding.

Some of the more sophisticated London hostesses started serving main courses of pasta and vegetables at luncheon, but this did not always appeal to the men, who still expected to eat meat at every meal. In ways like these, the country trailed several years, if not decades, behind the city. I remember the dismay on our country landlord's face when presented with kedgeree as a main course one evening in my mother's holiday cottage. This was in the early 1950s, when we were both learning to cook, but we had been living in London since the war, and had lost touch with the countryman's tastes.

Fish Pie

▎▎▎▎

This is a uniquely English dish, since it does not exist in quite the same form in any other country. It is just this sort of bland, comforting food that the English miss when living abroad.

1½ lb [680 g] haddock or cod fillet
½ pt [275 ml] milk
¾ oz [20 g] butter
1 Tbs flour
sea salt and black pepper
2 Tbs chopped parsley
3 large hard-boiled eggs, coarsely chopped
12 oz [340 g] tomatoes, skinned and thickly sliced (optional)

POTATO PUREE
1½ lb [680 g] floury potatoes
¼ pt [150 ml] milk
2 oz [55 g] butter, cut in bits
sea salt and black pepper

Put the fish in a broad pan and pour over the milk. Add enough cold water to barely cover the fish. Bring to the boil, cover and simmer for about 8 minutes, or until the fish is cooked. While it cooks, start boiling the potatoes for the potato purée. When the fish is ready, lift it out and strain the cooking liquor. Measure 7 fl oz [200 ml] and set aside. Flake the fish, chopping the large flakes in half, and discard all skin and bone. Make a sauce as usual with the butter, flour and measured fish liquor. Season well with sea salt and black pepper, then fold in the flaked fish and chopped parsley. When all is well mixed, turn into a soufflé dish which it fills by slightly more than half. Cover with the coarsely chopped eggs, and the sliced tomatoes, if used. Finish making the potato purée and spread it over the tomatoes so that all is covered. Reheat for 15 minutes at 325°F/170°C/gas 3. Alternatively, make in advance and reheat for 40 minutes at the same temperature, standing in a roasting tin half full of water. Do not overheat, or the sauce will boil and merge with the potato purée. Serves 4, with a green salad.

AB

Baked Cod

IIII

An excellent way of cooking a large piece of cod, an alternative to boiled cod with parsley sauce for Good Friday.

2½ lb [1.15 kg] cod, on the bone
4 oz [120 g] butter
juice of 1 large lemon
salt and black pepper
4–6 Tbs dry breadcrumbs

Lay the fish in a buttered fireproof dish and surround it with the butter cut in pieces. Pour the lemon juice over the fish, season with salt and pepper, and cover with a buttered piece of foil. Bake for 30 minutes at 350°F/180°C/gas 4. Take out of the oven and peel away the top layer of skin. Scatter the breadcrumbs over the top surface of the fish, making a thick layer. Baste with the butter and lemon juice in the dish, and return to the oven for a further 30 minutes, uncovered, or until the fish comes away from the bone easily. Baste once or twice during the second half of the cooking. Serve in the same dish, with boiled (or steamed) potatoes. Serves 4–6.

AB

Curried Cod

IIII

A simple dish for family meals, but good none the less.

1½ lb [680 g] cod
2 oz [55 g] butter
1 medium onion, chopped
8 oz [225 g] tomatoes, skinned and crushed to a pulp
1 Tbs curry powder
sea salt and black pepper
juice of ½ lemon

Boil the cod in salted water for about 15 to 20 minutes, till tender. Place in a colander and drain well. While the cod is cooking make the following sauce: melt 2 oz [55 g] butter in a frying pan. When hot, put in the chopped onion, and cook till slightly brown, then add the pulp of ½ lb [225 g] tomatoes, stir in 1 Tbs curry powder, salt and pepper. Cook this, stirring occasionally, while the cod is boiling. [*When it is cooked, drain it, then break into large chunks free from skin and bone.*] Place the fish, well-drained of all water, on a hot dish, pour the sauce over it, and add the juice of ½ a lemon. [*Serves 4, with rice.*]

Lightning Cookery by Countess Morphy

Sole Colbert

IIII

This is the best ever way of cooking Dover sole, in my opinion. Once a standby of Wheeler's Fish Restaurant – the original Wheeler's was an oyster bar in Old Compton Street, which opened in 1929 – the correct presentation does demand a degree of expertise, but even if the removal of the backbone is omitted, it still tastes just as good.

1 x 14 oz [400 g] Dover sole per person, minus head and skinned
seasoned flour
1 egg, beaten
dry white breadcrumbs
sunflower oil

MAITRE D'HOTEL BUTTER (ENOUGH FOR TWO)
½ oz [15 g] butter
1 tsp chopped parsley
½ tsp lemon juice

Make an incision down the centre of the thick side, between the two fillets, and cut through a section of the backbone about 2 inches [5 cm] long. Dip in seasoned flour and coat with egg and breadcrumbs. Fry till golden brown in sunflower oil, then part the fillets where they have been cut, and remove the section of bone. Have maître d'hôtel butter made in advance and chilled: mash the butter with the back of a wooden spoon, work in the chopped parsley and lemon juice, and chill until firm. Put a lump of the butter in the opening and serve straight away. Serves 1. Alternatively, for a simpler version, omit the cutting and removal of the backbone and serve the whole fish with a slice of maître d'hôtel butter lying on it.

Adapted from *A Year's Dinners* by May Little

Haddock Monte Carlo

▌||

One of the few fish dishes substantial enough to rate as a main course, this would probably have been served at a ladies' lunch, or for a light supper. Alternatively, it could have been served as a first course, with some cold meat and salad to follow.

2 large smoked haddock, or 2 lb [900 g] smoked haddock fillet
½ pt [275 ml] milk
4 tomatoes, sliced
¼ pt [150 ml] single cream
freshly ground black pepper
4 eggs, lightly poached

Cook the haddock in the milk [*mixed with an equal amount of water*] for about 10 minutes. Take the flesh from the bones, keeping it as far as possible in four large fillets and discarding the skin with the bones. Arrange the fillets in a buttered fireproof dish, slice the tomatoes over the top, season [*with freshly ground black pepper*]. Reduce the fish-flavoured milk [*by half*] by fast boiling, and add cream. Pour over the fish and tomatoes and finish quickly in the oven [*15 minutes at 375°F/190°C/gas 5*]. Arrange lightly poached eggs on top. [*Serves 4, with a lettuce salad.*]

Wheeler's Fish Cookery Book by Macdonald Hastings and Carole Walsh

Poached Salmon

The classic method for poaching salmon to eat cold is both simple and foolproof, providing you have a fish kettle that roughly fits the fish. Simply cover the fish with cold water, add salt, bring to the boil, turn off the heat and leave, covered, until it has cooled. Whatever its size, the fish will be perfectly cooked. (The only time this will not work is if the pan is much too big for the fish, or if the fish fits it too tightly, without leaving enough space for an adequate quantity of water.) Cold salmon was invariably served with mayonnaise, hot (or warm) new potatoes, and a cucumber salad. The fish was served simply, with its top skin removed, and garnished with thinly sliced cucumber, sprigs of parsley, and/or lemon slices.

Hot poached salmon is treated in much the same way. (Salmon is never cooked in a court bouillon, at least in Britain.) Cover the fish with lightly salted cold water and bring to the boil. Calculate the cooking time; this depends on the thickness of the fish rather than its weight, and will probably be from 15 to 25 minutes. Time it from the moment the water boils. When the time is up, drain it and transfer to a serving dish. Lift off the top skin; hot salmon is not garnished. Serve with hollandaise, new potatoes and green peas, or asparagus.

AB

Corn Meal Soufflé

IIII

This shows the relaxed American influence prevalent at the time, in some circles at least, and is a good example of the new style of entertaining. It is not a true soufflé, rising only an inch or so, and is equally good after it has sunk back. Mrs Lancaster suggests serving it with cold ham; it is also good with Parmesan bacon (see page 236), or bacon crisps (see page 236). A lettuce salad is almost obligatory.

16 fl oz [480 ml] milk
3 oz [85 g] corn meal, or polenta
½ oz [15 g] butter
3–4 Tbs freshly grated Parmesan
1 tsp sea salt
¼ tsp paprika
a few grains cayenne
3 eggs, separated

This is an excellent luncheon dish combined with cold ham and a green salad. Heat the milk to boiling point, then stir in the white or yellow corn meal and 1 tablespoon [*½ oz/15 g*] butter. Reduce the heat and stir in 3 tablespoons, or more, grated cheese. Cook these ingredients to the consistency of mush [*5 minutes*]. Season with 1 teaspoon salt, ¼ teaspoon paprika, a few grains of cayenne. Add 3 beaten egg yolks. Cook and stir for a minute longer to permit the egg yolks to thicken. Cool these ingredients, whip until stiff, then fold in 3 [*stiffly beaten*] egg whites. Bake the soufflé in an ungreased 7 inch [18 cm] baking dish [*it does not need to be more than 2 inches/5 cm deep*], in a moderate oven [*350°F/180°C/gas 4*] until it is slightly crusty, about 30–35 minutes. Serves 3.

Mrs Nancy Lancaster

Baked Chicken with Noodles

IIII

A useful dish for a party in that it can be prepared in advance, and needs nothing more than a green salad as accompaniment.

4 lb [1.8 kg] roasting chicken

FLAVOURING VEGETABLES
1 onion, halved
1 leek, halved

1 carrot, halved
2 stalks celery, halved
1 bay leaf
3 stalks parsley
salt and 8 black peppercorns

12 oz [340 g] noodles
sea salt and black pepper
2 oz [55 g] grated Gruyère or Emmenthal
½ oz [15 g] grated Parmesan
¼ oz [7 g] butter

CREAM SAUCE
1 oz [30 g] butter
2½ Tbs flour
½ pt [275 ml] chicken stock (from poaching chicken)
¼ pt [150 ml] single cream
2 egg yolks

GARNISH
1 oz [30 g] grated Gruyère, or Emmenthal

Boil a good, tender chicken [*about 1¼ hours, with flavouring veg-etables, herbs and seasonings*]. Boil noodles in one quart [1.2 litres] boiling salted water for fifteen minutes [*or less*]. Drain and season with salt, pepper, grated Swiss and grated Parmesan cheese. Butter a round baking dish and fill to three-quarters of its depth with the noodles. Place on top of the noodles, the chicken from which you have previously removed the skin, and cut into pieces about two to three inches [5–7.5 cm] long and an inch [2.5 cm] wide. Make a rich cream sauce with the bouillon of the chicken, and thick fresh cream. [*Melt butter, add flour and cook for 1 minute, stirring. Then add heated stock and bring to the boil, adding salt and pepper to taste. Stir in the cream and simmer gently for 4 minutes, stirring often.*] Thicken well with the yolks of eggs. [*Remove from the heat and allow to cool slightly, before stirring in the beaten egg yolks. Replace over the fire and stir over very gentle heat for 3 minutes, without allowing it to boil.*] Pour this sauce over the chicken and noodles. Sprinkle over the top a good covering of grated Swiss cheese and brown in a hot oven. [*Or under the grill. Or make in advance and reheat for 30–35 minutes at 350°F/180°C/gas 4. Serves 6.*]

Elsie de Wolfe's Recipes for Successful Dining

Pulled and Grilled Chicken

IIII

This is a fairly complex dish which was popular in grand households between the wars. This recipe comes from Polesden Lacey, Mrs Greville's house near Guildford.

4 lb [1.8 kg] chicken

VELOUTE SAUCE
1 oz [30 g] butter
2 Tbs flour
7 fl oz [200 ml] chicken stock
3 fl oz [75 ml] single cream
sea salt and white pepper

DEVIL MIXTURE
3 Tbs chutney, not too sweet
2 tsp English (made) mustard
2 tsp Dijon mustard
1 Tbs Worcestershire Sauce

1½ oz [45 g] dry white breadcrumbs
¼ oz [7 g] butter

Boil or roast the chicken as usual, then remove the white meat from the breast and wings and pull it into coarse shreds, using two forks. Make the velouté sauce, using some of the chicken stock if you have boiled the chicken. (If you choose to roast it, make a little stock in advance from the neck, wing tips, etc. You only need 7 fl oz/200 ml.) Keep warm, while you devil the brown meat. Carve the legs into 4 neat joints. Make the devil mixture: mix the chutney with the two mustards and the Worcestershire Sauce. Make small slits in the outside of the joints, through the skin, and rub all over with the devil mixture, then coat with crumbs. Dot with tiny bits of butter and grill until golden brown, turning to colour evenly.

To serve, stir the pulled chicken into the velouté sauce and reheat gently. Pour into the centre of a shallow dish and lay the grilled joints around the edge. Serves 4.

Adapted from *English Country House Cooking* by Fortune Stanley

Roast Chicken in Cream

IIII

This was one of Lord Berners' recipes, typical of the period; it also works well with roast pheasant. Lord Berners was inordinately fond of rich food, and liked to have cream in every course. This caused one of his friends and travelling companions, Siegfried Sassoon, much suffering, for his preferred diet was fried sole and milk puddings, eaten late at night, for he, like Proust, liked to work all night and spend the days in bed. I substitute Chambéry vermouth for the sherry.

2–3 onions, sliced
2 oz [55 g] butter
4 lb [1.8 kg] roasting chicken
sea salt and black pepper
¼ pt [150 ml] double cream
3 Tbs dry sherry or Madeira (or medium dry vermouth)
1 Tbs lemon juice

Cook the sliced onions slowly in the butter, allowing about 15 minutes for them to soften. Then add the chicken, sprinkle with salt and black pepper, and turn to brown on all sides. Then cover the casserole and cook for 1¼ hours at 325°F/170°C/gas 3. Lay the chicken on its side for the first ½ hour, then on the other side for ½ an hour, then turn it right side up for the last 15 minutes. Test to make sure it is done before removing to a carving platter; keep warm while you make the sauce. Strain the juices into a clean pan; skim off most of the fat, discard the sliced onions. Heat slowly, adding the cream, vermouth and lemon juice. Boil steadily for 2–3 minutes. Adjust seasoning to taste. Carve the chicken, lay on a shallow dish, and pour over a little of the sauce; serve the rest separately, in a sauceboat. Accompany the chicken with rice or noodles, and a green vegetable. Serves 4. For pheasant, allow 1 hour in the oven; the sauce will be plenty for a brace of pheasants. Serves 5–6.

Adapted from *The Alice B. Toklas Cook Book*

Roast Duck

IIII

One of the most classic of English dishes, served with new potatoes, green peas and apple sauce.

1 duck, 4–5 lb [1.8–2.3 kg] dressed weight
1 Tbs sea salt

Prick the skin here and there with a sharp fork and rub with sea salt. Lay the bird upside down in a roasting rack, in a tin. Roast for 45 minutes at 400°F/200°C/gas 6, then turn the bird right side up and pour off the fat in the tin. Turn down the oven to 350°F/180°C/gas 4, and roast the bird for another 45 minutes. (Or, 18–20 minutes per lb.) Transfer to a serving platter to serve, with the apple sauce with sage on page 172, and young vegetables simply boiled. Serves 3–4.

AB

Roman Pie

IIII

Roman pie was a popular dish which has completely disappeared. Formerly much in evidence at country luncheons, shooting parties, and other simple meals, it existed in various different forms. Usually made with chicken or rabbit, with additions of tongue or bacon, it was sometimes covered with pastry. A cold version was made with aspic instead of the cream sauce. This version is an amalgam of contemporary recipes.

1 x 4 lb [1.8 kg] roasting chicken
1 onion, halved
1 leek, halved
1 carrot, halved
2 stalks celery, halved
1 bay leaf
3 stalks parsley
salt and 10 black peppercorns
6 oz [180 g] sliced tongue or cooked ham, or thick rashers green
   streaky bacon
10 oz [285 g] macaroni

SAUCE
2 oz [55 g] butter
4 Tbs flour

¾ pt [450 ml] chicken stock (from poaching bird)
½ pt [275 ml] single cream
salt and pepper

1 oz [30 g] grated Parmesan

Start a day in advance. Poach the chicken as usual, with flavouring vegetables, herbs and seasonings. It will take about 1¼ hours. Then remove the flesh from the bones, put the carcase back in the pot, and boil for another 2 hours to make a good stock. Strain and cool, then chill overnight.

Next day, remove the fat, reduce if still weak in flavour, and measure ¾ pt [450 ml]. Cut the chicken in neat pieces about 2 x ½ inch [5 x 1 cm]. Cut the cooked tongue or ham in 1 inch [2.5 cm] squares. If using bacon, remove the rind, then fry until crisp. Drain on soft paper, then cut or break into 1 inch [2.5 cm] squares. Cook the macaroni for 14 minutes, or until tender, in lightly salted boiling water, then drain. While it cooks, make the sauce. Melt the butter, add the flour and cook 1 minute, stirring. Then add the heated stock and the cream, with salt and pepper to taste, and stir till blended. Simmer for 3 minutes, then set aside.

Choose a shallow baking dish holding about 3 pt [1.75 litres] and rub with butter. Divide each of the three main ingredients into three parts, and make alternate layers of chicken, tongue (or ham, or bacon), and macaroni, with a layer of sauce over the chicken and tongue (or ham, etc.) and over the macaroni. Season each layer of chicken and macaroni with salt and pepper; not too much salt because of the bacon. Finish with a thick layer of sauce and sprinkle the grated cheese over it. Bake for 40 minutes at 350°F/180°C/gas 4. Serves 6, with a green salad.

AB

Roast Squab

||||

Squab are pigeons that have been specially reared, or farmed as we would say nowadays. They have long been popular in the USA and have been raised in this country at different times. At present, they are imported from France; the French pigeons de Bresse are particularly delicious. Squab are much more tender than wild pigeon, and more delicate in flavour.

2 oz [55 g] butter
1 carrot, sliced
1 onion, sliced
sea salt and black pepper
4 squab (1 per person)
¼ pt [150 ml] good stock: veal, game or chicken
8–10 sprigs watercress
2 Tbs olive oil
1 Tbs lemon juice

Melt plenty of butter [*1 oz/30 g*] in a roasting pan and sprinkle on the bottom [*sliced*] carrot and onion. Salt and pepper the birds and spread a little butter [*1 oz/30 g*] on the breasts. Put them in the roasting pan and place in a hot oven [*400°F/200°C/gas 6*] to roast to a golden brown. When brown [*or after 10 minutes*], turn down heat [*to 350°F/180°C/gas 4*], and let them cook slowly for [*about*] half an hour [*35–40 minutes in all, basting carefully with the concentrated stock*]. Drain off all the juice in the pan, strain and reduce to a glaze by simmering. Pour over the birds and decorate them with watercress, which has been lightly mixed at the last minute with a little olive oil, salt and pepper, and lemon juice. [*Instead of reducing to a glaze, the pan juices may simply be served in a small jug, as gravy. Serves 4.*]

June Platt's Party Cook Book

Roast Grouse (and other game birds)

▌|||

Smear the grouse all over with softened butter and sprinkle with sea salt and freshly ground black pepper. Lay them on a roasting rack, or directly on the oven rack with a roasting tin on the shelf beneath. Roast for 25 minutes at 400°F/200°C/gas 6, turning them right way up halfway through. Move them to a warm place to rest for 5–10 minutes before serving, with bread sauce (see page 174), browned breadcrumbs (see page 185), game chips (see page 126), and a green vegetable like Brussels sprouts. Cut in half to serve: one bird will serve 2.

For roast pheasant, allow 45–60 minutes, depending on size.
For partridge, allow 20 minutes. For snipe and woodcock, allow 15
minutes. A hen pheasant will serve 2; a cock serves 3. Partridge,
snipe and woodcock serve 1 each.

AB

Cold Quails with Grape Salad

This was the sort of dish you might expect to find for a late supper after the theatre, or halfway through a ball.

‖‖

4 quails
1 pt [570 ml] veal or chicken stock
8 oz [225 g] white grapes, halved and seeded
2 small, crisp lettuces

SAUCE
¼ pt [150 ml] mayonnaise
3 fl oz [75 ml] double cream, lightly whipped
2 small onions, peeled and halved
1½ Tbs chopped parsley
1½ Tbs chopped chervil

Cook the quails lightly in veal [or chicken] stock. [Drop them into the
simmering stock and poach for 9 minutes.] Let them get quite cool in
it. Then drain and arrange neatly on a flat dish. Serve with a grape
salad arranged on lettuce leaves, and the following sauce. Mix
mayonnaise with some cream. Add small onions cut in halves.
These should remain in for an hour only just for flavouring. After
they have been removed, the sauce must be mixed again and
sprinkled with chopped parsley and chervil. This sauce should be
thick and very light. [Serves 2–4.]

June Platt in *Vogue*

Grouse Salad

This makes an elegant supper dish. An excellent way of using up cold grouse, it is even better when the birds have been cooked especially and are still

‖‖

warm. It is also good as a simple salad, without the grouse. Simply increase the eggs, beetroot and rocket, and serve with a lettuce and cucumber salad.

3–4 hard-boiled eggs, thickly sliced
3–4 small beetroot, freshly cooked and sliced
2 cooked grouse, cut in quarters (or remains of cold grouse)
12 sprigs rocket, or watercress

SAUCE

2 shallots, finely chopped
1½ Tbs chopped tarragon
1½ Tbs chopped chervil
¼ tsp castor sugar
2 egg yolks
sea salt and black pepper

a pinch of cayenne
6 fl oz [175 ml] olive oil
4 Tbs white wine vinegar
2–3 dashes Tabasco
¼ pt [150 ml] double cream,
   lightly whipped

Mix the chopped shallots with the chopped herbs, sugar, egg yolks and seasonings. Add the oil very gradually, almost as if making mayonnaise. Then stir in the vinegar, also slowly, adding a few dashes of Tabasco. Fold in the whipped cream, then pour into a bowl to serve. Make a border of sliced eggs and beetroot round the edges of a dish and pile the pieces of grouse in the centre. Decorate with rocket, or watercress. Serves 4.

Adapted from *The Gentle Art of Cookery* by Mrs C. F. Leyel and Miss Olga Hartley

Roast Haunch of Venison

IIII

Rarely seen nowadays, this is a wonderful dish, especially when made with the tender roe, or fallow, deer. It must be started 1–2 days in advance.

MARINADE

1 medium onion, sliced
2 shallots, sliced
2 cloves garlic, sliced
1 large carrot, sliced
1 stalk celery, sliced
3 Tbs olive oil

1 bottle red wine
3 large sprigs parsley
½ Tbs sea salt
8 black peppercorns
8 juniper berries
2 bay leaves

5–6 lb [2.3 kg–3 kg] haunch of roe (or fallow) deer
6 Tbs olive oil
1 tsp flour
¼ pt [150 ml] sour cream
approx. ¼ pt [150 ml] chicken stock
sea salt and black pepper

Make the marinade 1–2 days beforehand. While young roe deer may not actually *need* marinading, in this case the marinade becomes part of the dish, and forms the basis of the sauce. Cook the sliced onion, shallots, garlic, carrot and celery in the oil for 5 minutes, stirring now and then. Add the red wine, with parsley, sea salt, peppercorns, juniper berries and bay leaves. Bring to the boil, cover, and simmer for 45 minutes, then leave to cool. Lay the haunch in a large dish and pour the (unstrained) marinade over it. Leave for 1–2 days in a cool place, turning it over twice a day.

When ready to cook, drain the haunch and pat dry with soft paper. Lift the sliced vegetables out of the marinade with a slotted spoon (discard the herbs), and lay them in the bottom of a roasting tin. Rub the haunch all over with 2 Tbs olive oil then lay it on the sliced vegetables. Roast for 20 minutes at 425°F/220°C/gas 7, then reduce the heat to 350°F/180°C/gas 4 and roast for 20 minutes per lb [450 g] in all. Once the meat has gone into the oven, measure ¼ pt [150 ml] of the strained marinade and warm it in a small pan with 4 Tbs olive oil. Once the oven heat has been reduced, start to baste the meat with this mixture. When the meat has finished cooking, transfer it to a serving dish and cover loosely with foil and a thick towel. Rest for 15–20 minutes before carving.

Now make the sauce. Stir the flour into the sour cream and beat till amalgamated smoothly. Put the vegetables (except any that are burnt) from the roasting tin into the processor, adding the juices in the tin and about ¼ pt [150 ml] chicken stock – enough to make up to about ½ pt [275 ml]. Process, then add the sour cream and flour and process again. Pour through a coarse strainer into a pan and reheat, adding salt and pepper to taste, and stirring constantly. Simmer gently for 3–4 minutes, then pour into a heated jug and serve with the venison. Serves 8, with a purée of mixed root vegetables (potatoes, celeriac, turnips or swedes), and Brussels sprouts.

AB

Roast Ribs of Beef

||||

This is adapted from a recipe by June Platt that appeared in Vogue *in the 1930s. She specifies a three-rib roast, on the bone; this may be fore ribs, wing ribs or sirloin. I tend to buy the same cuts already boned, and ask the butcher to include the rib bones – plus one or two others if he has them. If the ribs are still joined together, you can use them as a roasting rack; otherwise lay them in the roasting tin and put the beef on them.*

3½ lb [1.7 kg] boned and rolled fore ribs, wing ribs, or sirloin,
    plus bones
¼ pt [150 ml] red wine

Heat the oven to 425°F/220°C/gas 7. While it heats, weigh the joint and calculate the cooking time. I allow 20 minutes per lb [450 g] for medium-rare beef, subtracting 10 minutes for rare beef, and adding on 10 minutes for reasonably well-done meat. Or, as June Platt says: 'Cook it in all 18 to 20 minutes per lb [450 g] for rare meat, 22 to 25 for medium-done – but please don't like it any more cooked than that.'

If using the joined ribs as a roasting rack, tie the beef on to them with string. Or, lay it in the roasting tin, fat side up, with the single ribs lying beneath it. Roast for 20 minutes at high heat – even hotter than the above temperature, if you can bear it, then reduce the oven heat to 350°F/180°C/gas 4. During the remainder of the cooking time, baste every 15–20 minutes with the fat in the pan. When the time is up, transfer the meat to a carving dish and cover loosely with foil and a thick towel. Pour off the fat in the tin, leaving the juices. Add the wine and bubble away over a moderate flame, scraping all the bits of sediment together. When it has reduced a little, pour through a strainer into a small pan and set aside. When ready to serve – the meat must be allowed to rest for at least 20 minutes before carving – pour the juices that have accumulated on the carving dish into the pan, and reheat. Serve with the beef, with horseradish cream (see page 59), and a good mustard. Don't carve the beef too thin. Serves 8. (If roasting a joint to eat cold, subtract 5 minutes from the roasting time.)

Adapted from June Platt in *Vogue*

Beef Olives

IIII

One of the best of the old dishes, rarely seen today. This would have been served for Saturday lunch in a country house.

6 thin slices buttock steak or topside
2 oz [55 g] shredded suet
1 oz [30 g] soft white breadcrumbs
2 rashers streaky bacon, chopped
½ tsp grated orange rind
1 Tbs chopped parsley
½ tsp fresh thyme, or ¼ tsp dried thyme
salt and black pepper
1 egg, beaten
1½ oz [45 g] butter
1 onion, thinly sliced
1 carrot, thinly sliced
1 leek, thinly sliced
1 stalk celery, thinly sliced
½ Tbs flour
½ pt [275 ml] beef or chicken stock

Lay the slices of beef on a sheet of cling film and cover with another sheet. Beat them out until very thin. Trim the edges to make a roughly rectangular shape; chop the trimmings and put them in a basin with the suet and breadcrumbs. Add the bacon, orange rind, parsley, thyme, salt and pepper. Mix well, adding the beaten egg, then divide the stuffing between the 6 slices of beef. Roll each one up and tie with string.

Melt the butter in a casserole and brown the sliced vegetables quickly, stirring constantly. When they have coloured, take them out and put in the beef olives. Brown them on all sides, then remove them also. Shake the flour into the casserole and blend with the butter. Cook for 1 minute, stirring, then add the heated stock and stir till blended, adding salt and pepper to taste. Put the vegetables back into the pan, and lay the olives on them. Cover and cook gently for 1½ hours, either on top of the stove or in a low oven, 325°F/170°C/gas 3.

To serve, remove the string and lay the olives on a bed of mashed potato. Spoon the vegetables over the top, moistening with the sauce. Serves 6.

AB

Cottage Pie, or Shepherd's Pie

||||

At a time when so many roast joints of meat were being consumed, dishes like these were constantly being made to use up the remains. In the big houses they were more likely to appear in the nursery than in the dining-room. Strangely enough, I don't remember them often in my own home, where we used to eat up rare roast beef, cold, without ever tiring of it. When made with beef, this is called cottage pie; when made with mutton or lamb, it becomes shepherd's pie.

6–8 oz [180–225 g] carrots, thinly sliced
10–12 oz [285–340 g] cold cooked beef, mutton or lamb
1 small onion, chopped
½ oz [15 g] butter
2 tsp flour
salt and black pepper

POTATO PUREE
1½ lb [680 g] potatoes
4 Tbs milk
1 oz [30 g] butter

Cook the sliced carrots for 5 minutes in very lightly salted boiling water, then drain, reserving the water. Have the meat trimmed of all fat and neatly chopped by hand. Fry the chopped onion in the butter for 5 minutes, then add the meat and cook for a further minute or two, stirring. Then add the flour and cook for 1 minute, stirring to blend with the fat. Measure ¼ pt [150 ml] of the carrot water, substituting any meat gravy or good stock you happen to have, and add to the pan, stirring until it has blended. Simmer gently for 4 minutes, adding salt and pepper to taste. Then turn the contents of the pan into a greased pie dish, or soufflé dish. Lay the sliced carrots over the meat. Make a potato purée as usual, but be careful not to make it too moist or it will merge with the meat below. Make rough ridges in the surface and bake until nicely browned, 30–35 minutes at 375°F/190°C/gas 5. Serves 4, with a green vegetable. This can also be made with raw meat, minced or finely chopped in a food processor. Simply allow an extra 5 minutes initial frying with the onion, then proceed as above.

AB

Sea Pie

IIII

I love this simple version of steak pudding, where the suet crust is merely laid on top of the meat for cooking, instead of all around it.

2 lb [900 g] best stewing steak
salt and black pepper
2 medium carrots
2 small onions

SUET PASTE
4 oz [120 g] shredded suet
8 oz [225 g] self-raising flour
approx. 4 fl oz [120 ml] water

Cut the steak into thin slices about 3 inches [7.5 cm] square, put them into a shallow stewpan, season with salt and pepper, barely cover the slices with boiling water, put on the lid and simmer gently. Slice the carrots thinly, cut the onions into small pieces, and add them to the meat. Make the suet paste [*according to the directions on the packet*], roll into a round rather less than the top of the stewpan [*using the lid as a guide*]. Lay the paste on top of the meat when it has simmered for about ½ an hour, replace the lid and continue the cooking for about 1½ hours longer. When the pie is done, cut the paste into 4 pieces, and remove them carefully from the stewpan to a plate; arrange the meat and vegetables neatly on a hot dish, and place the crust on top. Sufficient for 4 persons.

Mrs Beeton's All About Cookery

Boiled Silverside

IIII

One of the best of the traditional dishes, not often seen nowadays. You may have to order the salt beef from your butcher a few days in advance. The French also love boiled beef, but their bouilli is made with fresh beef.

3–4 lb [1.5–1.8 kg] salted silverside
1½ lb [680 g] large carrots
2 leeks, halved
2 onions, halved
4 cloves
2 bay leaves
4 stalks parsley
10 black peppercorns

Put the beef in a large pan and surround it with 2 of the carrots cut in half, the leeks, onions stuck with cloves, bay leaves, parsley and peppercorns. Cover generously with cold water and start to bring slowly to the boil. As it approaches boiling point, skim carefully, removing all the grey scum that rises to the surface. When only a light white foam remains, cover and cook steadily for 1½–2 hours, or 30 minutes per lb [450 g]. Towards the end of the time, cook the remaining carrots separately; they may be left whole, or, if very large, cut in halves or quarters lengthwise. When the meat is ready, lift on to a serving platter and carve in fairly thick slices. Taste the stock to make sure it is not too salty, then use some to moisten the slices. Lay on a platter, surrounded with the carrots. Serve with a bowl of boiled potatoes sprinkled with chopped parsley. Serves 6.

AB

Spiced Beef

IIII

Cold spiced beef (it can also be eaten hot, but rarely was at that time) was a popular joint for the sideboard, also for shooting and picnic lunches, and for summer holidays. Since saltpetre, which was used in the pickling mixture, is now unobtainable by law, I have had to go back to a Victorian recipe for spicing beef with common (or sea) salt and spices. I have doubled the quantity of salt to be on the safe side. The cooking instructions are based on those of Elizabeth David, as given to Harrods' meat department in 1958, when they first started selling spiced beef according to Mrs David's recipe. (They still do, for Christmas.)

5–6 lb [2.3–3 kg] beef: topside, round, silverside or brisket, boned and rolled
1 tsp ground mace
1 tsp coarsely ground black pepper
1 oz [30 g] juniper berries, roughly crushed
2 tsp ground cloves
½ small nutmeg, grated
⅛ tsp cayenne
3½ oz [100 g] dark-brown muscovado sugar
8 oz [225 g] Maldon sea salt

Mix all the spices and seasonings except the salt and rub the beef all over. Lay it in an earthenware crock with a lid (I use a bread crock, unless it is a long sausage-shaped joint when I use an oval earthenware dish covered with foil). Leave it for 3 days, then add half the salt. Rub it well with the spice and salt mixture and put back in the crock, or dish. Rub it or turn it every day for 12 days, adding half the remaining sea salt on the 4th day, and the remainder on the 8th day.

When the time is up, wipe off the spices, rinsing the meat briefly if necessary, but on no account soak it. Put it in a casserole that fits it as closely as possible and add ½ pt [275 ml] water. Cover with 2 sheets of foil and the lid and cook for 45–50 minutes per lb [450 g] in the bottom of a low oven – 275°F/140°C/gas 1. When it is cooked, unless you are going to eat it hot, take out of the oven and leave to cool for 2–3 hours in its pot. Then lift out the meat and lay it on a flat surface. Weigh down with a board with 3 x 2 lb [1 kg] weights standing upon it, and leave overnight. Next day, wrap in foil and keep in the refrigerator. It should keep for 10–14 days, replaced in the refrigerator after use. To serve, carve in thin slices and serve with baked potatoes and a mixed salad.

Adapted from *Modern Cookery* by Eliza Acton

Beef Stew

IIII

This recipe has evolved over the years in my kitchen, based originally on recipes of the period.

2½ lb [1.15 kg] chuck steak, or topside, thickly sliced
1 large onion, sliced
1 oz [30 g] butter
4 Tbs olive oil
2 large carrots, cut in thick strips
½ celeriac, or 3 stalks celery, cut in thick strips
1 large parsnip, cut in thick strips
2 large cloves garlic, crushed
about 1½ Tbs seasoned flour
½ pt [275 ml] beef or chicken stock
½ pt [275 ml] red wine
1 Tbs tomato purée
juice of 1 orange

strip orange peel 2 inches x ½ inch [5 x 1 cm]
1 large bay leaf
3 shakes Tabasco
sea salt and black pepper
3 Tbs coarsely chopped parsley

Trim the beef, cutting away all gristle and membrane, then cut it in neat rectangles. Cook the sliced onion gently in the butter and half the olive oil, for about 3 minutes, then add the root vegetables which you have cut in strips like thick matchsticks about 1½ inches long by ⅓ inch square [3.5 cm x 7.5 mm]. (In spring and summer, substitute fennel for the celeriac, and green pepper for the parsnip.) Cook all together gently for about 5 minutes, adding the crushed garlic halfway through. Then lift out the vegetables with a slotted spoon, add the remaining 2 Tbs oil, and put in the sliced beef which you have coated lightly with flour at the last minute. Brown the meat on both sides, doing it in 2 or 3 batches. Then remove it and put the vegetables back in the pan. Heat the stock and wine together and pour on to the vegetables, stirring to blend with the flour. When all is smooth, put back the meat and add the tomato purée, orange juice and peel, bay leaf and Tabasco. Add sea salt and black pepper, bring to the boil, then cover the pan and cook for 1 hour in a low oven, 300°F/150°C/gas 2. Then remove the lid and cook for another hour, basting the surface of the stew 2 or 3 times with the juice. This produces a really excellent dish, for the reduction of the sauce increases the flavour, at the same time causing the surface of the casserole to become almost caramelised. It must be transferred to a clean dish for serving, however, for the evaporation of the meat juices will have discoloured the casserole. Sprinkle with parsley and serve with a purée of potatoes and a boiled vegetable, or a green salad. Serves 6.

AB

Braised Oxtail

IIII

A wonderful winter dish, sustaining without being too expensive. It takes two days to make properly.

1ST DAY	2ND DAY
2 oxtail, cut in 2 inch [5 cm] sections	1 oz [30 g] butter
2½ Tbs flour	1 Tbs olive oil
salt and black pepper	1 leek, cut in thick strips
2 Tbs olive oil	2 medium carrots, cut in thick strips
1 oz [30 g] butter	2 small turnips, cut in thick strips
2 cloves garlic, crushed	2 stalks celery, cut in thick strips
2 Tbs tomato purée	1 parsnip, cut in thick strips
1 large onion, halved	2 Tbs coarsely chopped parsley
1 large carrot, halved	
1 stalk celery, halved	
1 bay leaf	
3 stalks parsley	
1¼ pt [720 ml] beef stock	
¼ pt [150 ml] red wine	

Start 1 day in advance. Trim excess fat off oxtail. Season flour with salt and pepper and shake over the meat, turning so that it is lightly and evenly coated. Heat oil and butter in a heavy casserole and brown the oxtail on all sides, lifting them out as they are done. Put the garlic and tomato purée in the pot and replace the meat, adding the halved vegetables and herbs. Heat stock and wine together and add to the pan. Bring to the boil slowly, adding more salt and pepper, then cover and cook for 4 hours in the oven, at 300°F/150°C/gas 2. Remove and leave to cool overnight.

Next day remove the fat from the surface and transfer the pieces of meat to a shallow earthenware dish. Discard the flavouring vegetables and herbs. Heat fresh butter and oil in a sauté pan; put in the vegetable strips and fry gently for 8 minutes, then add ½ pt [275 ml] of the oxtail stock taken from the stew, and simmer gently for 15 minutes. Then lift out the vegetable strips with a slotted spoon and scatter them over the surface of the oxtail. Pour their stock, and the rest of the oxtail stock, over them, and cook for 1 hour at 350°F/180°C/gas 4, basting from time to time. When the time is up, they should have acquired a slightly crisp, caramelised exterior from the evaporation of the meat juices. Sprinkle with coarsely chopped parsley and serve in the same dish, with boiled or baked potatoes, and a green salad. Serves 6.

AB

Roast Rack of Lamb

IIII

This is a good, simple dish, typical of the best cooking of the time. I have adapted it from contemporary recipes.

1 x 8-bone rack of lamb, trimmed for roasting, with chine bone removed
½ oz [15 g] butter
1 small onion, thinly sliced
1 carrot, thinly sliced
6 fl oz [175 ml] meat stock, heated

Rub a piece of foil with half the butter and lay over the rack of lamb. Rub the rest of the butter over the bottom of a roasting tin and lay the sliced onion and carrot in it. Stand the lamb in the tin, on a rack if you have one, and roast for 15 minutes at 375°F/190°C/ gas 5. Then remove the foil and baste with some of the heated stock. Continue to roast for 25 minutes (40 minutes in all), basting two or three times, then rest in a warm place for 10 minutes before carving into cutlets. While it rests, lay the roasting tin over a low flame and stir up the juices. Let them bubble all together for a few minutes, adding a drop more stock if you have it, or a drop of red wine, then strain into a sauceboat. Serves 3. For two people, buy a 5-bone rack of lamb and cook for 35 minutes. These times will give you meat that is slightly pink; add an extra 5 minutes, if you must, for well-done meat.

AB

Roast Saddle of Lamb

IIII

Rarely seen nowadays except at Guildhall dinners, this is one of the glories of the English kitchen. In pre-war days it would often have been a saddle of mutton, which has a character all of its own. But a saddle of well-reared lamb is also a marvellous dish. It is carved in long rectangular strips, quite thick and slightly wedge-shaped, which look very good on the plate. Allow roughly 1 lb [450 g] per person.

saddle of British lamb, approx. 6 lb [3 kg]
3 Tbs best olive oil
1 Tbs lemon juice
freshly ground black pepper
6 branches tarragon (optional)
8 branches chervil (optional)
½ pt [275 ml] lamb, beef, veal or chicken stock

Virtually nothing needs to be done to this joint, except paying for it, before putting it in the oven. In spring and summer, when the lamb is young, I merely rub a little virgin oil all over it, sprinkle over a few drops of lemon juice and some freshly ground black pepper, and lay branches of tarragon and chervil all over. In winter, when the lambs are older and fresh herbs hard to come by, I merely rub it with oil, lemon juice and pepper. Lay on a roasting rack and cook for 1¼–1½ hours, whatever its weight, at 350°F/180°C/gas 4. (The weight merely extends its length, while the cooking time should be calculated according to its thickness.) It doesn't need basting, since it is completely covered with its own fat. When the time is up, move on to a carving platter and cover loosely with foil and a heavy cloth. Stand in a warm place for 15–20 minutes to rest before carving; this is very important. While the meat rests, make the gravy. Heat the stock in a small pan and pour off the fat in the roasting tin. Stand the tin over a moderate flame. Add the hot stock to the tin, scraping and stirring with a wooden spoon until all the caramelised meat juices amalgamate with the stock. Let it all bubble away and reduce for a few minutes, then pour through a strainer into a sauceboat. Although the saddle is a good-looking joint, it is perhaps easiest to carve it in the kitchen. It must be cut parallel to the bone, in long strips, about ¼ inch [5 mm] thick on the outside, tapering slightly as they meet the bone. If too long, they may be cut in half to serve. Sometimes the whole saddle is slightly concave, making it very hard to carve. In this case, cut the whole joint across in half with a strong knife, then carve as above, in shorter strips. Serves 6. This is good served with the grilled slices of potatoes on page 125, mint sauce and/or redcurrant jelly, or the sauce soubise on page 179, and as many simple vegetables as you can manage.

AB

Grilled Rack of Lamb

||||

This was a favourite dish of Edward VII, still popular between the wars. Twice-cooked meat can be very good, when done with that end in view. The little cutlets are very tender, and are also good cold, for eating in your fingers: perfect picnic food. The caper sauce is optional, certainly not for taking on a picnic. Allow 2–3 cutlets per person, remembering that the end ones will not be so perfect in shape as the others. Start a day in advance.

8-bone rack of lamb, in one piece, chined
approx. 2 pt [1.2 litres] light beef or chicken stock
1 leek (or onion), thickly sliced
1 carrot, thickly sliced
1 stalk celery, thickly sliced
sea salt and 6 black peppercorns
¼ bay leaf
1 oz [30 g] butter, melted
dry white breadcrumbs

CAPER SAUCE (OPTIONAL)
½ pt [275 ml] reduced stock (see above)
1 Tbs capers, chopped
1 Tbs chopped pickled gherkin

Put the rack of lamb in an oval pan and add enough stock to almost cover it. Remove the meat and put in the sliced vegetables, salt and peppercorns, and bay leaf. Bring slowly to the boil, then replace the meat. Bring back to the boil then simmer gently, covered, for 1 hour. Remove the meat and leave to cool overnight. Continue to boil up the stock, uncovered, until reduced to a good flavour. (You only need just over ½ pt/275 ml.) Strain and cool, then chill overnight.

Next day, divide the meat into cutlets and trim off most of the fat. Dip each one in melted butter, then in breadcrumbs. To make the sauce, remove the fat from the surface of the reduced stock. Heat the stock in a small pan, adding roughly chopped capers (if small, they can be left whole) and gherkins. Grill the cutlets for about 4 minutes on each side, just until nicely browned. (They are already cooked and only need warming through.) Serve them on a flat dish, with the caper and gherkin sauce, if used, in a sauceboat.

If serving without a sauce, they may be garnished with a few capers
and thinly sliced gherkins. Serves 3.

Adapted from *Kitchen Essays* by Lady Jekyll

Pâté Don Pedro

IIII

*This oddly named dish is one of my favourites,
and typical of its genre. Its essence lies in its
simplicity: a style of cooking where nursery and
dining-room meet.*

12 cutlets, middle end of neck of lamb, trimmed
sea salt and black pepper
1 medium carrot, thinly sliced
1 medium onion, thinly sliced
2 stalks parsley
½ small bay leaf
1 pt [570 ml] beef or chicken stock

POTATO CRUST
1½ lb [680 g] floury potatoes, peeled and halved
6 Tbs milk
½ oz [15 g] butter
sea salt and black pepper

Trim 1 dozen cutlets as for Irish stew, place in circular order in a
stewpan. Season with salt, pepper, carrot, onion, and herbs, and 1
pint [570 ml] of good stock. Cook by the side of the stove fire till
tender [*about 1 hour on top of the stove*]. Remove cutlets into pie-
dish, skim all grease from gravy, reduce it [*to 6 fl oz/175 ml*], and
pour over the cutlets, cover with a potato crust [*mash the freshly
boiled and drained potatoes with the milk and butter which have been
heated together, with plenty of sea salt and black pepper*], brown, and
serve hot. [*Serves 4–5.*]

Lady Sysonby's Cook Book

Côtelettes Soubises

IIII

*An appetising dish of lamb cutlets masked with a
thick onion sauce under a coating of egg and
breadcrumbs. Also good cold, this makes an elegant dish for a picnic.*

8 lamb cutlets, trimmed of excess fat

SAUCE SOUBISE
6 oz [180 g] onions, thinly sliced
½ oz [15 g] butter
½ Tbs flour
¼ pt [150 ml] veal or chicken stock
sea salt and black pepper

WHITE SAUCE
¾ oz [20 g] butter
1 Tbs flour
¼ pt [150 ml] milk
4 Tbs thick cream
a pinch each ground cloves and mace
¼ bay leaf
sea salt and black pepper

COATING
1 large egg, beaten
1 Tbs milk
approx. 2 oz [55 g] dry white breadcrumbs
1 oz [30 g] butter, melted

Cook [*grill*] your cutlets lightly [*4 minutes*] the side on which the sauce is to be. Then press them flat between two plates to get cold. Prepare a sauce half soubise, half white sauce. [*Cook the sliced onions gently in the butter in a non-stick pan for 5 minutes, stirring now and then, stir in the flour. Add the heated stock, salt and black pepper, and simmer gently, covered, for 10 minutes, stirring occasionally. Set aside. In another pan make the white sauce. Melt the butter, stir in the flour, and cook for 1 minute, stirring. Then add the heated milk and bring to the boil, stirring. Add cream, ground cloves, mace, bay leaf and salt and pepper and simmer for 4 minutes, stirring often. Then mix the two sauces together and set aside to cool. If you prefer a smooth purée, they can be put briefly in the food processor. Once cool, chill in the refrigerator for an hour or two.*] Then spread thickly over the cooked side of the cutlets, egg and breadcrumb them both sides, and finish cooking in a hot oven. [*Lay them on a greased baking tray and dribble the melted butter over them. Bake for 25 minutes at 375°F/190°C/gas 5, then brown briefly under the grill. Serves 4.*]

Lady Sysonby's Cook Book

Boiled Leg of Mutton with Caper Sauce

IIII

Before the war, lamb was a seasonal dish, only to be had in the spring. For the rest of the year they ate mutton, and this was one of the best ways of cooking it. Mutton is beginning to regain its popularity, especially in the West Country.

1 leg of mutton, trimmed of excess fat
2½–3 pt [1.5–1.75 litres] light meat or chicken stock
1 stalk celery
1 medium onion, halved
3 carrots
20 black peppercorns

Start 1 day in advance: Place the leg in a large saucepan or casserole. Cover with the stock [*add the vegetables and peppercorns*] and bring slowly to the boil. Simmer for 2 hours, then leave to cool overnight.

Next day, remove any excess fat from the top of the pan and discard the vegetables. Bring slowly back to the boil and simmer for another hour. You can add some fresh root vegetables to the pan for the last half hour. Any mutton left over can be kept in the juice in a cool place overnight. Reheat thoroughly just before serving. Serves 6–8, depending on the breed of sheep.

Caper Sauce

1 oz [30 g] butter
¾ oz [20 g] flour
½ tsp dry mustard
¼ pt [150 ml] mutton stock
   (see above)

salt and black pepper
2 Tbs capers, drained
½ Tbs caper juice
1 Tbs double cream

Melt the butter in a pan, add flour and mustard, and mix well. Add ¼ pt [150 ml] stock from the mutton, and season well with salt and pepper. Simmer for 2 to 3 minutes. Add a good quantity of capers to taste, plus 1 dessertspoon of their juice. Simmer a few moments more, and add a tablespoon of cream just before serving.

Caroline Blackburn

Cold Roast Loin of Pork

IIII

This is a combination of two recipes of June Platt's, published in Vogue *in 1938. Like many young American women living in England at that time, she was ahead of her time, and was constantly urging her readers to be more adventurous and to break with the conventions. She starts her recipe by saying: 'Try serving a well-cooked roast of pork cold, accompanied by a big bowl of mayonnaise and a delicious French bean salad with French dressing.'*

4 lb [1.8 kg] loin of pork, on the bone
1 Tbs sunflower oil
sea salt and black pepper

Preheat the oven to its maximum. Rub the crackling lightly with oil, and sprinkle with salt and pepper. Lay it on a rack in a roasting pan. If there are bone ends, cover each one with a twist of foil. Roast 15 minutes in a very hot oven, then turn down the heat to 375°F/190°C/gas 5, and cook more slowly, basting now and then, for 1 hour 50 minutes, 2 hours 5 minutes in all. Or, 28 minutes per lb plus the initial 15 minutes. If it starts to get too brown, lay a piece of foil loosely over it. When it is done, take out of the oven and leave to cool. Pour off the juices in the pan and reserve for another dish. Leave the joint in a cool place overnight – preferably not in the refrigerator. Next day, cut out the bone carefully; with a small sharp knife this is not hard to do, and makes carving very much easier. Then remove the crackling in one piece, and discard most of the fat between the crackling and the meat. Carve the meat in neat slices, not too thin, and lay them on a serving dish. Break the crackling into strips and lay around the meat. Serves 6–8, with an apple sauce, or mayonnaise, or a cherry salad (see page 175); a new potato salad, and another of string beans.

Adapted from June Platt in *Vogue*

Escalopes de Veau aux Concombres

A typical dinner-party dish, this also works well on a small scale, for two – or even one.

▌|||

½ cucumber, peeled and cut in oval lozenges about 1 inch
    [2.5 cm] long
2 oz [55 g] butter
4 thin veal escalopes
½ pt [275 ml] double cream
salt and pepper
a pinch paprika

Drop the cucumber lozenges into lightly salted boiling water and cook for 2 minutes, then drain and refresh under the cold tap. Keep warm while you cook the veal. Heat half the butter in a broad frying pan. When very hot, put in 2 escalopes and cook until nicely coloured, about 2 minutes on each side. Remove them as they are done and keep warm while you fry the others. When all four are done, add the cucumber lozenges to the dish and make the sauce. Pour the cream into the frying pan, scraping all the juices and caramelised bits of sediment together. Let it boil briskly for a few minutes to reduce, adding salt and pepper and a pinch of paprika. Then swirl in the remaining 1 oz [30 g] butter cut in small bits. Once it has melted, pour the sauce over the veal and cucumber and serve at once. Serves 4, with noodles, or new potatoes, and a green salad.

Adapted from *What Shall We Have Today?* by X. Marcel Boulestin

VEGETABLES

Vegetables

One of the great culinary advances during this period was in the treatment of vegetables. As Mrs Martineau recalls in the introduction to her book *Caviare to Candy*, published in 1927: 'My own mother gave each of her daughters a recipe book on their marriage, and though filled with many good dishes, there is not a single vegetable dish nor salad therein.' This illustrates clearly the cook's priorities pre-World War I. Once that war was over, however, the vegetable began to grow in favour. This was due in part to the American influence which was spreading among sophisticated London folk, but not entirely. An old family friend recalled going to lunch with King George V and Queen Mary, and being struck by the meal, for a dish of green peas was served on its own, after the main course, and the old King remarked how much he liked to eat vegetables in this way.

Many households, even the most conservative and old-fashioned, took to serving a vegetable dish alone, usually after the main course. Mrs Martineau describes the vegetable soufflés made by Lady Wilton's chef at Melton: 'a soufflé of small Brussels sprouts, boiled very soft with well-beaten eggs and cream one night, the next a soufflé of white (Jerusalem) artichokes or asparagus, and the third night one of spinach which, boiled with cream and whipped up with eggs was a delicate green colour with a brown top.'

In 1931 a whole book devoted to the subject of vegetables appeared, something that would have been unthinkable before the First World War. This was *Vegetable Cookery* by Elizabeth Lucas, who speaks with authority, as her strictures on butter show: 'One thing is essential – the use of good butter. Delicious butter with a faintly nutty flavour is rarely to be found in private houses. To use too much is as great a crime as to use none. Vegetables swimming in butter are nauseating. They should be turned over in it at the last moment (enrober is the good French word) and be eaten before it has lost its freshness.'

As the twenties and thirties progressed, the enthusiasm for vegetables continued to grow. 'Get as many vegetables as you can,' wrote Lady Sysonby, 'and a simple dinner will at once become elegant if you have a vegetable served as a separate course.' An alternative use of vegetables was serving as many as four or five, each cooked separately, with a simple meat dish, like grilled chicken, or lamb cutlets. This custom can be traced back to the United States where it had long been popular with elegant hostesses. Lady Cunard took it to extremes, sometimes serving as many as six different vegetables at one meal, while Englishwomen like Lady Aberconway, then Mrs Henry MacLaren, followed suit.

Few people today realise just how strong the American influence was at that time. One dish that displays this trend was the composite salad, which had not appeared until then on English menus, where 'a salad' was always made with green leaves. The American salad is well described in *Vogue* in 1927, in an article on current trends in suppers, as served at balls. (Despite the fact that the guests had all been included in dinner parties beforehand, it was thought necessary to provide both supper and breakfast at the ball itself.) 'American salads are a good deal served. These are salads in which lettuce, fruit finely cut up, and sliced nuts are delicately mixed with some variety of mayonnaise, hollandaise or tartare sauce, and put in the same bowl as the straw-sliced chicken, tongue, ham or shredded lobster or prawn, or whatever the principal ingredient may be.'

The new fashion for serving vegetables very small – another American idea – provoked running battles between cooks and gardeners, who were outraged at being asked to pick their produce before it had reached its prime, regarding it as infanticide. The head gardener was vital to the cook, for he provided all the vegetables for the house, and most of the fruit, except for a few exotic things like bananas.

In her book *Cottesbrooke*, Susan Campbell has provided us with a valuable document in the history of kitchen gardens. Cottesbrooke belonged to the Macdonald-Buchanans, and until Lady Macdonald-Buchanan's death in 1987, the three-acre kitchen garden was still run on precisely the same lines as it had been since the family acquired it in 1935. The author describes a typical garden of this sort: 'The traditional garden would be enclosed by high walls, with possibly an orchard alongside. It would have hothouses capable of supplying its owner with figs, grapes, peaches, melons, and nectarines, as well as forced vegetables and exotic pot plants. It would have potting sheds, vegetable and fruit stores, and a work-force big enough to keep a fair-sized household in fruit, cut flowers, vegetables and indoor plants all the year round. Gardens like this were the rule, rather than the exception in

all proper country establishments before the Second World War.'
One of the nicest things about having your own garden was that
it enabled you to have special varieties of fruit and vegetables on
your table. At our home in Scotland, I remember yellow tomatoes,
and yellow raspberries; one of the specialities at Cottesbrooke was
white carrots.

Broad Beans with Artichoke Bottoms

||||

This is an utterly delicious dish, quite capable of standing alone. It would probably have been served on its own, after the main course, but it works well today as a first course.

1 lb [450 g] shelled broad beans (allow 3–4 lb [1.5–1.8 kg] in their pods)
3 artichokes
1 oz [30 g] butter
¼ pt [150 ml] chicken, veal or vegetable stock
sea salt and black pepper
1½ Tbs chopped chervil (optional)

Cook the two vegetables separately in salted water. [*Cook the beans as usual. Boil the whole artichokes for 40–45 minutes, then drain well. Discard the leaves and choke.*] Cut up the artichoke bottoms into small dice. Melt 1 oz [30 g] butter in a pan. Add the vegetables. Cook for a moment or two, then add a very little [¼ pt/150 ml] good stock, and seasoning. Simmer for ten minutes [*covered*], shaking the pan from time to time. Do not stir the contents, or you will break the beans. [*Turn into a serving dish, sprinkle with chopped chervil when available, and serve as soon as possible. Serves 4 as a first course or vegetable accompaniment, or 3 as a light main dish, with rice.*]

Vegetable Cookery by Elizabeth Lucas

Endives au Jus

||||

Our chicory is called endive in French, and vice versa, which is very confusing. I love cooked chicory, which is seldom seen in this country, and this recipe is quite exceptional.

1½ lb [680 g] chicory
1 oz [30 g] butter
1 Tbs flour
8 fl oz [250 ml] good veal or chicken stock
salt and black pepper
½ tsp sugar
2 Tbs double cream

Blanch the chicory by throwing them, whole, into a pan of fast-boiling water. Cook for 6 minutes then drain in a colander. Run the cold tap over them, then drain again and squeeze out the moisture between the hands. Chop by hand, then tie in a cloth and squeeze out once more. Melt half the butter in a sauté pan that can go in the oven, or a deep frying pan with lid. Cook the chopped chicory for 5 minutes over gentle heat, stirring often. Then add the flour and stir for 1 minute. Pour on the heated stock and stir till blended. Add salt and black pepper and sugar, then cover closely with a buttered piece of foil and the lid, and cook in the oven for 1 hour at 300°F/150°C/gas 2.

When the time is up, take out of the oven and pour off the remaining liquid through a strainer into a small bowl. Put the pan over gentle heat and stir in the cream, and the remaining butter, and 2 Tbs of the cooking juices. Add more salt and pepper as required, and simmer gently for 3–4 minutes, then tip into a serving dish. Serves 4. This delicious dish goes well with dry dishes of roast or grilled chicken, game, veal, lamb cutlets, or grilled steak.

Adapted from *Vegetable Cookery* by Elizabeth Lucas

New Carrots with Curry

IIII

This is a surprisingly modern dish in that it can be served either with a meat dish, or alone, or with other vegetable dishes, as part of a vegetarian meal.

12 oz [340 g] new carrots, cut in ¼ inch [5 mm] slices
½ pt [275 ml] chicken stock
1 oz [30 g] butter
½ small bay leaf
2 stalks parsley

1 sprig thyme
salt and black pepper
a pinch of sugar
1 onion, finely chopped
1 Tbs curry powder
½ tsp flour
8 fl oz [250 ml] milk
6 oz [180 g] rice
1½ Tbs chopped coriander, or parsley (optional)

Scrape the carrots and cut them across. Put them in a pan with
[½ pt/275 ml] stock, a little [½ oz/15 g] butter, a bouquet [bay leaf,
parsley and thyme], salt, pepper and a pinch of sugar. [Cook till the
carrots are tender, then drain, reserving the liquid for soup.]
    Chop a large onion and fry it in [the remaining ½ oz/15 g] butter
and when it is pleasingly browned, add a tablespoonful of curry
powder and a big pinch of flour. Continue to fry the onion gently
for two or three minutes. Then add a little [8 fl oz/250 ml] milk. Put
it through a sieve [or medium food mill] and back into the pan. Add
the drained carrots. Simmer for five or six minutes and serve in a
border of rice. [Boil the rice as usual and drain well, then pack into a
greased 1 pt/570 ml ring mould and stand in a very low oven for 10–15
minutes. When the carrots are done, unmould the rice on to a flat dish
and tip the carrots into the centre. Sprinkle the chopped coriander or
parsley over all. Serves 3–4.]

    Vegetable Cookery by Elizabeth Lucas

Savoury Lentils with Rice

||||

*An unusually modern dish, except that in the
original recipe the lentils were sieved before
adding to the rice. This is a useful vegetarian dish,
good for serving with other vegetables, like grilled
tomatoes, or alone, with a dash of soy sauce.*

5 oz [140 g] green or brown lentils
5 oz [140 g] long-grain rice
6 oz [180 g] onions, chopped
1 oz [30 g] butter
sea salt and black pepper

Boil the lentils as usual; drain. Cook the rice as usual, and drain well. Fry the chopped onions in the butter until they are brown; about 12 minutes. Then add the lentils and rice to the onions and stir well. Cook gently until all is well mixed and hot, adding sea salt and black pepper to taste. Serves 4.

Adapted from *The Gentle Art of Cookery* by Mrs C. F. Leyel and Miss Olga Hartley

Glazed Onions

IIII

The delicious sweetness of these little onions makes a wonderful accompaniment to a grilled steak of beef or lamb, or a joint of roast meat.

1 lb [450 g] very small onions, or pickling onions, trimmed and wiped
2 oz [55 g] butter
1 tsp castor sugar
6–8 fl oz [175–250 ml] veal, beef, or chicken stock

Prepare a number of small onions as directed. Let them be all the same size. Melt some butter in a pan and when it is hot, add the onions and sprinkle them with a teaspoonful of castor sugar. Cook very gently in a covered pan, shaking them occasionally, for ten minutes, by which time they should be evenly coloured. Add enough stock to cover the onions and cook them, still with the lid on, until the liquid is reduced to a glaze. [*About 20 minutes. Serves 4.*]

Vegetable Cookery by Elizabeth Lucas

Onions au Gratin

IIII

This is a useful supper dish which can be served as an adjunct to cold meat, or on its own.

1½ lb [680 g] onions, peeled
salt
2 oz [55 g] coarse breadcrumbs
1 oz [30 g] butter
2 oz [55 g] grated Parmesan
freshly ground black pepper

CREAM SAUCE
½ pt [275 ml] milk
¼ bay leaf
2 cloves
pinch of mace, or nutmeg
1 oz [30 g] butter
2 Tbs flour
4 Tbs double cream
salt and pepper

Put the whole onions in a pan and cover with cold water. Bring to the boil, then throw away the water. Cover the onions with fresh cold water, add salt, and bring to the boil. Cook steadily till the onions are very tender, 20–30 minutes. While they are cooking, toss the breadcrumbs in butter until light golden, then set aside. When the onions are cooked, drain them well, then slice thickly. Butter a shallow gratin dish and make a layer of half the onions, covered with half the breadcrumbs and ⅓ of the grated cheese. Fill up the dish with alternate layers of onions, breadcrumbs and parmesan, keeping back ⅓ of the parmesan. Season the onion layers with salt and black pepper.

To make the sauce, heat the milk in a small pan with the bay leaf, cloves and mace (or nutmeg). When it reaches boiling point, remove from the heat and stand, covered, for 20 minutes. Then strain the milk and reheat. Melt the butter, stir in the flour, and make your sauce as usual, using the flavoured milk and cream, salt and pepper. Pour over the dish, scatter the reserved cheese over the top, and bake for 20 minutes at 400°F/200°C/gas 6, or until the top has browned. Alternatively, make in advance, leaving the sauce still in its pan. Then reheat the sauce at the last moment, pour over the dish, and bake for 30 minutes at 350°F/180°C/gas 4. Serves 4. Serve with hot or cold roast lamb, or vegetarian dishes, or as a dish in its own right, with a green salad.

Adapted from *Cantaloup to Cabbage* by Mrs Philip Martineau

Onion Rings

IIII

Deep-fried onion rings were perhaps more American than English, but they appeared in the pages of English Vogue *during the 1930s. Extremely delicious, they are equally good served with meat or other vegetables.*

2 large Spanish onions
1 egg white, lightly beaten
1 generous Tbs flour
½ tsp salt
frying oil

Peel the onions, cut into ½ inch [1 cm] slices and separate into rings. Place in a bowl of ice water for 1 hour. Make a batter by mixing the egg white with the flour and ½ teaspoon salt. Dip the rings in the batter, fry them in deep fat [*or oil*] until brown and crisp, drain on crumpled paper, and serve. These rings are excellent with beefsteak or with lamb chops. [*Serves 6.*]

Vogue's Cookery Book edited by Hilda Powell

Jugged Peas

▋|||

'Jugging' was once a common method of cooking in England, as in jugged hare. This also makes the base for a superb green pea soup (see page 55).

3 lb [1.5 kg] green peas
½ oz [15 g] butter
¼ tsp sea salt
¼ tsp sugar
12 small leaves mint
black pepper

Shell your green peas and put them into a jar or bottle with a screw lid or anything with a closely-fitting top. [*I use a Kilner jar.*] Put in with the peas a tablespoonful of butter, a saltspoonful of salt, ¼ teaspoonful of powdered sugar; a dozen mint leaves, and a very little black pepper. Cover the vessel tightly and put in a saucepan of boiling water to reach half-way up the jar. Put the saucepan on the fire and boil quickly for half an hour. If the peas are old they may take more than half an hour to cook. Take out the mint leaves before serving. Lettuce leaves and young onions may be used for flavouring instead of mint if preferred. These should be tied together and removed when the peas are dished up. [*Makes about 12 oz/340 g; serves 4.*]

The Gentle Art of Cookery by Mrs C. F. Leyel and Miss Olga Hartley

Mousse of Green Peas

IIII

This is a wonderful summer dish, good for serving alone, as a first course, or with other cold dishes. When served on its own, it is improved by a fresh tomato sauce. Also good made with broad beans, for serving with a cold roast leg of lamb.

1 pt [570 ml] shelled green peas (about 2 lb/900 g unshelled)
1 Little Gem lettuce, or heart of round lettuce
1 tsp chopped onion

BECHAMEL SAUCE
½ oz [15 g] butter
1 Tbs flour
¼ pt [150 ml] chicken or veal stock
sea salt and black pepper
a pinch of sugar (optional)
½ oz [15 g] gelatine
¼ pt [150 ml] double cream, lightly whipped

Cook the freshly shelled peas, a pint [570 ml] or so, in salted boiling water, together with the heart of a lettuce [*roughly chopped*] and a teaspoonful of chopped onion. When they are tender, strain off the water and put the vegetables through a sieve. [*Or purée in food processor with the béchamel sauce.*] Mix the purée, to which you have added seasoning and a very little sugar, with a gill [150 ml] of béchamel sauce made with chicken or veal stock. Melt some aspic jelly or a jelly made from a veal knuckle bone. [*Or, melt ½ oz/15 g gelatine in 4 Tbs of the reserved pea stock.*] Strain it into the purée. Pour the mixture into a bowl. Whisk it [*over ice*] till it begins to cool. Then add a small cupful of whipped cream. Season and beat together until it begins to set. Pour into a mould or bowl. Serve very cold. [*Serves 4. If making with broad beans, allow 2½ lb/1.15 kg unshelled.*]

Vegetable Cookery by Elizabeth Lucas

Grilled Slices of Potatoes

IIII

This unusual recipe is quite delicious, when made with firm, waxy potatoes. It is also very practical for a dinner party, in that most of the cooking is done in advance. An excellent dry potato dish for serving with grilled or roast meat or game.

4 large waxy potatoes, weighing about 6 oz [180 g] each, freshly
  cooked and cut in ¼ inch [5 mm] slices
6 Tbs olive oil
1 small onion, finely chopped
1 oz [30 g] butter
sea salt and black pepper

Slices of cooked potatoes can be marinaded for half an hour [*or
longer*] in oil with a little chopped onion. They should then be
drained [*leaving most of the chopped onion*]. Put a tiny piece of butter
with pepper and salt on each slice and grill. [*For 8–10 minutes, lying
on a baking sheet. Serves 4.*]

   Vegetable Cookery by Elizabeth Lucas

Game Chips

▌||||

*The traditional accompaniment to roast game,
together with bread sauce and browned breadcrumbs. It is worth making your own game chips
now and then, instead of buying them, for the cost
is minimal and they do not take long. I like King
Edwards best for frying, and I prefer them left
unsalted.*

4 medium potatoes, peeled and very thinly sliced
frying oil
salt (optional)

Slice the peeled potatoes as thinly as possible, either by hand or
with a mandoline. Rinse well in cold water, then dry them very
thoroughly between two layers of cloth. Heat the oil to
380°F/190°C, as for chips, then lower in the potatoes carefully,
about ¼ of the total at a time. Cook them for 2–2½ minutes, until
they are light-golden. There is no need to turn them, but they
should be moved about from time to time. When they have reached
a perfect shade, lift them out and drain on soft paper. Allow the oil
to come back to the correct temperature before lowering in the next
batch, then transfer the first lot to a warm dish and keep hot. A
pinch of salt may be sprinkled over them at this stage if you wish.
They are at their best eaten soon after frying, but they can be kept
hot for an hour or two without losing their crispness. Serves 4.

   AB

Roast Potatoes

||||

Roast potatoes are usually cooked in the same tin as the joint they are to accompany, but I prefer to cook them separately, while the joint 'rests'.

1½–2 lb [680–900 g] potatoes, preferably King Edwards
3–4 Tbs [1½–2 oz/45–55 g] dripping, fat or olive oil
sea salt

Peel the potatoes and cut in halves or quarters, depending on size. Put them in a pan, cover with lightly salted cold water and bring to the boil. Cook for 5 minutes, uncovered, then drain in a colander. When cool enough to handle, dry them in a cloth and rough up the cut surfaces with a fork. If a joint is already cooking, take some of the fat from the tin and put in a shallow baking dish. Heat this in the oven for 5 minutes, then lay the potatoes in it, turning them to coat with fat. (If no joint is cooking, use goose or duck fat, beef dripping or olive oil.) Roast them uncovered, for 35–40 minutes, turning frequently, at 425°F/220°C/gas 7. When golden brown and crusty all over, drain them on soft paper and sprinkle with sea salt. Serves 4–6.

AB

Steamed Spring Vegetable Pie

||||

Lord Berners was well known for the excellence of his food at Furingdon, and this is an adaptation of one of his recipes. It was probably served as a first course, or as a separate vegetable dish, but today it makes a good main dish for a light meal. I have substituted shortcrust for the puff pastry in the original, as I find it almost impossible to fasten the unbaked lattice on to the fragile shell which has already been baked.

PASTRY
8 oz [225 g] flour
a pinch of salt
4 oz [120 g] butter
a little iced water

FILLING
3–5 oz [85–140 g] of any 4 or 5 of the following:
baby carrots
leeks
small courgettes
pickling onions, or shallots, or large spring onions
asparagus tips
shelled broad beans, or peas
cherry tomatoes
1 oz [30 g] butter, melted, or 2 Tbs virgin olive oil
sea salt and black pepper

GLAZE
1 egg yolk, beaten

Make the pastry as usual. Chill for 20 minutes, then roll out and use two-thirds of it to line a 9 inch [23 cm] pie tin. Prick with a fork and weigh down with foil and dried beans, then bake for 8 minutes at 375°F/190°C/gas 5. Remove the foil and beans and bake for another 5 minutes at 350°F/180°C/gas 4. While the tart is baking, prepare the vegetables. If the carrots are really tiny, leave them whole, otherwise cut across into 1 inch [2.5 cm] chunks. Cut the leeks and the unpeeled courgettes in like-sized pieces. Peel the pickling onions or shallots, leaving them whole, or trim the spring onions to within 1 inch [2.5 cm] of the bulbs. Trim the asparagus to about 1½ inches [3.5 cm] of the tender tips; leave the broad beans, peas and cherry tomatoes whole, unpeeled. Steam them (except for the tomatoes) in separate groups until just tender; allow about 10 minutes for the carrots and 5 minutes for the rest. Leave the tomatoes raw.

When the shell is baked, lay the steamed vegetables in it in little clumps, and lay the cherry tomatoes over them. Pour the melted butter over all, and sprinkle with sea salt and black pepper. Cut the remaining pastry into long strips about ¼ inch [5 mm] thick. Brush the edges of the pie with beaten egg, then lay the strips of pastry over the vegetables to form a lattice, pressing the ends firmly on to the sides of the pastry case. Then brush the lattice with egg yolk and bake for about 10 minutes at 350°F/180°C/gas 4, until the lattice is nicely browned. Serve as soon as possible, as a first course or light main dish. Serves 5–6 as a first course or 3–4 as a main dish. No other accompaniment is needed.

Adapted from *The Alice B. Toklas Cook Book*

Vegetable Soufflés

IIII

In some houses, a vegetable soufflé was served after the main course, as a dish on its own. Nowadays it is more likely to be served as a first course.

8 oz [225 g] vegetable, weighed after trimming: broccoli, shelled broad beans, carrots, cauliflower, celery, onions, spinach or tomatoes
2 shallots, finely chopped
½ oz [15 g] butter

THICK WHITE SAUCE
1 oz [30 g] butter
1 oz [30 g] flour
¼ pt [150 ml] milk
salt and pepper
mace, or nutmeg (with spinach or onions)
3 eggs

Cook the vegetable as usual. Broccoli, broad beans, carrots, cauliflower and spinach should be cooked quickly in lightly salted boiling water, then drained thoroughly. Celery cut in chunks, or roughly chopped, skinned tomatoes, should be softened in 2 Tbs butter or olive oil for 10 minutes, while onions should be quartered and blanched for 5 minutes in boiling water, then drained and chopped, and stewed gently in 1 oz [30 g] butter for 10 minutes.

After draining well, the cooked vegetable should be roughly puréed in a food processor, or by pushing through a coarse food mill, together with the shallots which have been softened in butter. Make a thick white sauce with the butter, flour and heated milk, season carefully with salt and pepper, and mace, or nutmeg, in the case of spinach and onions. Then weigh 4 oz [120 g] of the vegetable purée and mix it with the sauce, stirring over low heat till amalgamated. Remove from the fire and stir in 2 egg yolks, one at a time, then 1 whole egg. Cool for a little, then fold in 2 stiffly beaten egg whites. Turn into a greased 1½–2 pt [825 ml–1.2 litres] soufflé dish and bake for 20 minutes at 400°F/200°C/gas 6. Serve alone, after the main course, or as a first course. (The onion soufflé makes a good accompaniment to roast or grilled lamb.) Serves 3 on its own, or 4 as a vegetable accompaniment to a meat dish.

Adapted from *Vegetable Cultivation and Cookery* by Eleanour Sinclair Rohde

Tomato and Rice Pie

||||

A surprisingly modern dish, this would probably have been served as a vegetable accompaniment to a meat dish, at a simple family meal. Nowadays, it could serve as a light main dish, together with one or more other vegetables.

5 oz [140 g] rice
1 medium onion, sliced
1 oz [30 g] butter
2 Tbs chopped mixed herbs: basil or tarragon, parsley, etc.
salt and black pepper
12 oz [340 g] tomatoes, skinned and sliced
4–6 Tbs dry white breadcrumbs
1½ Tbs freshly grated Parmesan

Boil the rice as usual and drain well. Fry the sliced onion in half the butter. Mix with the rice, adding the chopped herbs and salt and pepper to taste. In a buttered gratin dish, make alternate layers of rice and sliced tomatoes, seasoning the tomatoes with salt and pepper. Make two layers of each, finishing with tomatoes. Mix the breadcrumbs and Parmesan; the amount you need will depend on the shape of the dish. Scatter them over the tomatoes and dot with the rest of the butter cut in tiny bits. Bake for 40 minutes at 350°F/180°C/gas 4. Serves 4.

Adapted from *Vegetable Cultivation and Cookery* by Eleanour Sinclair Rohde

Fried Tomatoes in Cream

||||

This is good made with large ripe tomatoes, and served with rice, or with other vegetable dishes, or with bacon, gammon, or ham.

6 large, ripe tomatoes, unskinned, cut in ½ inch [1 cm] slices
sea salt and black pepper
a pinch of sugar
2 Tbs flour, sifted
1 oz [30 g] butter
2 Tbs bacon fat, melted (or 4–5 rashers fatty bacon)
4 fl oz [120 ml] double cream
1 Tbs chopped chervil, parsley or chives

Pat the sliced tomatoes with kitchen paper, then sprinkle them on both sides with sea salt, black pepper and sugar. Dip them in the flour, shaking off the excess. Heat the butter and bacon fat in a broad frying pan. (If you don't have any bacon fat, cook a few fatty bacon rashers very slowly beforehand, turning them until they have given out all their fat.) When the fat is hot, put in as many of the sliced tomatoes as the pan will hold in one layer and cook briskly, until lightly browned and soft. Turn them and cook the second side, then remove to a hot dish while you cook the rest. When all are done, pour the cream into the pan and swirl around. Let the juices and the cream bubble together for a couple of minutes, then pour over the tomatoes and sprinkle with chopped chervil, parsley, or chives. Serves 4.

Adapted from *Vogue's Cookery Book* edited by Hilda Powell

᷐ced Tomatoes and ᷐Horseradish Sauce

▐▐▐▐

This has become my favourite dish for serving with a cold roast of beef or lamb, or a cold roast duck. (It is also wonderful with cold boeuf en gelée.) When I can get them, I use a mixture of red and yellow cherry tomatoes; I always prefer to use small ones, rather than the large ones specified in the original recipe.

1 lb [450 g] small tomatoes, skinned

HORSERADISH SAUCE
¼ pt [150 ml] mayonnaise
¼ pt [150 ml] double cream, lightly whipped
2–3 Tbs grated horseradish
1–2 Tbs milk

Very good to serve as a salad on a hot summer day are large tomatoes, skinned and put in the ice chest [*or refrigerator*] till very cold, and at the last moment some good creamy horseradish sauce poured over them. The sauce to be just slightly iced. With a joint of cold lamb this is excellent. The best horseradish sauce to use is made by grating some horseradish into a mayonnaise to which has been added some cream. [*At the last moment, thin the sauce with a drop of milk to achieve a spooning consistency. Serves 6.*]

Food for the Greedy by Nancy Shaw

Salade aux Truffes

IIII

An interesting example of the comestibles that were available at the time, for those that could afford them. This recipe was published by X. M. Boulestin in Vogue *in 1926, when he was their regular food writer. It is a wonderful dish, one of the best ways of appreciating a small fresh truffle, or a tin of truffle peelings. It is also good without the truffle. Truffle oil may be used as a flavouring, or omitted altogether.*

4 oz [120 g] thinly sliced celery heart
12 oz [340 g] new potatoes, freshly boiled in their skins
4 Tbs extra virgin olive oil
½ Tbs white wine vinegar
sea salt and black pepper
1 black truffle, fresh or tinned, cut in thin strips (or peelings)

This salad is prepared with celery cut very thinly, slices of boiled potatoes [*skinned after boiling, while still hot*], and a sprinkling of fresh truffles cut en julienne. Quite plain seasoning, and not too much vinegar.

I would, once more, remind my reader that for this, as well as for all salads, the olive oil must be the very best, and the vinegar wine vinegar, either made with red or white wine. [*Best eaten within the hour, while the potatoes are still warm. Serves 3–4, as a separate course. Or, without the truffle, served with other dishes of cold meat or vegetables.*]

Vogue's Cookery Book *edited by Hilda Powell*

Mimosa Salad

IIII

A simple and delicious salad, good for serving with a meat or chicken dish, or as a course on its own.

2 Little Gem lettuces

DRESSING
sea salt and black pepper
¼ tsp Dijon mustard
a pinch of sugar
3 Tbs olive oil

1½ Tbs white wine vinegar
2 hard-boiled egg yolks, chopped
1 heaped Tbs chervil leaves

Season crisp lettuce salad with a vinegar and oil sauce. Sprinkle thickly over it, before serving, chopped yolks of hard-boiled eggs, and leaves of chervil. [*Serves 4.*]

Elsie de Wolfe's Recipes for Successful Dining

Watercress Salad

IIII

This is a truly delicious dish, and quite unusual. I serve it alone, as a first course, or as part of a spread of salads.

1½ lb [680 g] waxy (or new) potatoes, freshly boiled
4 fl oz [120 ml] single cream
sea salt and black pepper
1 lb [450 g] tomatoes, skinned and sliced
2 Tbs chopped parsley (optional)
½ large bunch watercress, tender sprigs only
2 Tbs best olive oil
1 Tbs white wine vinegar

Dice [*or slice thickly*] even, waxy new potatoes and drop into a very little salted cream. Cover the bottom of a flat dish with sliced tomatoes. Take a small bunch of parsley and shred finely over the tomatoes. On this green bed lay a layer of the white potatoes, and finally cover the whole with watercress sprigs. [*Season each layer well with sea salt and freshly ground black pepper, except for the watercress which needs no seasoning. Mix the olive oil and vinegar and spoon over all. Serves 3–4.*]

Food in England by Dorothy Hartley

PUDDINGS

Puddings

English puddings have been famous for hundreds of years, and rightly so. Both at home and abroad, they are acknowledged as excellent and uniquely English. There are an immense number of them, falling within a relatively limited range. Within each group a few examples still survive, while many more have been forgotten. Probably the most typical are the hot steamed and baked puddings that only exist in this country. These are made with varying combinations of suet, flour and, sometimes, breadcrumbs. Some are made with fresh fruit, usually apples, while others contain dried fruit. Many are flavoured with jam, marmalade, syrup, treacle, or ginger. They may be steamed, boiled or baked; those containing suet are always cooked in steam, or water. Nowadays, these are made in pudding basins standing within a large covered saucepan half filled with boiling water. Until Victorian times, however, these same puddings were simply wrapped in a cloth and submerged in boiling water. This explains the traditional 'cannon-ball' shape of plum puddings in old prints. In some parts of the country, people continue to boil their puddings in the old way, maintaining that they taste better.

Puddings made with fat instead of suet may be baked or steamed according to taste. Baking gives a light, crisp pudding, rather like a hot cake, while steaming produces a softer, moister texture. Most of these puddings were served with a custard sauce, or with cream, or both. Some had sauces relating to their fillings. A canary pudding was accompanied by a hot jam sauce, sometimes laced with brandy, while castle puddings were served with a sauce of golden syrup warmed and sharpened with a dash of lemon juice.

Then we come to the sweet pastry dishes, the fruit pies and tarts. Unlike the Continental and American fruit pies, which were made with two crusts, the English version was made in a deep china or glass dish filled with sweetened fruit, usually sliced apples or whole gooseberries, and covered with a pastry lid. Even the traditional apple pie was capable of variation, as in Lady Portarlington's version, where a dollop of Devonshire cream was slipped under the lid before serving. Another remarkable pastry dish was Bakewell tart; this was an old Derbyshire dish not far removed from the almond tart often seen today in fashionable restaurants. Bakewell tart is especially good when made with fresh raspberries, instead of jam, and served with clotted cream.

English apple puddings are legion. Indeed, we are the only country to grow cooking apples commercially; Continental dishes like the French tarte aux pommes and the Viennese apfelstrudel are made with dessert apples. And for these sorts of dishes the dessert apple is best, but for others where a soft fluffy mass is desired, only the Bramley will do. Apples were often combined with pastry; with suet, as in apple hat; with bread, as in apple Charlotte and brown Betty; with sponge, as in Eve's pudding; or on their own, as in baked apples, compotes and purées. The combination of crisp fried bread, caramelised sugar, and tart, juicy apples is unbeatable; a good example is Elsie de Wolfe's caramel apples.

Also very English are the bread puddings. Two are still much in evidence: summer pudding and bread and butter pudding. Both had many variations which have been long forgotten: paradise pudding, made with alternate layers of bread soaked in milk, and soft fruit; and satisfaction pudding, made like bread and butter pudding, with jam added, and a meringue topping. Best of all is probably Constance Spry's toffee pudding, whereby fingers of white bread are soaked in milk, then dipped in toffee sauce and served hot, with cream.

With few exceptions, milk puddings are viewed askance today, by grown-ups and children alike. Yet before the Second World War they were very popular indeed, at all levels of society. Most favoured by the upper classes, especially the men, were the steamed and baked puddings, also rice pudding. The Bath Club's speciality was a cold rice pudding set almost solid with a little gelatine, and cut in slices like a cake. An elaborate form of creamed rice was tête de nègre: set inside a round mould, encased within a chocolate shell, and topped with a turban of whipped cream. Milk puddings were most popular lower down the social scale, but these too were enjoyed at all levels, in a slightly more elaborate form. Lady Cunard used to serve tapioca beaten up with cream at her luncheon parties, while Lady Mendl offered a blancmange with orange sauce, or semolina with currant sauce.

Fortunately, the English love for custard survived the invention of Bird's Custard Powder which was already in existence by 1920, at least in the upper-middle classes. In working-class homes, Bird's Custard soon ousted the real thing in popularity, and was much used in trifles, or with tinned fruit. But there is nothing quite so good with hot fruit puddings as a true boiled custard, sometimes called sauce à la vanille. Often it would be served with cream as well, or with a proportion of whipped cream incorporated within it. Sometimes it formed part of the dish, in combinations of custard and meringue, like floating island and bombe favorite. Variations of the former are still found on the dessert trolleys in old-fashioned hotels and restaurants; a modern innovation is the golden thread of caramel dribbled over the meringue.

Lastly come the ices, on which the country houses prided themselves. With superlative fruit grown to order in their greenhouses, cream from the home farm, and obliging kitchen maids to crank the churn, these set few problems, and the results were often exquisite. They were always freshly made, since domestic freezers did not exist. Refrigerators appeared in 1925, but by 1939 only one house in fifty had one. Yet ice was not a problem. Most of the big country houses had their own ice house, where great blocks of ice were stored all year round. In the big towns, the ice-cart would deliver two or three times a week. The ice came in a huge block and was stored in a chest; pieces were hacked off and used as required.

In the grand houses, the pudding was followed by cheese at lunchtime, and a savoury at dinner. After the cheese, or savoury, the table was cleared and dishes of fresh fruit were handed round. It was very carefully arranged, each variety kept separate, piled high on sets of matching porcelain dessert dishes, often Sèvres or Meissen. There would be four or even five to choose from, at certain times of year: figs, peaches, nectarines, melons, grapes, apricots, strawberries, raspberries and giant dessert gooseberries, as well as apples and pears. All were grown in the garden, and came under the jurisdiction of the head gardener, rather than the cook. In some houses, he would indicate which pear was to be eaten next. The hothouse muscat grapes were often a special source of pride. At Cottesbrooke, the Macdonald-Buchanans' garden, it took a gardener up to twenty minutes to thin a bunch of grapes, so that each individual grape could grow extra large.

Apple Charlotte

A classic English pudding, and one of the very best.

▌|||

2 lb [900 g] cooking apples, peeled, cored and thickly sliced
4 oz [120 g] granulated sugar
4 oz [120 g] butter
4 Tbs water
juice of ½ lemon
2 Tbs apricot jam
approx. 8 thin slices dry white bread, crusts removed

Put the sliced apples in a heavy pan with the sugar, 1 oz [30 g] butter and 4 Tbs water. Cook gently, covered, until soft. Then uncover the pan and continue to cook, uncovered, over low heat until you have a thick purée. Stir in the lemon juice and apricot jam; set aside.

Cut the bread to fit a mould or soufflé dish about 3 inches [7.5 cm] deep. Melt the remaining 3 oz [85 g] butter and dip the pieces of bread in it so that they are coated on both sides, then replace them in the dish. Fill the lined dish with the apple purée and cover with a lid of more bread dipped in butter, cut to fit neatly into the top of the dish. Bake for 35–40 minutes at 350°F/180°C/ gas 4, or until the top layer of bread is crisp and golden brown. Turn out on to a flat dish to serve, fairly hot but not scalding, with a jug of thick cream, or creamy custard sauce (see page 187). Serves 4–6.

Adapted from *Come Into the Garden, Cook* by Constance Spry

Apple Hat

Suet and apples go together like bread and cheese, but for this great English dish I prefer to use crisp dessert apples, like Granny Smiths, rather than Bramleys. Custard sauce is almost obligatory with this pudding, or thick cream.

▌|||

1½ oz [45 g] butter
8 oz [225 g] self-raising flour
a pinch of salt
4 oz [120 g] shredded suet

4 Granny Smiths, or other crisp apple, peeled, cored and sliced
4 Tbs brown sugar
grated rind of 1 lemon

Grease a 2 pint [1.2 litres] pudding basin with some of the butter.
Sift the flour with the salt and cut in the suet with the blade of a
knife; mix lightly. Stir in enough cold water to make a firm dough,
and cut in 2 pieces, one larger than the other (75/25). Roll out the
larger piece to line the greased bowl. Put the apples in it, sprinkling
with brown sugar and lemon rind. Roll out the remaining suet and
lay over the bowl. Damp the edges, press together to seal and trim.
Cover with a piece of buttered foil, doming it slightly to allow for
expansion. Tie with string around the rim of the bowl. Steam over
(or in) boiling water for 2 hours. Serves 5–6. Serve with creamy
custard sauce (page 187), or cream.

AB

Lady Portarlington's Apple Tart

IIII

This is an unusual two-crust apple pie, with a generous dollop of whipped (or clotted) cream slipped under the lid before serving. Lady Portarlington served it 'iced'; I assume this meant chilled, but I prefer to serve it warm.

PASTRY
12 oz [340 g] flour, sifted
1½ tsp castor sugar
6 oz [180 g] butter, cut in bits
1 egg yolk
about 6 Tbs iced water

FILLING
3–4 crisp dessert apples, Cox or Granny Smith, peeled, cored
  and sliced
2 tsp castor sugar
1 Tbs lemon juice

GLAZE
1 egg yolk
1 Tbs milk

GARNISH

½ pt [275 ml] double cream, lightly whipped, or clotted cream
icing sugar, sifted

Make the pastry as usual and chill for 20–30 minutes. Divide it in
two pieces, one slightly larger than the other. Roll out the larger
one and line a 9 inch [23 cm] pie tin. Weigh down with foil and
dried beans and bake blind for 8 minutes at 375°F/190°C/gas 5,
then remove the foil and beans and bake for another 5 minutes.
Remove from the oven and leave to cool.

Lay the sliced apples in the pastry case, sprinkling with sugar
and lemon juice. Brush the edges of the pastry case with the egg
yolk beaten with the milk, then roll out the remaining pastry and
lay over the base. Trim the edges and seal. Decorate with some
pastry leaves, then brush all over with the egg glaze. Bake for 10
minutes at 375°F/190°C/gas 5, then for a further 30 minutes at
350°F/180°C/gas 4. Remove from the oven and leave to cool for 30–
60 minutes. Just before serving, cut round the edge carefully and
lift off the lid. Do not worry if it breaks into 2 or 3 pieces. Spread
the lightly whipped cream over the surface of the apples and
replace the lid. Sprinkle very lightly with icing sugar and serve
straightaway. Serves 6.

Adapted from Lady Portarlington in *Vogue*

Caramel Apples

The combination of tart apples, crisp fried bread and thick cream is unbeatable.

IIII

3 Granny Smith dessert apples, peeled, cored and thickly sliced
2½ oz [70 g] butter
approx. 3 oz [85 g] castor sugar
4 Tbs apricot jam, warmed and sieved
4 slices dry white bread, ⅓ inch [7.5 mm] thick, crusts removed

Fry the sliced apples in half the butter. Do them in batches, in a
broad frying pan. As each batch is done, transfer them to a shallow
(or flat) serving dish and sprinkle each layer with 1 Tbs castor sugar
and brush with the sieved apricot jam. Keep in a warm place while
you fry the rest of the apples, piling them in a level mound.

Then prepare the bread. Cut each slice in 1½ inch [3.5 cm]

squares, then cut each square into 2 triangles. Fry these in the remaining butter until lightly coloured, then drain on soft paper and lay on a baking sheet. Sprinkle them with half the remaining sugar, then place under the grill just until the sugar has melted and lightly coloured. Then remove from the grill, turn the bread over, sprinkle with the remaining sugar and replace under the grill. When lightly browned on both sides lay them over the apples and serve, hot, with a jug of thick cream. Serves 6.

Adapted from *Elsie de Wolfe's Recipes for Successful Dining*

Bread and Butter Pudding

IIII

This is my own recipe for an old favourite among puddings, and one that is fairly typical of the period. A delicious accompaniment, although not authentic, is home-made vanilla ice cream. Between the wars this pudding would have been served with a jug of cream, or, for a simple meal, alone.

3 oz [85 g] dry white bread, crusts removed, sliced
approx. 1 oz [30 g] unsalted butter
¾ oz [20 g] raisins
½ pt [275 ml] milk
¼ pt [150 ml] single cream
3 eggs
3 oz [85 g] vanilla sugar, or castor sugar

Butter the slices of bread, cut each one in half diagonally, and lay them in a buttered china dish holding 1 pt [570 ml]. Scatter the raisins between each layer of bread and over the top. Heat the milk with the cream in a small pan. Beat the eggs with the sugar, using an electric hand-beater or wire whisk. When the milk is about to boil, pour it on to the eggs continuing to beat. Then pour on to the bread through a strainer. Bake for 40–45 minutes at 325°F/170°C/gas 3, until the custard has set and the top has become crisp and golden brown. Serves 4. This pudding is best served warm, about 45 minutes after taking out of the oven. Accompany it with a jug of thick cream, or some vanilla ice cream.

AB

Bakewell Tart

||||

Jam puddings of this sort are once again fashionable, I am glad to say. I make this with short pastry instead of puff, as stated in the original recipe.

SHORT PASTRY
4 oz [120 g] flour
2½ oz [70 g] unsalted butter
½ tsp castor sugar
a little iced water

FILLING
4 Tbs each strawberry and apricot jam
2 Tbs ground almonds
3 oz [85 g] unsalted butter
2 oz [55 g] castor sugar
3 egg yolks
1 large lemon
2½ oz [70 g] soft white breadcrumbs
1 egg white
a pinch of salt

Line a round tin with pastry, roll out the bottom quite thin, put on it a layer of two sorts of jam, strawberry and apricot, sprinkle on it a thin layer of ground almonds. Beat to a cream three ounces [85 g] real butter and add to it two ounces [55 g] castor sugar. Then add the yolks of three fresh eggs, the grated rind and juice of 1 large lemon, two and a half ounces [70 g] of fine breadcrumbs, and the white of one egg well beaten with a pinch of salt. Pour on this mixture [*into the pastry case*] and bake carefully [*for about 40 minutes, or until set, at 350°F/180°C/gas 4*]. The mixture *must* set and the jam must *not* boil up and show. Eaten as a rule cold. [*Even better warm.*] Enough for six people.

Lovely Food by Ruth Lowinsky

Castle Puddings

||||

These little individual puddings like tiny sand castles are made in dariole moulds. They may be either baked or steamed, and are usually served with a golden syrup sauce. If you don't have dariole moulds, make one big pudding in a bowl and steam it. In this case it is called canary pudding, and is usually served with a hot jam sauce.

4 oz [120 g] unsalted butter
4 oz [120 g] castor sugar
4 oz [120 g] self-raising flour, sifted
2 large eggs, lightly beaten
1 tsp grated lemon rind
2 Tbs milk, or as needed

SAUCE
6 Tbs golden syrup
2 Tbs lemon juice

The sponge mixture may be made in a food processor or mixed by hand. Cream the butter and sugar, then mix in the sifted flour and beaten eggs alternately, a little at a time. Add the lemon rind and, lastly, enough milk to give a soft dropping consistency. Pour into small dariole moulds which have been well buttered. Do not fill them more than ¾ full. They may be baked for 20 minutes at 350°F/180°C/gas 4, or steamed over boiling water for 30 minutes.

When the time is up, make the sauce. Warm the syrup in a small pan, adding the lemon juice, and pour into a small jug or sauce-boat. Turn out the puddings to serve, cutting a slice off the top of each one to make a level base. Serve with the warm sauce and a jug of thick cream. Serves 6.

AB

Canary Pudding

||||

This is made with exactly the same mixture as castle puddings, but instead of using individual moulds the mixture is turned into a greased pudding basin holding about 1½ pt [825 ml]. (If to be served with a jam sauce, 2 tablespoons of the same jam may be put in the bottom of the bowl before adding the sponge mixture.) The bowl is covered with foil and tied as usual, then steamed for 2 hours. If made with jam, serve with the apricot jam sauce on page 186 or the mixed jam sauce on page 188. Alternatively, make without jam and serve with the golden syrup sauce above. Serves 5–6.

AB

Seven-Cup Pudding

IIII

My mother was given this receipt by her Scottish mother-in-law when she married. It is an old favourite: like a simpler version of plum pudding, made on the 'cup' principle instead of using scales. On a cold grey day it is very good indeed, served with a creamy custard sauce (see page 187), or lemon and vanilla sauce (see page 187). Use a teacup holding 6 fl oz [175 ml] as your measure.

1 teacupful soft white breadcrumbs
1 teacupful shredded suet
1 teacupful sultanas
1 teacupful currants
1 teacupful castor sugar
1 teacupful plain flour
2 oz [55 g] chopped mixed peel
2 oz [55 g] coarsely chopped almonds
2 tsp ground ginger
1 tsp ground cinnamon
1 tsp mixed spice, or allspice
a pinch of salt
1 egg
approx. ¼ pt [150 ml] milk
1 tsp bicarbonate of soda
1 tsp wine vinegar

Mix all the ingredients together except for the egg, milk, bicarbonate of soda and vinegar. Break the egg into a measuring jug and make up to 6 fl oz [175 ml] with milk. Stir into the mixture. Dissolve the bicarbonate of soda in the vinegar for a few moments, then stir in also. Mix all together very well, then turn into a buttered pudding basin and steam for 4–6 hours. Turn out to serve, with creamy custard sauce (page 187), lemon and vanilla sauce (page 187), plain custard, or cream. Serves 6–8.

Lady Moray

Christmas Pudding

IIII

Everyone has their own recipe for plum pudding; this is a good one, less rich than some, but light and full of flavour. In the old days, the puddings were kept from one year to the next, or made months ahead of time. The old houses had cool airy larders in which to store them, however, and anyone who tries to keep a plum pudding for long in a centrally heated flat is in for a nasty surprise, as it is sure to grow a coating of mould. Ideally, I would make the Christmas puddings about six weeks in advance.

1½ lb [680 g] seedless raisins
8 oz [225 g] cut mixed peel
8 oz [225 g] glacé cherries, halved
4 oz [120 g] coarsely chopped almonds
12 oz [340 g] shredded suet
12 oz [340 g] soft white breadcrumbs
8 eggs, beaten
¼ pt [150 ml] Guinness
6 Tbs brandy

Mix the raisins, peel, cherries, almonds, suet and breadcrumbs in a large bowl. Stir in the beaten eggs, Guinness and brandy. Leave for a few hours at this stage, or even overnight if convenient, for the flavours to develop. When ready to cook, pack the mixture into three 1½ pt [825 ml] pudding basins which have been well buttered. (If adding charms, put them in now, and remember to indicate which bowl has the charms.) Do not fill them too full; there should be at least 1 inch [2.5 cm] left empty at the top. Cover with a buttered piece of foil, doming it slightly to allow extra room for the pudding to swell. Then wrap in a square piece of clean linen – part of an old sheet will do – knotting the four corners over the top to form a handle, useful for lowering the pudding in and out of the water. Have a very large pan ready with boiling water to come halfway up the side of the bowls. Lay each bowl on an upturned saucer or small cake tin, and cover the pan. Boil steadily for 6 hours, adding more boiling water from time to time, as needed. When the time is up, lift out the puddings and leave to cool; one can be eaten straightaway if you like. The others should be stored in a cool place. If giving one or two as presents, wrap them in clean cloth after cooling.

Before serving, they should be boiled again in the same way, for 4–6 hours. To serve on Christmas Day itself, turn out on to a flat dish and stick a sprig of holly in the centre. Warm 3 Tbs brandy gently in a soup ladle, then set light to it with a match, and pour – flaming – over the pudding just before you set it on the table. Each of these puddings will serve 6–8 people; but two larger ones – or one giant – can be made if preferred.

AB

Gentleman's Pudding

IIII

A fine example of a steamed sponge pudding, made without suet or breadcrumbs. Light, delicate in flavour, and with an outstanding sauce, it is one of the best.

5 oz [140 g] butter
2½ oz [70 g] castor sugar
5 oz [140 g] self-raising flour
3 large eggs
3 Tbs raspberry jam

SAUCE
2 egg yolks
1 Tbs castor sugar
2½ fl oz [70 ml] dry sherry
1½ Tbs raspberry jam

Cream butter and sugar, add sifted flour and eggs [*one at a time*] alternately. Beat well, then add jam. Turn into a buttered bowl [*holding about 1¾ pt/1 litre*] and steam for 1½ hours. Turn out and serve with the following sauce: Whip egg yolks with sugar over hot water. Add sherry, then jam. Serve hot, either poured around the pudding, or separately, in a sauceboat. Cream may be served as well, if you wish. Serves 6.

Lady Colefax in *Vogue*

Marmalade Pudding

This pudding uses a mixture of equal parts suet and breadcrumbs, with no flour.

‖‖

4 oz [120 g] soft white breadcrumbs
4 oz [120 g] shredded suet
4 oz [120 g] castor sugar
2 heaped Tbs marmalade, chopped
1 egg, lightly beaten

SAUCE
4 Tbs marmalade, chopped
2 Tbs orange juice
¼ pt [150 ml] double cream

Mix the breadcrumbs, suet and sugar in a bowl. Mix the marmalade with the beaten egg and stir into the suet mixture. Turn into a greased pudding basin holding about 1½ pt [825 ml]. Cover with greased foil, slightly domed, and tie with string around the rim of the bowl. Steam over boiling water for 2 hours, or stand in a large covered saucepan with boiling water coming halfway up the sides of the bowl. Check now and then to see that it is not boiling dry, adding more boiling water as needed. When the time is up, make the sauce. Put the marmalade and orange juice in a small pan, add 2 Tbs water, and heat gently. Add the cream, stirring till blended. When all is hot, pour into a sauceboat. Unmould the pudding on to a round dish and serve with the marmalade sauce. Serves 4–5.

AB

Pudding Louise

‖‖

I am told by a mutual friend that this was Lord Berners' favourite pudding. It is very good indeed, rather like Bakewell tart without the almonds. I have adapted it from the original, which was brief, but very precise. I tend to use Tiptree Raspberry Seedless, or Blackberry Jelly, instead of redcurrant jelly.

PASTRY
6 oz [180 g] flour
3 oz [85 g] unsalted butter
a little iced water

FILLING
4–5 Tbs redcurrant (or other fruit) jelly
3½ oz [100 g] unsalted butter, at room temperature
3½ oz [100 g] castor sugar
2 oz [55 g] flour, sifted

Make the pastry as usual. Chill for 20 minutes, then roll out to line a 9 inch [23 cm] pie tin. Chill again, then bake blind, weighed down with foil and dried beans, for 8 minutes at 375°F/190°C/gas 5. Remove the foil and beans, and bake for a further 5 minutes at 350°F/180°C/gas 4. Remove from the oven and leave to cool.

Later, spread the jelly over the bottom of the pastry case. Cream the butter and sugar, either by hand or in a food processor. Mix in the sifted flour and spread over the jelly. Bake for 1 hour at 325°F/170°C/gas 3. Serve soon after coming out of the oven, with cream. Serves 6. This tart is utterly delicious served hot or warm, but it is not good cold, nor will it reheat well.

Adapted from *The Alice B. Toklas Cook Book*

Two-Tier Lemon Pudding

IIII

This is a good hot pudding, simple and quick to make, that has been all but forgotten. It separates into two parts on baking: a solid cakey top, with a lemon sauce lying underneath the surface. I like to serve it with fresh raspberries and thick cream.

½ oz [15 g] unsalted butter
2 oz [55 g] castor sugar
2 eggs, separated

½ pt [275 ml] milk
juice of 1 lemon
2 heaped Tbs flour

Cream butter and sugar. Beat yolks and add to creamed mixture. Add milk, lemon juice, and flour. Add stiffly beaten whites and put in buttered [2 pt/1.2 litres] dish. Put dish in a bigger one [or a roasting tin] containing hot water and cook until nicely brown for about 45 minutes in a moderate oven [375°F/190°C/gas 5]. This is enough for about 3 [or 4] people.

Mrs Arthur James

Pain Perdu with Raisin Sauce

▌▌▌▌

Pain perdu was originally a French pudding which became popular in England, where it was sometimes known as 'eggy bread'. This is a more elegant version, such as might have been served at a lunch party, with a hot raisin sauce.

½ pt [275 ml] milk
2 Tbs vanilla sugar, or castor sugar and ½ vanilla pod
6 large slices stale white bread, crusts removed
2 eggs, beaten
2 oz [55 g] butter

HOT RAISIN SAUCE
4 Tbs seedless raisins
2 Tbs sugar
½ oz [15 g] butter
¼ pt [150 ml] water
1 Tbs brandy
4 Tbs double cream

Have the sauce made in advance. Put the raisins in a small pan with the sugar, butter and ¼ pt [150 ml] water. Simmer gently for 10 minutes, until the raisins have swelled and become soft. Stand, covered, at the back of the stove while you make the pudding.

Heat the milk with the vanilla sugar. (If you don't have vanilla sugar, use ordinary castor sugar with half a vanilla pod to flavour the milk.) Bring slowly to boiling point, then reduce the heat and cook gently until the sugar has melted, then leave to cool. (If using a vanilla pod, remove it once the milk has cooled completely.) Cut each slice of bread in four, and lay in a shallow dish. Pour over the milk, turning the pieces of bread over to absorb the milk without allowing them to become too soft. Beat the eggs and dip each slice in them. Heat the butter in a broad frying pan and fry the bread on both sides, until golden. Lay on a serving dish and sprinkle with castor sugar. Reheat the sauce, adding the brandy and cream, and serve in a sauceboat, with the pain perdu. Alternatively, you may omit the raisin sauce and simply serve it with a bowl of lightly whipped cream. Serves 6.

AB

Paradise Pudding

IIII

This is an early variant of the well-known summer pudding. It was served in its dish, with a layer of lightly whipped cream spread over the top, but I prefer to turn it out and serve the cream separately. When soft fruit is plentiful, I cook a second lot and spoon it around the pudding before serving. My favourite fruit combination is raspberries, blueberries and redcurrants.

1½ lb [680 g] soft fruit: mixed berries and currants
2 Tbs castor sugar
8–10 thick slices dry white bread, crusts removed
¾ pt [450 ml] milk

GARNISH (OPTIONAL), TO BE MADE ON 2ND DAY
12 oz [340 g] soft fruit (as above)
2 Tbs castor sugar

Start 1 day in advance: Cook the fruit very lightly indeed: put the berries in a large bowl beside the stove. Put the sugar in a heavy pan with 4 Tbs water; heat slowly until the sugar has melted. Then put in the blackcurrants, if used, and cook gently for 2 minutes. Then add redcurrants and blueberries. Cook for another 2 minutes, then pour the contents of the pan, still simmering, over the berries in their bowl. (Raspberries, blueberries and blackberries are best; strawberries are not ideal, being too watery. If used, they are best added raw, after the rest of the fruit has cooled.)

When the fruit has cooled to room temperature make a layer of it in the bottom of a bowl. Cut pieces of bread to fit the bowl, then dip each one in milk and press gently. Then lay them over the fruit. Continue to make alternate layers of fruit and bread in this way, until the dish is full. Finish with a layer of bread cut to fit exactly, so the fruit is completely covered. Cover with foil and a small plate, and lay a 1½ lb [680 g] weight on the plate. Stand overnight in the refrigerator. Next day, if adding a fruit garnish, cook the second lot of fruit exactly as you did the first lot the previous day. Leave it to cool, then shortly before serving unmould the pudding on to a shallow dish and spoon the extra fruit around it. Serve with a jug of thick cream, or a bowl of lightly whipped cream. Serves 6–8.

Adapted from *Lady Sysonby's Cook Book*

Toffee Pudding

IIII

This is the best of all the hot, rich English puddings, perfect for a weekend lunch party on a winter day.

4 oz [120 g] unsalted butter
4 oz [120 g] light brown demerara sugar
8 oz [225 g] golden syrup
½ pt [275 ml] milk
fingers of (white) bread, 1 day old

Put the butter, demerara sugar, and syrup into a frying pan, stir until melted over slow heat, then boil more rapidly until golden brown, stirring continuously. Bring the milk up to boiling point. Arrange the fingers of bread in a large dish, pour over the milk. Lift out the fingers at once and put them into the toffee sauce to coat them well. Pile them up in a fireproof dish, and if necessary pour over a little extra toffee sauce. Serve with whipped cream. [*Serves* 6.]

The Constance Spry Cookery Book by Constance Spry and Rosemary Hume

Cream of Rice
(As made at the Bath Club)

IIII

A cold rice pudding, set almost solid by the addition of a small quantity of gelatine, was popular with men, who seemed to prefer it to the softer creamier version which was sometimes served.

1½ pt [825 ml] milk
4 oz [120 g] pudding rice
2 Tbs castor sugar
¼ oz [7 g] gelatine, or ½ a packet
1 egg yolk, beaten
3 Tbs lightly whipped cream

Bring the milk to the boil and shake in the rice. Bring back to the boil and cook for 20 minutes, half covered. Add the sugar and cook for another 20 minutes, then turn into a basin, keeping back about 4 Tbs of the hot milk. Pour this into a cup and dissolve the gelatine in it. Once melted, stir it into the rice, mixing well. Then stir in the beaten egg yolk and leave to cool. When it has reached room temperature, fold in the whipped cream and turn into a serving dish. Chill for a few hours, or overnight. Serve very cold, with a dish of lightly cooked fruit still slightly warm or at room temperature. Cream may be served as well, if you like. Serves 6. A useful dish in that it keeps well in the fridge, may be prepared well in advance, and is quite sustaining.

Adapted from *The Perfect Hostess* by Rose Henniker Heaton

Rice Meringue

IIII

This is based on a recipe in Minnie Lady Hindlip's Cookery Book, *but I have substituted a tart purée of apples for the layer of jam in the original.*

6 oz [180 g] pudding rice
1½ pt [825 ml] milk
2 inch [5 cm] strip lemon peel
2 oz [55 g] vanilla sugar, or castor sugar
2 egg yolks, beaten
2 Tbs double cream

APPLE PUREE
3 Bramley cooking apples, peeled, cored and thickly sliced
3 Tbs sugar

MERINGUE
3 egg whites
2½ oz [70 g] castor sugar

Put the rice in a pan with the milk and lemon peel. Bring to the boil and cook slowly, half covered, until the rice is tender and all the milk has been absorbed: about 25 minutes. Then remove the lemon peel and leave to cool. Then stir in the sugar, and the egg yolks beaten with the cream. Cook the sliced apples with 3 Tbs sugar and 6 Tbs water until soft, then push them through a medium food mill and leave to cool.

Spread half the rice in the bottom of a buttered fireproof dish – a soufflé dish does well – and spread the apple purée over it. Cover with the rest of the rice. Beat the egg whites until they become stiff, then add most of the sugar bit by bit. Fold in the last spoonful by hand, and pile on top of the rice. Bake for 30 minutes at 275°F/140°C/gas 1, until lightly set and golden brown. This dish is good at any temperature: hot, warm, cool, or straight from the fridge. Serves 4–6.

Adapted from *Minnie Lady Hindlip's Cookery Book*

Tête de Nègre

▌▌▌▌

This was a popular pudding in the thirties, now rarely seen. The combination of the crisp chocolate shell with the creamy rice within is very good indeed.

3 oz [85 g] long-grain rice
¾ pt [450 ml] milk
3 egg yolks
2 oz [55 g] vanilla sugar
½ pt [275 ml] double cream

CHOCOLATE SAUCE
3 oz [85 g] plain chocolate
2 oz [55 g] unsalted butter

Drop the rice into boiling water and cook for 10 minutes; drain well. Heat ½ pt [275 ml] milk, shake in the drained rice, and cook for another 10 minutes, then drain again.

Make a custard by beating the egg yolks with the vanilla sugar. Then heat the remaining ¼ pt [150 ml] milk until almost boiling and pour on to the egg yolks, beating well. Stand over a pan of simmering water and continue to stir for 6–8 minutes, until it has thickened slightly, just enough to coat the back of the spoon. Stir the hot custard into the cooked rice, and leave to cool. Then stir in 2 Tbs cream and turn into a round pudding basin rinsed out with cold water, which it fills nicely. (About ¾ pt/450 ml.) Chill for several hours, or overnight.

Some hours later, make the sauce. Grate the chocolate into a bowl standing over a pan of simmering water. Add the butter cut in small bits, and 1 Tbs hot water. Once the chocolate has melted, beat well. Unmould the rice pudding on to a flat dish and pour the hot chocolate sauce over it so that it is completely covered. The sauce will set to a hard shell immediately on contact with the cold rice. Chill again before serving, or stand in a cool larder.

Just before serving, whip the remaining cream and pile on top, like a turban. Serves 4–5.

Adapted from *Personal Choice* by Ambrose Heath

Lady St Just's Raspberry and Redcurrant Compote

This is an exquisite dish, both in flavour and in appearance. I cook the currant purée for a couple of minutes, just long enough to sweeten it.

▌║

1 lb [450 g] raspberries
8 oz [225 g] redcurrants
1½–2 oz [45–55 g] castor sugar

Press but do not pulp some raspberries. [*Put them under a 3 lb/1.5 kg weight for 1 hour.*] Put them into a glass bowl [*reserving 2 oz/55 g*] and cover with some of the redcurrants [*again reserving 2 oz/55 g*]. Continue with layers [*four in all*] of pressed raspberries

156

and whole redcurrants until the dish is nearly full. Sugar each layer [*with 1 Tbs castor sugar*]. Make a purée of the remaining raspberries and redcurrants. [*Heat 4 Tbs water with 4 Tbs sugar in a heavy pan until the sugar has melted, then add the currants and cook gently for 2 minutes. Pour them, still simmering, over the reserved raspberries in a bowl and leave to cool. Then purée and spread over the surface of the dish.*] Put in the refrigerator for several hours [*or overnight*]. Serves 4.

English Country House Cooking by Fortune Stanley

Sliced Peaches in Plum Juice

||||

An unusual fruit dish, elegant and delicious, yet quickly made. I add eau-de-vie de framboise, when I have it, instead of kirsch, to the plum juice before serving.

5 oz [140 g] sugar
5 Tbs water
6 large red (ripe) plums
4 perfectly ripe peaches, white flesh for preference
1 Tbs kirsch, or eau-de-vie de framboise

Make a syrup of the sugar and ¼ cup [5 Tbs] water. When thick pour it over the plums in a saucepan, place on the fire, and cook gently until the plums burst and the syrup becomes red. Strain the juice of the plums and put part [*half*] of the plums through a sieve [*or medium food mill*] and add to the juice. Place this juice on ice to chill. [*Add spirits at this point if you prefer not to hand it round at table.*] Peel and slice the peaches, which should be very ripe, pour the plum juice over, and serve with a bottle of kirsch [*or eau-de-vie*] separately, to be added to the fruit as desired. Serves 4. [*This looks pretty served in individual glass bowls, or in one large one.*]

Vogue's Cookery Book edited by Hilda Powell

Pekin Dust

||||

This excellent dessert is an old favourite in my family, but the name of this version is new to me. The cream may be omitted if preferred or served separately.

6 medium oranges
castor sugar (optional)
4 oz [120 g] loaf (or granulated) sugar
¼ pt [150 ml] water
¼–½ pt [150–275 ml] double cream

Peel the oranges and slice them, removing all skin and pips and taking care to lose none of the juice. Mix the juice with a little castor sugar to taste [*I leave it unsweetened*], adding a little more juice if necessary, and pour over the oranges.

Put the loaf [*or granulated*] sugar in a saucepan, add the water and boil quickly till [*light golden*] brown, being careful not to let it get too dark. Pour it out onto a tin to let it get cold and set. When it is hard, crush it coarsely with a rolling-pin and shake it all over the fruit. Whip the cream and pile it on top. [*Serves 6.*]

When The Cook Is Away by Catherine Ives

Compote of Oranges with Orange Jelly

||||

An orange jelly was a favourite with children and grown-ups alike. This one is particularly good, served with a compote of sliced oranges in a light orange syrup.

JELLY
9 oranges
1 lemon
4 oz [120 g] granulated sugar
4 Tbs water
½ oz [15 g] gelatine (1 packet)

COMPOTE
6 oranges
1 oz [30 g] granulated sugar

Make the jelly a day in advance. Pare the rind of 1 orange; squeeze the juice of all nine, and the lemon. Heat the sugar with 4 Tbs water until it boils, and the sugar has melted, then pour it over the rind and leave to cool. Dissolve the gelatine in 4 Tbs hot water, then add to the fruit juices, with the sugar syrup. Mix well, then pour through a strainer into a shallow bowl. Chill overnight.

Next day, squeeze the juice of 2 oranges into a bowl. Dissolve the sugar in 2 Tbs water, then add to the juice and leave to cool. Peel the remaining 4 oranges, removing all the white pith, and cut in fairly thick slices. Arrange them overlapping in a shallow round dish and pour the syrup over them. Chill for at least 2 hours before serving, with the jelly in a separate bowl. Serves 6. (The jelly will probably be very soft. If firm, it may be roughly chopped with the edge of a palette knife, then turned back into the clean bowl.)

Adapted from *Kitchen Essays* by Lady Jekyll

Red Wine Jelly

IIII

This was a popular dessert in England in Stuart times, but was later forgotten. It survived in the United States, however, and from there was reintroduced to England in the 1920s.

4 oz [120 g] castor sugar
¾ oz [20 g] gelatine (1½ packets)
½ pt [275 ml] good red wine
4 Tbs brandy
2 Tbs orange juice
2 Tbs lemon juice
½ pt [275 ml] double cream, lightly whipped

Bring ½ pint [275 ml] water to the boil, add the sugar and stir until it has melted. Remove from the heat, cool slightly, then shake in the gelatine. When this also has melted, add the wine, brandy and fruit juices. Mix well, then pour into a (1¼ pt/720 ml) ring mould through a strainer. Cool, then chill overnight, or for several hours, in the refrigerator. Turn out on to a flat dish to serve, filling the centre with lightly whipped cream. Serves 4.

AB

Plum Croutons

IIII

This uncomplicated dish is based on a recipe in Mrs Leyel's classic, The Gentle Art of Cookery. *It must be made with plums ripe enough to eat.*

4 slices dry white bread cut ½ inch [1 cm] thick
1 oz [30 g] unsalted butter
4 large ripe plums, or 6 medium ones
1 oz [30 g] castor sugar

Cut the bread in neat rectangles, removing the crusts. Butter on both sides and lay them on a baking sheet. Cut the plums in half and remove the stones. Do this over the bread so that the juice that runs out is not wasted. Lay 2 or 3 plum halves on each piece of bread. Sprinkle them thickly with sugar and dot each plum half with a tiny bit of butter. Bake for 45 minutes at 325°F/170°C/gas 3, sprinkling them once or twice with the rest of the sugar during the baking. Take out of the oven and cool for 10–15 minutes before serving, on a flat dish, with a jug of cream. Serves 4.

Adapted from *The Gentle Art of Cookery* by Mrs C. F. Leyel and Miss Olga Hartley

Floating Island

IIII

This is one of the few old-fashioned puddings to have remained popular, for it is still sometimes seen today in the restaurants of grand hotels like Claridge's. Nowadays, a thin stream of caramel is often trickled over the mound of meringue, which is also rather delicious.

MERINGUE
4 egg whites
6 Tbs vanilla sugar, or castor sugar

CUSTARD SAUCE
¾ pt [450 ml] milk
½ vanilla pod
4 egg yolks
3 Tbs vanilla sugar, or castor sugar

CARAMEL (OPTIONAL)
4 oz [120 g] granulated sugar

If using caramel, make this first. Put the granulated sugar in a heavy pan with 4 Tbs water and heat slowly. Boil steadily, watching constantly, until the sugar melts and starts to caramelise.

When it has turned pale golden, remove from the heat and pour it into a wetted mould or fireproof dish. (This may be either a tin charlotte mould, or a fireproof glass or china bowl holding about 1½ pt [825 ml].) Turn the mould quickly as you pour in the caramel so that the sides are evenly coated. Set aside to cool.

Beat the egg whites until stiff, then add 3 Tbs vanilla (or castor) sugar, little by little, as you continue to beat. Finally fold in the remaining 3 Tbs sugar, then turn into the caramel-lined mould and bake for 20 minutes at 325°F/170°C/gas 3.

Make the custard sauce while it bakes. Heat the milk with the vanilla pod in a small pan. Bring slowly to the boil, then remove from the heat, cover, and stand for 20–30 minutes. Then remove the pod and reheat the milk slowly. Beat the egg yolks in a bowl, adding the 3 Tbs vanilla (or castor) sugar. When the milk boils, pour it on to the egg yolks, continuing to beat. Then stand the bowl over a saucepan of simmering water, making sure the water does not touch the base of the bowl, and stir constantly until it has thickened very slightly, just enough to coat the back of a spoon. This may take 7 or 8 minutes. Remove from the heat and stand in a sink half full of very cold water, stirring now and then as it cools to prevent a skin forming.

When both meringue and sauce have cooled, chill them for 2–3 hours in the refrigerator. Shortly before serving, turn out the meringue by running a sharp knife round the inside edge of the mould. Pour the custard sauce around it. Serves 6. (If you prefer the old-fashioned version without the caramel, simply leave it out, and oil the mould lightly with sunflower or almond oil.)

AB

Prune Whip

IIII

This is like a simple soufflé, delicious served hot, with a bowl of whipped cream flavoured with brandy.

8 oz [225 g] prunes
½ pt [275 ml] cold (Indian) tea
2 oz [55 g] castor sugar
3 egg whites

GARNISH
½ pt [275 ml] double cream
1 Tbs brandy

Stew the prunes [*which have been soaked for a few hours in cold tea*] until the stones come out easily. Crush [*by chopping, then pushing through a food mill*], add the sugar and well beaten egg whites; [*spoon into a soufflé dish and*] place in a pan of warm water and bake in a moderate oven. [*25 minutes at 350°F/180°C/gas 4.*] Serve with whipped cream flavoured with brandy. [*First whip the cream, then fold in the brandy little by little. Serves 4.*]

Caviare to Candy by Mrs Philip Martineau

Bombe Favorite

‖‖

This is known as cream bomb in my daughter-in-law's family, where it is made with undiluted whipped cream mixed with broken meringue. This is how it was always made before the war, but during the food restrictions an egg custard often replaced some of the cream. I prefer it made this way, for the other is very rich indeed. It was usually served with a raspberry sauce, or with stewed fruit. I like it with a garnish of very lightly cooked mixed berries.

CUSTARD
2 egg yolks
1 Tbs cornflour
1 Tbs castor sugar
½ pt [275 ml] milk

½ pt [275 ml] double cream, whipped
5–6 oz [140–180 g] meringues, broken in large pieces

FRUIT GARNISH
2 Tbs castor sugar
12 oz [340 g] blueberries
8 oz [225 g] raspberries

Start several hours in advance. Make the custard as usual, adding a little cornflour mixed to a paste with 3 Tbs water to the egg yolks, to assist the thickening. Cool quickly in a sink half full of cold water, stirring often to prevent a skin forming. When it has cooled almost to room temperature, whip the cream and fold into the custard. Fold in the pieces of meringue, trying to avoid breaking them up too much. Add as many as are needed to make a fairly stiff mixture that will hold its shape. Turn into a bowl and freeze for 2 hours.

While it is freezing, make the fruit garnish. Put the sugar in a heavy pan with 2 Tbs water. When the sugar has melted, add the blueberries and cook for 2 minutes, then pour them over the raspberries which are standing beside the stove in a bowl. Leave to cool.

Shortly before serving, turn out the 'bombe' on to a shallow dish and pour the fruit compote around it. Serves 5–6. Very popular with children.

Alternatively, make a fruit sauce with 1 lb [450 g] raspberries (fresh or frozen), puréed in a food processor and rubbed through a coarse sieve or food mill to hold back the pips. Sweeten to taste, and pour around the iced pudding.

Kate Boxer

Raspberry Ice

IIII

This excellent dish is based on one prepared by Mrs Woodman, the Mildmays' cook, for a dinner party at their house in Berkeley Square. In the original version, which I have simplified, the ice was served on a base of sponge cake, with a dish of fresh raspberries handed separately, together with cream, and cigarette wafers. Raspberry makes the best of all ice creams, for the acidity of the fruit cuts through the bland mass of cream. The ice is also very good served alone.

ICE CREAM
1 lb [450 g] raspberries
1 Tbs castor sugar
2½ oz [70 g] granulated sugar
3 egg yolks, beaten
½ pt [275 ml] double cream, lightly whipped

MIXED BERRY SAUCE (OPTIONAL)
8 oz [225 g] raspberries
2 Tbs castor sugar
1 Tbs eau-de-vie de framboise, or kirsch
8 oz [225 g] strawberries, cut in quarters

163

Purée the raspberries in a food processor, then rub through a sieve, or push through a fine food mill; add the castor sugar. Put the granulated sugar in a small pan with 4 fl oz [120 ml] water and heat slowly. When the sugar has melted, increase the heat and boil rapidly until it will form a thread between finger and thumb. Then take it off the heat and leave for a moment to cool, then pour it on to the beaten egg yolks, beating constantly with a wire whisk until the mixture is thick and foamy. Set aside to cool, then mix with the raspberry purée and fold in the lightly whipped cream. Freeze as usual. Makes just over 1 pint [570 ml], or 1¼ lb [570 g].

While it is freezing, make the sauce. Simply purée the raspberries in a food processor and rub through a coarse sieve, or fine food mill. Add the sugar, and a drop of eau-de-vie de framboise, or kirsch, if you have it. Then mix with the strawberries which you have cut in quarters, and turn into a shallow bowl. Serve with the ice cream, and a plate of home-made sponge fingers (see page 230). Serves 6; the ice alone serves 4.

AB

Caramel Ice Cream

‖‖

This recipe comes from Joyce Molyneux, chef/ proprietor of the Carved Angel in Dartmouth. Joyce is wholly English, despite her name, and this is just the sort of ice cream that was being made before the war, cranked by hand in wooden pails packed with ice and rock salt, in the English country houses. Joyce Molyneux is an inspired cook, and this ice cream cannot be bettered. Made with plain sugar instead of muscovado, it is simply a superlative vanilla ice cream.

1 vanilla pod
3 egg yolks
4 oz [120 g] light brown muscovado sugar (or castor sugar)
½ pt [275 ml] milk
¼ pt [150 ml] double cream

Slit the vanilla pod down its length. Beat the egg yolks with the sugar in a bowl until pale and fluffy. Pour the milk into a pan and add the vanilla pod. Bring slowly to the boil. Remove from the heat and pour on to the egg yolks, stirring constantly. Set the bowl over a pan of simmering water, and stir for about 5 minutes, until the custard is thick enough to coat the back of a spoon. Do not let it boil. Stand the bowl in iced water to cool quickly. Remove vanilla pod.

When cool, add the double cream and mix well. Churn or beat by hand as it freezes. Move the ice cream from the freezer to the fridge about 15 minutes before serving. Serves 4–6.

The Carved Angel Cookery Book by Joyce Molyneux

Brown Bread
Ice Cream

‖‖

To make brown bread ice cream, an old English favourite, first make toasted breadcrumbs as follows. Lay 3 oz [85 g] soft brown breadcrumbs on a baking sheet and bake in the oven at 300°F/150°C/gas 2, for 30–40 minutes, until light golden brown. Turn on to a plate to cool. Then make vanilla ice cream as above, using vanilla or castor sugar instead of muscovado, and fold in the breadcrumbs when it is two-thirds frozen. Continue to freeze until thick. Serves 4–6.

AB

Cream of Roses

‖‖

One of Mrs Leyel's enchanting recipes, a timely reminder that English food could be exotic as well as homely. I have substituted milk for half the cream to make it less rich, more in tune with current tastes.

½ pt [275 ml] milk
½ pt [275 ml] single cream
1–1½ oz [30–45 g] fresh rose petals, preferably old-fashioned roses
3 egg yolks
4 Tbs castor sugar
a few drops cochineal (optional)

Boil a pint [570 ml] of cream [*or milk and cream mixed*], and put into it when it boils two handfuls of fresh rose petals, and leave them for two hours, well covered. Then pass this through a sieve [*or strain it*], and mix [*or make into a custard*] with the well-beaten yolks of eggs, and sugar to taste. Add a little cochineal [*optional*], and put it on the fire, stirring all the time, but do not let it boil on any account. [*Beat the egg yolks with the sugar, then pour on the boiling milk and cream, after straining. Stir over a pan of simmering water for 6–8 minutes, or until it has very slightly thickened, then cool quickly in a sink half full of cold water. Freeze as usual. Makes approx. 1 pt/570 ml.*]

The Gentle Art of Cookery by Mrs C. F. Leyel and Miss Olga Hartley

Rhubarb Sorbet

||||

This is an unusual sorbet, delicious in flavour and a lovely shade of pink. It is best made with early (forced) rhubarb which does not need peeling, as the flavour is more delicate and the skin gives it its colour. This could very well be used as a sorbet halfway through a long meal; in this case use less sugar.

1½ lb [680 g] forced rhubarb, cut in chunks
2 dessert apples, or 1 Bramley, peeled, cored and roughly chopped
6 oz [180 g] sugar
juice of 1 orange

Put the rhubarb and apple in a pan with the sugar and add enough water to come barely level with the contents of the pan, about ½ pint [275 ml]. Cook gently until both rhubarb and apples are soft, then drain off the juice into another pan and boil up until it is reduced by about one third; this will take about 5 minutes. Leave to cool. Later, put the cooked fruit in a food processor with the orange juice and the cooled syrup. Process until blended, then freeze as usual. Serves 6–8.

Jane Longman in *Vogue*

SAUCES

Sauces

English and French sauces differ fundamentally in that they are constructed on totally different principles. Whereas a French sauce is an intrinsic part of the dish it accompanies, often made with the juices that result from its cooking, the English sauce is a thing apart. There is no English equivalent to the sauce served with a canard pressé, for example, which is made from the blood and juices of the pressed duck. Our traditional sauce for duck is made with stewed apples. Whereas in France a sauce is used to implement and reinforce the main flavour of the main element, in England the sauce is used to give a contrast: in taste, texture and – sometimes – temperature.

Almost every main dish had its accompanying sauce, and in most households these were rarely, if ever, deviated from. To eat roast lamb without mint sauce, or at least redcurrant jelly, would have been unthinkable. Duff Cooper described such a fiasco in a letter to his wife in 1938: 'My dinner for eight was quite successful last night except when Mrs Blackman sent up roast partridge without bread sauce. I nearly had a stroke.' Roast beef was invariably accompanied by horseradish in some form; boiled mutton by caper or onion sauce. Parsley sauce was always served with boiled ham, egg sauce with boiled cod, bread sauce with roast chicken, mustard sauce with grilled herrings and cheese sauce with macaroni, cauliflower and hard-boiled eggs.

In addition to the sauces, there was also a range of traditional garnishes that were often served with the sauce, or instead of one. These included fruit jellies, either redcurrant, rowan or crab-apple, to accompany hot or cold roast mutton or lamb. Cumberland sauce is like a cross between a fruit jelly and a sauce; this was served with hot or cold ham, game pâté and terrines. Fruit garnishes were sometimes served with cold meat, especially pork, or duck. These might be composed of chopped apples, onions and celery, like an uncooked chutney. Breadcrumbs fried in butter were always served with roast pheasant and grouse, at the same time as the bread sauce. Fried parsley was the traditional garnish for fried fish, either whole, like smelts or whiting, or cut in strips, like goujons of Dover sole. It was also served with fish cakes and egg croquettes. Whole sprigs of parsley were dropped into very hot oil for a few seconds, and emerged bright emerald green, crisp and fragile as the fried seaweed (actually shredded spring greens) that we eat today in Chinese restaurants.

Typical of the thirties were the chilled or even semi-frozen sauces that were often served with hot dishes. Since refrigerators were the newest thing in kitchen technology, iced dishes were considered very smart. Ices were made with the most surprising ingredients, ranging from Camembert cheese to horseradish, and a sorbet-like tomato mush was often served with hot fried goujons of sole. This sort of extreme contrast demanded care and precision; the plates had to be cool and the service speedy or a soupy mush was the end result.

Bottled sauces had been manufactured in Britain since the mid-nineteenth century. Firms like Lea & Perrins, Crosse & Blackwell and Burgess had been producing such things as Worcestershire Sauce, Harvey's Sauce, Anchovy Essence and Mushroom Ketchup for almost a hundred years, and they were still as popular as ever. Their appeal was for the typical Englishman who liked to combine a strong sharp taste with the basically bland flavour of English food, and who preferred to add it himself, at table. (Worcestershire Sauce and Anchovy Essence both show a similarity to the ancient Roman sauce garum, which was made with pickled anchovies and asafoetida, and used for adding to dishes.)

Some of these sauces can still be bought today – Worcestershire Sauce is still in demand for making bloody Marys – but their popularity has been usurped by the tomato- and pepper-based sauces like tomato ketchup and Tabasco. In my own kitchen, I find that soy sauce, Maggi Liquid Seasoning and Tabasco have replaced the heavier sauces mentioned above, that I remember so well from my childhood. I never ate them myself, of course, for they are anathema to children, but my father was fond of them. In the great country houses bottled sauces were never seen, for the cook preferred to make her own.

Sweet sauces for puddings were also important at this time, when hot steamed and baked puddings were popular. For these really need a complementary sauce to realise their full potential. The most usual was the excellent boiled custard, sometimes called sauce à la vanille. (Bird's Custard Powder had been around since 1846, but I found no mention of it in any of the cookery books of the inter-war period. It may be that it was only the convenience foods of recent development, like American breakfast cereals and tinned petits pois, that caught the fancy of the upper and middle classes. Certainly in working-class homes Bird's Custard was much in use, and was served with tinned fruit, or in trifle.) True custard makes the perfect accompaniment for English fruit puddings; cream was sometimes served as well, or incorporated into the custard. Hot jam sauces were popular with steamed and baked puddings. These were simply made, either with one jam or two, heated and sieved and sometimes spiked with a dash of spirits. Golden syrup was already in existence; this made an easy sauce for hot sponge puddings: just warmed through and sharpened with a squeeze of lemon juice.

A contrast in temperature was definitely the dernier cri among fashionable hostesses. In the sweet course, the contrast was reversed, with a hot sauce accompanying an ice cream. One of the most popular came from the U S A: a hot butterscotch sauce which set to a hard shell when poured over a vanilla ice.

Good as they are, English sauces are rather primitive, and help to explain the term 'nursery food' used in this context. In the field of sauces our cuisine seems simplistic, especially when compared with the French. In this realm at least, we find ourselves closer to the Americans, whose cranberry sauce with roast turkey we were soon to adopt, and whose hot sauce for ice cream had already caught on.

Savoury Sauces and Garnishes
‖‖

‖‖

Apple Sauce with Sage
‖‖

This is an unusually good apple sauce for serving with roast pork, duck or goose.

1 medium onion [about 4 oz/120 g], quite finely chopped
½ oz [15 g] butter
2 tsp chopped sage
1 lb [450 g] cooking apples, peeled, cored and thickly sliced
½ tsp sugar

Cook the chopped onion slowly in the butter until it has softened, without allowing it to brown much: about 10 minutes, covered. Then add the chopped sage and cook all together for another couple of minutes, uncovered, then set aside. Put the sliced apples in a heavy pan with just enough water to cover the bottom. Add the sugar and bring slowly to the boil. Simmer gently, uncovered, until the apples are soft, then push them through a medium food mill into a clean pan. Reheat gently, adding the sage and onion mixture. Once it is hot, remove from the heat and stand, covered, for 10–15 minutes, or until ready to serve, with roast pork, duck or goose. Serves 6. Best served warm.

Mrs Arthur James

Aspic Jelly
‖‖

By the end of the thirties, compromises were being made in the kitchen. With fewer assistants, if any, cooks could not afford to spend hours making aspic in the traditional way, as was customary before the First World War. This was how our cook in London made her simplified version.

1 medium onion, chopped
1 medium carrot, chopped
1 Tbs gelatine
sea salt and black pepper
1 pt [570 ml] chicken, veal, beef or fish stock
1 egg white, lightly beaten
1 egg shell, crushed

Put in a saucepan 1 chopped onion, 1 chopped carrot, 1 Tbs powdered gelatine, salt and pepper. Add 1 pint of stock and bring slowly to the boil, stirring all the time. Strain. When gelatine has dissolved, drop in the white of one egg and crushed egg shell. Whisk over the flame until it boils, then put on one side and leave to settle. Strain through muslin.

Winnie, our cook

Celery Sauce

IIII

This is a useful sauce for serving with game birds of all sorts. Roast pheasant in particular benefits from a sauce to counteract its potential dryness.

8 stalks celery
1 small onion, finely chopped
1 bay leaf
¾ pt [450 ml] light stock, game or chicken
1 oz [30 g] butter
1 Tbs flour
salt and freshly ground pepper
4 Tbs chopped parsley

Cut the celery in small pieces and put in a saucepan with the finely chopped onion, bay leaf, and stock. Simmer over low heat until the celery is cooked, about 20 minutes. Remove the bay leaf and put the celery and stock into a blender or food processor. Purée for about 20 seconds, then rub through a sieve. Make a roux with the butter and flour and gradually add the celery purée to make a sauce. Season well and add freshly chopped parsley. Good with all game. Serves 4–6.

Jane Longman in *Vogue*

Bread Sauce

||||

This was the traditional accompaniment to roast chicken, grouse and pheasant. It is one of those English foods which can be the best or the worst thing in the world, depending on how it is made. It is vital to flavour the milk with care, and to get the right consistency: not too smooth, or too lumpy.

12 fl oz [340 ml] milk
½ medium onion
2 cloves
½ bay leaf
sea salt and black pepper
a pinch of mace, or nutmeg
about 6 Tbs soft white breadcrumbs, made from 1-day-old
    bread, crusts removed
½ oz [15 g] butter
2 Tbs cream (optional)

Put the milk in a small pan with the onion stuck with the cloves, bay leaf, salt, pepper, and mace, or nutmeg. Bring slowly to the boil, then turn off the heat, cover the pan, and stand for 20–30 minutes. Strain and reheat. As it approaches boiling point, shake in the crumbs gradually, stirring all the time, and stop as soon as it approaches the right consistency, remembering that it will thicken slightly on cooling. Simmer for 3 minutes, stirring often, adding more salt and pepper if required. Just before serving, stir in the butter, and a drop of cream if you have it. Serve with roast chicken, turkey, pheasant and grouse. Serves 4–5. This should be made soon before serving if possible; otherwise, keep warm over hot water.

AB

Cumberland Sauce

||||

This is an old English sauce, especially useful at Christmas time, for serving with cold turkey, ham, game pâtés and terrines. It was often made with port, which I rarely buy, so I use a dash of brandy. It may be thickened – slightly – with arrowroot, if desired.

1 orange
1 lemon
12 oz [340 g] redcurrant jelly
2 tsp arrowroot (optional)
2 Tbs brandy

Pare the rind of the orange and lemon thinly, then cut in julienne strips. Blanch in boiling water for 5 minutes, then refresh under the cold tap. Squeeze the juice of the orange and lemon and add to the jelly in a small pan. Heat gently, stirring, until the jelly has melted, then push through a sieve or small food mill and return to the clean pan. Reheat slowly until it reaches boiling point. If using arrowroot, slake it in 2 Tbs cold water, beating to a smooth paste with the back of a spoon, then stir into the simmering sauce and remove from the heat. Stir until smooth, then add the blanched rind. Later, when it has cooled slightly, add the brandy. Pour into a jam jar; once it has cooled, seal tightly and leave for 1 week before eating. Serves 6–8.

Adapted from *A Book of Scents and Dishes* by Dorothy Allhusen

Cherry Salad

IIII

Dorothy Allhusen, the author of A Book of Scents and Dishes, *recommends serving this unusual side dish with a cold fillet of beef, but I find it is even better with the cold roast loin of pork on page 112.*

8 oz [225 g] red cherries
1 Tbs brandy
1 Tbs light olive oil, or sunflower oil
1 tsp tarragon vinegar
salt and pepper
1 tsp chopped parsley

A delicious salad to eat with cold fillet of beef is made as follows: Stone ½ lb [225 g] of fresh red cherries, put them in a basin and pour over 1 tablespoonful of brandy, 1 tablespoonful of oil, 1 teaspoonful of tarragon vinegar; add salt and pepper to taste and 1 teaspoonful of chopped parsley. Serve very cold. [*Serves 3–4; easily made in double quantities. Also good with cold duck.*]

A Book of Scents and Dishes by Dorothy Allhusen

Harvy-Scarvy

IIII

This is a good, simple relish to eat with cold meat. It comes from Norfolk, by way of American writer M. F. K. Fisher, who quotes it in one of her books. She recommends serving it with a cold, grilled pork chop; I find it excellent with the cold roast loin of pork on page 112.

4 Tbs red or white wine vinegar
4 Tbs olive oil
4 oz [120 g] finely chopped celery
4 oz [120 g] finely chopped apples, cored but not peeled
4 oz [120 g] finely chopped onions
salt and freshly ground pepper to taste

Add vinegar and oil to celery, apples, and onion, and stir well. Chill for 1 or 2 hours, and stir again just before serving. Good with any cold meats, but preferably pork chops. [*Serves 6.*]

With Bold Knife and Fork by M. F. K. Fisher

Devil Sauce

IIII

A popular way of using up left-over game (or chicken) was to reheat it in a devil sauce. Usually made with undiluted whipped cream, this was too rich for my taste, but this recipe, which I have adapted from three contemporary ones, uses a mixture of milk and cream.

1 oz [30 g] butter
1½ Tbs flour
½ tsp English mustard (powder)
½ tsp curry powder (optional)
½ pt [275 ml] milk, heated
¼ pt [150 ml] double cream, heated
½ tsp sea salt
a pinch of cayenne
1½ Tbs Worcestershire Sauce
½ Tbs Mushroom Ketchup
a dash of Tabasco

Melt the butter, stir in the flour, mustard and curry powder, if used, and cook for 1 minute, stirring. Then add the milk and cream which you have heated together, and stir constantly until the sauce starts to bubble. Simmer gently for about 8 minutes, until slightly reduced, adding the other flavourings as it cooks. This is a basic devil sauce, for serving with grilled or fried chicken, egg or chicken croquettes, or hard-boiled eggs. Serves 4.

To devil game (or chicken), cut the cooked bird in neat joints and spread them all over with a layer of Dijon mustard. Lay them in a shallow dish and pour over 3–4 Tbs game (or chicken) stock. Cover with foil or a lid, and reheat in the oven for 15 minutes at 325°F/170°C/gas 3. Then drain off the stock and turn up the oven to 400°F/200°C/gas 6. Pour the hot devil sauce over the joints and put back in the oven, uncovered, for 10 minutes, or until it has browned nicely. (Alternatively, it may be browned under the grill for 4–5 minutes.) Serve with boiled rice and a green salad, as a main course.

AB

Piquant Sauce

IIII

Rather like a gazpacho, this excellent cold sauce is quickly made and very adaptable. I serve it over warm hard-boiled eggs, warm asparagus, or artichoke bottoms, either as a first course, or as part of a summer buffet.

½ pt [275 ml] fresh tomato pulp (approx. 12 oz [340 g] tomatoes)
1 Tbs finely chopped green pepper
1 Tbs finely chopped peeled cucumber
1 Tbs finely chopped celery
1 Tbs wine vinegar
a pinch of sugar
sea salt and black pepper to taste
a pinch each paprika, ground allspice and nutmeg

Peel ripe tomatoes and cut in pieces. Put them in a food processor and purée. Add the chopped vegetables, vinegar and seasonings, then purée again. Serve at room temperature, or chilled, over poached fish, vegetables, or hard-boiled eggs. Serves 4.

Gladys Stewart-Richardson

Sauce Duglèré

||||

This is a delicious sauce, quite thin, made with fish stock, white wine and cream, with crushed tomatoes and herbs added. It is excellent served with poached fish. (See also sole Duglèré on page 61.)

1 shallot, finely chopped
1 oz [30 g] butter
2 tomatoes, skinned, seeded and finely chopped
1 level Tbs flour
¼ pt [150 ml] dry white wine
¼ pt [150 ml] fish stock
salt and black pepper
¼ pt [150 ml] double cream
½ Tbs each finely chopped chervil, chives and parsley

Cook the chopped shallot in the butter for 3–4 minutes, then add the chopped tomatoes and cook for a further 2 minutes. Then add the flour, cook 1 minute, stirring, then add the white wine and fish stock which have been heated together. Bring to the boil and simmer for 4 minutes, stirring now and then, adding salt and pepper to taste. Finally, add the cream and cook for another 1–2 minutes, then remove from the heat, stir in the chopped herbs, and pour into a sauceboat. Serve with a large piece of poached white fish, preferably turbot or halibut, or the filets de sole pochés on page 60. Serves 6.

Adapted from *The Complete Hostess* by Quaglino

Egg and/or Parsley Sauce

||||

I like to combine these two traditional English sauces, both of which go so well with boiled fish, gammon, fish cakes, etc., but either can be made separately if preferred.

1 oz [30 g] butter
1½ Tbs flour
½ pt [275 ml] chicken, fish or ham stock, or ¾ pt [450 ml] milk
5 Tbs single cream (if using stock)
sea salt and black pepper

ground mace, or nutmeg
4 Tbs chopped parsley
2 hard-boiled eggs, roughly chopped

Melt the butter, add the flour, and cook for 1 minute, stirring. Then add the hot stock, or milk, gradually, stirring till blended, and simmer gently for 3 minutes. Then add the cream, salt and black pepper (unless using ham stock, in which case omit the salt), and a little mace, or nutmeg. If using milk instead of stock, omit the cream, and increase the milk to ¾ pt [450 ml]. Stir in the chopped parsley and/or hard-boiled eggs, and tip into a sauceboat to serve. This is good with boiled cod, boiled ham, gammon steaks, fish cakes and egg cutlets (in this case use parsley alone). Serves 4–5.

AB

Sauce Soubise

▌‖‖

A creamy onion sauce lightly flavoured with nutmeg was often served with roast lamb, or a boiled leg of mutton. It is also delicious served over hard-boiled eggs, as a light supper dish.

3 large onions
salt
½ pt [275 ml] milk
1½ oz [45 g] butter
2 Tbs flour
2½ fl oz [70 ml] cream
nutmeg

Peel the onions and cut them into small pieces. Put them in a saucepan, cover them with hot water and a little salt, and boil them till tender [*about 15 minutes*]. Heat the milk. Melt the butter in another saucepan, stir in the flour, then stir in the hot milk gradually. Add the onions and stir till the sauce boils. Place the sieve over a basin and rub the sauce through it with the back of a wooden spoon [*or blend in a food processor*]. Put it back in a clean saucepan, add the cream and a few grains of grated nutmeg. Heat well, but do not let it boil again. [*Serves 4–5, or 2 with hard-boiled eggs.*]

When The Cook Is Away by Catherine Ives

Hollandaise Sauce

||||

This exquisite sauce was much in use, largely as a hot alternative to mayonnaise. It accompanied poached fish, especially salmon and salmon trout, also artichokes and asparagus, and was part of the popular American dish, eggs Benedict (see page 66). In pre-war days it demanded skill in the making, but today it can be made with ease in a food processor.

4 egg yolks
a pinch of sea salt
6 oz [180 g] unsalted butter
1½ Tbs lemon juice

First warm the container of the food processor by filling it with very hot water. Stand for 4–5 minutes, then drain and dry well. Put the egg yolks with the salt into the processor and cover with the lid, leaving the funnel open. Heat the butter in a small pan until it is almost boiling, then process the egg yolks for 30 seconds, and start adding the hot butter through the lid, while continuing to process. Once all the butter has been added, stop the machine. The sauce should have thickened slightly; if not, pour it into a small bowl sitting over a saucepan of simmering water and stir until this has happened. Add the lemon juice. Serve as soon as possible, in a warm bowl. It does not need to be hot, just warm. Serves 3–4.

Sauce Mousseline: shortly before serving, fold 4 Tbs lightly whipped cream into the hollandaise sauce. Serves 4. This luxurious sauce is particularly delicious with asparagus.

AB

Fried Parsley

||||

This is my favourite garnish for goujons of fried fish, egg croquettes, and other fried dishes. Alas, it now seems to have been forgotten.

Take your little sprigs of parsley, picked off the main stem, wash them, if it is really necessary, dry them well, and keep them covered with a cloth until you are ready for them; at any rate, do not let them wilt. Have ready your deep-frying oil on the fire and, when the blue smoke begins to rise, which shows that it is very hot [*about 360°F/180°C*], plunge your parsley in. It is ready almost immediately; it is a matter of seconds. I find it best to use a frying basket. It should come out crisp, bright green and neither greasy, limp, nor brown. If you fry it too long, it is apt to break to pieces. [*Use as a garnish for any crisp fried food, especially fish.*]

Come Into the Garden, Cook by Constance Spry

Mayonnaise

▌|||

This was very much used between the wars, both in its own right – as an accompaniment to cold salmon, lobster, asparagus, artichokes and hard-boiled eggs – and as an ingredient in other dishes: cold sauces, sandwiches, savoury ices, etc.

2 egg yolks
a pinch of sea salt
¼ tsp Dijon mustard
½ pt [275 ml] olive oil
3 tsp white wine vinegar
3 tsp lemon juice

Have all the ingredients at the same temperature, i.e. take the eggs out of the refrigerator 1 hour in advance. The eggs should be very fresh. Drop the yolks into a large bowl standing on a damp cloth so that it cannot slip around. With an electric hand beater, or a wire whisk, beat the egg yolks for a minute or two, adding the salt and mustard. Have the olive oil in a jug and hold it in the left hand while you beat with the right. Start adding the oil literally drop by drop, beating constantly. After a short while you can add it a little more quickly, but only a few drops at a time. When about half the oil has been added, you can start to add it in a thin trickle, then a stream, beating all the time without stopping. When all the oil is finished, beat in the vinegar and lemon juice. Taste and adjust the seasoning as you prefer. Turn into a clean bowl, cover with cling film, and store in the refrigerator until needed. Take out well in advance of serving, as it should be eaten at room temperature. Makes ½ pt [275 ml]; serves 6 as a sauce.

Variation: A proportion of lightly whipped cream may be folded into the mayonnaise before serving: roughly half as much cream as mayonnaise.

AB

181

Mint Sauce

||||

This was the traditional accompaniment to hot roast lamb; redcurrant jelly could be provided as well, or as an alternative. With cold lamb a mint jelly was sometimes served. The best variety of mint to use is the old-fashioned English spearmint, Mentha spicata.

4 Tbs chopped mint
1 Tbs castor sugar
4 Tbs lemon juice

Put the chopped mint in a bowl with the sugar and lemon. Add 6 fl oz [175 ml] boiling water, stirring. Stand for 1 hour before serving, at room temperature. Serves 6.

AB

Sauce Tartare

||||

This excellent sauce was often served with fried Dover sole, or with fried whitebait – indeed almost any fried fish. It also figures in the shooting sandwiches made with cold roast beef or game, on page 200.

½ pt [275 ml] mayonnaise (see page 181)
2 Tbs chopped parsley
2 Tbs chopped gherkins
2 Tbs chopped capers

Add chopped parsley, chopped gherkins and chopped capers – about 2 tablespoons of each – to half a pint of mayonnaise. [*Serves* 6.]

Wheeler's Fish Cookery Book by Macdonald Hastings and Carole Walsh

Iced Tomato Sauce

||||

This is an ideal sauce for light summer dishes, simple and quick to make, and very adaptable. It is best served semi-frozen, frozen thick but not yet solid. It goes well with hot fried goujons of Dover sole, or egg croquettes, or fish cakes, as well as cold dishes.

¼ pt [150 ml] mayonnaise (see page 181)
¼ pt [150 ml] double cream, lightly whipped
6 oz [180 g] tomatoes, weighed after skinning and de-seeding,
    pulped
1½ tsp onion juice, made in a garlic press
salt and pepper

Mix together equal parts of mayonnaise, [*lightly whipped*] cream,
and tomato pulp. Add onion juice, salt and pepper. Freeze and
serve with cold fish or with cucumber salad. [*Serves 4.*]

     Come Into the Garden, Cook by Constance Spry

Horseradish Sauce with Apple

||||

This unusual combination of grated apple with horseradish makes a most delicious sauce for serving with cold roast beef or duck. It is based on a recipe in Alice B. Toklas' last book, but it also turns up in a few English cookbooks of the period. The best horseradish to use, failing the fresh root, comes from Germany in small jars, called Kochs or Scandia.

1 Granny Smith, or other tart green apple, peeled and grated
1½ Tbs grated horseradish, or ½ a jar
3 Tbs sour cream
¼ tsp sea salt
¼ tsp lemon juice
a pinch of cayenne
½ tsp brandy

Mix grated apples with grated horseradish. Add [*sour cream*], salt,
lemon juice, a pinch of cayenne, and brandy. [*Serves 4.*]

    Aromas and Flavors by Alice B. Toklas

Scraped Horseradish

||||

Rarely seen nowadays, this is the best possible way of eating horseradish, almost Japanese in its simplicity. Good for people who grow their own, since fresh horseradish is not often seen in shops.

Get a nice large single root of horseradish, peel it, and with a sharp knife scrape it so that each shaving is a long thin sliver. This is placed all down the centre of the roast beef and the carver puts a small portion on each plate with a slice of beef. It should be scraped only a few minutes before it is required, otherwise it will lose its flavour and become dry. Scraped horseradish is only eaten with roast beef, and is a most delicious adjunct.

Kitchenette Cookery by G. F. Scotson-Clark

Yorkshire Pudding

IIII

In the country houses, bastions of tradition, roast beef was always served with Yorkshire pudding, roast potatoes, gravy, horseradish sauce and a green vegetable. The pudding is best made after the beef has finished cooking, since it demands a very hot oven.

5 oz [140 g] white bread flour
½ tsp salt
1 large egg, lightly beaten
8 fl oz [250 ml] milk
1–2 Tbs beef dripping, from the joint

Sift the flour into a food processor with the salt. Add the lightly beaten egg and process, then pour the milk slowly through the lid, while continuing to process. Rest for 30–60 minutes before baking, if possible.

Five minutes before the joint is ready, extract 1–2 Tbs dripping from the roasting tin and spread it round a shallow baking dish. Heat this in the oven for 5 minutes, then remove the beef to rest in a warm place and turn the oven up to 425°F/220°C/gas 7. Process the batter once more, then pour into the dish and bake for 35 minutes, until well-risen and golden brown. Cut in sections to serve, with the beef. Serves 6.

AB

Bread Stuffing

▌▌▌▌

Before the war, a roast bird was almost invari-
ably stuffed. Nowadays, with the emphasis on
low-fat food, stuffings are rarely seen except at
Christmas time. This is my favourite stuffing,
excellent with chicken, turkey, duck or goose.

6 oz [180 g] shallots, peeled and chopped
2 oz [55 g] butter
6 oz [180 g] soft white breadcrumbs
¾ oz [20 g] chopped parsley
sea salt and black pepper

Cook the chopped shallots gently in the butter until light golden,
then add the crumbs and mix well. Remove from the heat, stir in
the chopped parsley, and add plenty of sea salt and black pepper.
Allow to cool before using. This makes enough to stuff a large
chicken or capon; double the quantities for a 12 lb [6 kg] turkey.

AB

Browned Breadcrumbs

▌▌▌▌

This was the classic accompaniment to roast
game, together with bread sauce and (home-
made) game chips. The bread sauce was served in
a sauceboat, and the browned breadcrumbs in
another sauceboat, or bowl.

1 oz [30 g] butter
6 Tbs fairly coarse dry (white) breadcrumbs

In a thick frying pan, preferably non-stick, heat the butter until
very hot. Just before it turns colour add the breadcrumbs and cook
for about 2½ minutes, turning constantly, until they have browned
evenly to a golden mid-brown. Remove from the heat, tip into a
bowl or sauceboat, and keep warm until ready to serve. Serves 4.

AB

SAUCES

Sweet Sauces

‖‖‖

‖‖‖

Apricot Jam Sauce

‖‖‖

This hot jam sauce is excellent served with plain sponge puddings.

8 oz [225 g] apricot jam
3 Tbs kirsch
4 Tbs water

Heat together to boiling point, in a small enamel pan, ½ cup of apricot jam, 3 tablespoons of kirsch, and ¼ cup of water. Pour into serving bowl and serve at once. [*Serves 4.*]

June Platt's Plain and Fancy Cookbook

Brandy Butter

‖‖‖

This used to be called senior wrangler sauce, or hard sauce – it is still called hard sauce in the USA. It is the traditional accompaniment to Christmas pudding.

4 oz [120 g] unsalted butter
4 oz [120 g] castor sugar
3–4 Tbs brandy

Cream the butter until pale and smooth. (Or blend in food processor.) Add the sugar gradually, beating (or processing) continuously. When amalgamated, start to add the brandy very slowly, beating (or processing) all the time. Taste after adding the third tablespoon, then add the rest – if needed – very slowly indeed, for it can separate easily at this stage. Once done, pile into a small jar and store in the refrigerator until needed. It can be made several days in advance, as it keeps very well indeed. Serve very cold, with the Christmas pudding. Makes 8 oz [225 g].

AB

Creamy Custard Sauce

▮|||

A jug of cream was often served at the same time as a custard sauce, with hot puddings made with fruit, bread, suet or sponge. I have chosen to combine the two in a delicious creamy custard sauce. To make a simple custard, omit the cream and increase the milk to ¾ pt [450 ml].

½ vanilla pod
½ pt [275 ml] milk
3 large egg yolks
2½ Tbs vanilla sugar, or castor sugar
¼ pt [150 ml] double cream

Put the vanilla pod in a small pan with the milk. Bring slowly to the boil, then remove from the heat, cover the pan and stand for 20 minutes. When the time is up, reheat the milk gently and remove the vanilla pod. (Rinse, dry and store in a jar of castor sugar.) Start beating the egg yolks with the sugar. When the milk is just about to boil, pour it on to the egg yolks, still beating. Then stand the bowl over a pan of simmering water and stir constantly until it has slightly thickened. This may take 7 or 8 minutes.

Once it has thickened enough to coat the back of a wooden spoon, remove the bowl from the heat and stand in a sink half full of cold water to cool quickly. Stir now and then while it cools to prevent a skin forming. While it cools, whip the cream until just thickened, stopping before it becomes solid or it will be hard to blend with the custard. When the custard is warm, fold in the whipped cream.

If possible, serve while still warm, or at room temperature; do not chill. Excellent with hot or cold puddings of all sorts, or with compotes of fruit. Serves 4–6.

AB

emon and Vanilla Sauce

▮|||

This is an unusual sauce for serving hot with steamed or baked puddings. It goes well with the seven-cup pudding on page 146. I like to serve a jug of thick cream at the same time.

2 oz [55 g] vanilla sugar
1 Tbs cornflour
½ pt [275 ml] boiling water
2 oz [55 g] unsalted butter, cut in bits
juice and grated rind of 1 lemon

Mix together sugar with cornflour. Add boiling water gradually, stirring constantly. Cook five minutes. Remove from fire. Add butter [*cut in small bits*]. Stir until melted. Add the juice and grated rind of 1 lemon. Serve hot [*with a baked or steamed pudding, or plum pudding. Makes ¾ pt/450 ml; serves 4–6*].

June Platt in *Vogue*

Mixed Jam Sauce

Jam sauces were often served with sponge or suet puddings, with pancakes or even ice cream.

‖‖

4 Tbs raspberry jam
4 Tbs redcurrant jelly
1 Tbs orange juice
1 Tbs lemon juice
½ Tbs brandy

Warm the jam and jelly together over low heat, until the jelly has melted. Then push through a small food mill into a clean pan. Heat again, adding fruit juices and brandy, but remove from the heat well before it reaches boiling point. Serve warm; enough for 4.

Adapted from *More Lovely Food* by Ruth Lowinsky

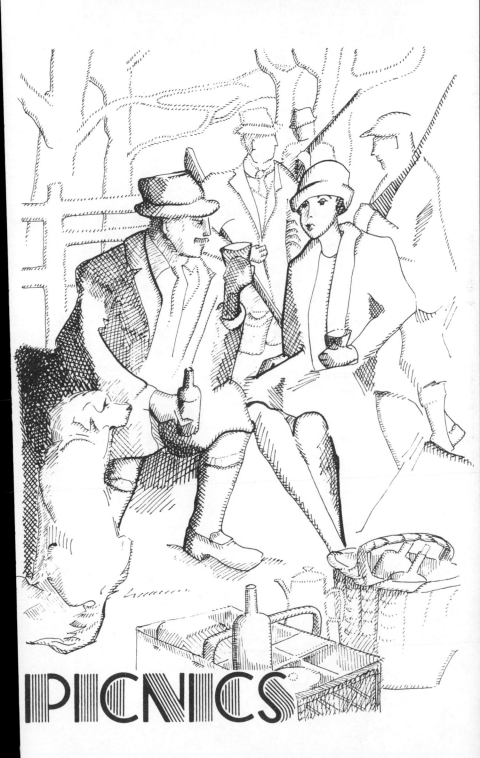

PICNICS

Picnics and
Shooting Lunches

IIII

Picnics had been popular in Britain since Victorian times, and even earlier; they varied widely to suit the occasion. Perhaps the favourite sort, and one that is still much loved today, was the seaside picnic, with as wide a mixture of ages as possible. Many prosperous families sent their children to the sea for a summer holiday, even if they lived in the country all year round. Some lucky ones lived close to the sea, in which case they were inundated with summer visitors, cousins and friends, for a period of weeks throughout July and August. Other families took houses at resorts like Seaview, Cromer or Littlehampton; sometimes a family would take over a small hotel for a few weeks each summer. In some cases, like our own, the children were sent to stay in lodgings at a resort like Bognor, accompanied by nanny or governess, while their parents stayed at home, or did something more amusing.

Seaside picnics were simple affairs, not unlike those of today. The food might consist of hard-boiled eggs, bread and butter, or simple sandwiches – my favourite were jam sandwiches made with thin white bread – followed by a cake, with milk or tea to drink. At Mothecombe, the little bay where the Mildmays swam, a few miles from Flete, Helen Mildmay's grandfather had built a small stone tea-house on the edge of the beach. This had a fireplace, so that they could picnic from April onwards. (It also provided a cosy spot for the children to dress after bathing.) The Mildmay picnics sound delicious: small pasties (to rhyme with nasty), little profiteroles filled with chicken, lettuce and mayonnaise, with meringues and cake to follow, and cider or ginger beer to drink.

In Scotland, our favourite picnics were by the river, or on the moors. Our grandfather had built a small wooden fishing hut on the banks of the River Findhorn, with a fireplace, where we could shelter from bad weather. When it was fine, we would sit on the steep banks watching the river tear through narrow gorges far below, dark peaty brown and foaming like Guinness. Here my father would join us for lunch after fishing for salmon in one of the pools. We would eat little hot pies of mutton or lamb, brown bread and butter, raw tomatoes and lettuce leaves, with a piece of cheese, or cake, to follow.

Like most children's lives, ours seemed very uneventful. The highlight of the year as far as I was concerned, better by far than Christmas or birthdays, was the week we spent en famille, camping out in a small shooting lodge on the moors. This was the only time in the whole year when we were alone with our parents for any length of time, without nanny or governess, or even a cook. My mother and sisters struggled with the meals, which were erratic, despite the hampers of pre-cooked food sent up from the big house. I remember my mother trying to clean a grouse with a silver teaspoon, and my father's face of dismay on being told dinner was ready at six thirty, just as he was about to set off for a quiet evening's walk. Our bicycles were sent up on a lorry, so we could cycle to a nearby farm each morning to get milk. One of my sisters kept bees, and her beehives came up with the bicycles. The bees were left up on the moors for some weeks, so that they could make heather honey.

Our shooting lunches were much like picnics on the river: fairly simple stuff. There might be cold game, or game pie, roast beef sandwiches or cold ham in aspic, and salad. To follow, we often had jam puffs. Grand shooting lunches were a different affair altogether, especially in the great English houses. At the Duke of Westminster's shoot, a lunch was laid on for thirty guests in a small Elizabethan house in a river valley in north Wales, an hour and a quarter's drive from Eaton Hall. Here two cooks would labour in the kitchen, finishing off dishes that had been brought up from the main house at dawn. A superlative lunch would follow, served by footmen, with hot mulled claret to drink.

This degree of grandeur was unusual; each house varied in its style, but most liked to keep the food very simple, in order not to distract from the shooting. At Bolton Abbey, the Duke of Devonshire's shoot in Yorkshire, a donkey loaded with two panniers was used to carry the food up on to the moors. Mrs Shimwell, who succeeded her mother as cook to the Devonshires in the 1930s, tells me that there was always a hot soup and one other hot dish, usually a stew, packed in hayboxes. At Flete, there were always two hot courses: a stew with hot baked potatoes and another vegetable, and a hot luncheon pudding, usually steamed, or rice. Towards the end of the thirties the lunches at Flete grew simpler, and the hot pudding was replaced by a sticky ginger cake, served with a hard English cheese like Cheddar. The Mildmays drank beer or cider, with sloe gin afterwards.

Each house had its customary locale for the shooting lunch,

which never varied from year to year. It might be a barn, or cottage, pavilion, folly, or small hut equipped for the purpose. They rarely returned to the big house for lunch, even when it was within reach, as it made the meal too lengthy; by the time the ladies had gone upstairs to tidy themselves, and everyone had trooped into the dining-room, half the afternoon would have been wasted.

Some houses made a habit of packing individual shooting lunches; this worked well for less grand shoots, where the lunch was more in the nature of a picnic. Ruth Lowinsky describes these in *Lovely Food*; they sound like a more elaborate version of the packed lunches we used to take out hunting, in a jointed silver case hanging from the saddle. 'Shooting lunches are best packed separately for each person, with his name written on the outside. A small aluminium box, preferably jointed at sides, back and lid, is lined with greaseproof paper. Then half a grouse is put in, some thinly cut bread and butter, a couple of savoury sandwiches, a jam puff, cheese, biscuits, and an apple, salt and pepper, each item wrapped separately in greaseproof paper.'

Elaborate shooting lunches still go on today, in a very few houses. At Lambton Park, in Durham, Lady Lambton is famous for the originality and perfection of her shooting lunches which take place every weekend from the end of October to the beginning of February, and which she organises down to the smallest detail. They are held under a tarpaulin in a walled garden about a mile from the house. A rectangular table to seat eighteen has been built over a charcoal brazier. The centre of the table is made of stainless steel, and is hot enough to cook on; the surround is made of earthenware tiles. Dishes are prepared in the kitchens of the big house and brought down to be finished off, or cooked from scratch, in the centre of the table. The food varies constantly; there are usually seven or eight different things, all hot. Sardines are grilled on wire racks; kidneys, steaks, lamb cutlets and patties of corned beef hash likewise. Marrow bones are kept hot, as is a saddle of lamb. Individual cauliflower cheeses are made in small bread tins; a pot of fondue bubbles away on the side. By each place is a tiny frying pan, for making blinis perhaps, should anyone produce some caviare, or just for frying eggs. Purées of root vegetables, or succotash, are served inside a giant pumpkin; roast parsnips are also popular. Tomatoes and mushrooms are filled with duxelles or herb stuffing, then cooked directly on the table. In a cool hut nearby the cold dishes are laid out: a huge ham, a tongue, Stilton, celery and puddings. Bullshots or bloody Marys are served before lunch, while the butler serves mulled claret during the lunch, assisted by two footmen.

This is not all that is laid on to encourage the guns, for at some point during the morning they are joined by the ladies bringing with them hot soup in thermos flasks, and sandwiches, or hot sausages, for a mid-morning snack.

The catering arrangements at the Lambton shoots are hardly typical, being a product of Lady Lambton's fertile imagination, rather than indicative of what is general practice. On a less exalted plane, the food at shooting lunches is supposed to be very simple fare, and any deviation is viewed askance. I went to a shooting lunch recently where the hostess had provided a cassoulet. Perfect food, I should have thought, for a cold day, but it did not meet with approval from the other guests, being considered too exotic.

Potage à l'Ecossaise

IIII

A sophisticated version of Scotch broth, this is recommended by Lady Jekyll for a hot picnic lunch, to take on a 'motor excursion' in a haybox. It is equally good eaten at home, in the comfort of one's own kitchen. Quite substantial, it is really more of a stew than a soup.

2¼ pt [1.25 litres] stock: beef, chicken or lamb
2 Tbs pearl barley, washed
1 carrot, thickly sliced
1 small turnip, quartered and sliced
1 leek, thickly sliced
1 onion, quartered and thickly sliced
1 stalk celery, thickly sliced
¼ heart of a small green cabbage, sliced, or 3 or 4 Brussels
    sprouts
1½–2 lb (680–900 g) best end of neck of lamb, divided into
    cutlets and trimmed, excess fat removed
2 Tbs chopped parsley
2 Tbs double cream
salt and black pepper
4 oz [120 g] shelled peas, fresh or frozen, cooked
12 oz [340 g] small new potatoes, skinned and cooked

Put into rather more than a quart [*1.2 litres*] of good light stock some 2 tablespoonfuls of pearl barley [*previously washed in cold water*], a carrot, turnip, leek, onion, celery, a little cabbage or 3 or 4 Brussels sprouts, and let them cook gently together with the required number of nice cutlets from a well-selected and trimmed neck of mutton or lamb. Season [*after cooking gently, on top of the stove, for 2 hours*] with a little chopped parsley, cream, salt and pepper to taste, some green peas [*cooked separately*], and some tiny new [*cooked*] potatoes. [*Serves 4–5.*]

Kitchen Essays by Lady Jekyll

Irish Stew

▌|||

A simple dish of this sort was popular for shooting lunches, or for Saturday lunch in the country. This old-fashioned method of dividing the potatoes in two parts works well.

2½ lb [1.15 kg] middle end of neck of lamb
salt and black pepper
2 lb [900 g] potatoes
1 lb [450 g] onions

Cut and trim the meat into cutlets, put in the pot, cover with hot water, add the salt, boil up and skim. Peel the potatoes, cut about one third of them in slices, and add to the pot. Peel and slice the onions. Add these with the pepper and stir up. Then lay the rest of the [*whole*] potatoes on top and stew 2 or 3 hours, stirring occasionally. The sliced potatoes should thicken the liquid and prevent the stew being watery. [*Serves 4.*]

Irish Cookery Recipes by Florence Irwin

ancashire Hotpot

▌|||

This sort of traditional dish was often served in country houses, either for a shooting lunch or for a simple family meal.

2 lb [900 g] middle end of neck of lamb, divided into cutlets
1½ lb [680 g] potatoes, peeled and sliced
12 oz [340 g] onions, sliced
salt and black pepper

$\frac{1}{4}$ pt [150 ml] light stock
$\frac{1}{2}$ oz [15 g] butter, melted
chopped parsley

Trim the meat, removing all excess fat. Butter a fireproof casserole
– it does not need to have a lid – and make a layer of sliced potatoes
in the bottom. Scatter some of the sliced onion over them, and
sprinkle with salt and black pepper. Lay the meat on top, in one
layer. Then add more salt and pepper, and the remaining onions.
Pour the stock over, then cover with the remaining potatoes, the
slices neatly overlapping like tiles on a roof. Brush the potatoes
with melted butter, cover with the lid, or a piece of foil, and bake
for 2 hours at 325°F/170°C/gas 3. Then remove the lid (or foil), and
continue to cook for another 30 minutes, by which time the
potatoes should be nicely browned. I like to serve this with a small
bowl of chopped parsley on the table. Serves 4.

AB

Small Mutton (or Lamb) Pies

IIII

*Small mutton pies, served hot, used to be a feature
of shooting-party lunches on the moors when I
lived in Scotland, as a child. They were small
enough to hold in the palm of your hand, and very
delicious. Nowadays they may be made with
lamb, and are a useful way of using up the
remains of a joint.*

1 lb [450 g] cooked mutton or lamb, chopped
6 oz [180 g] mushrooms, chopped
1$\frac{1}{2}$ oz [45 g] butter
$\frac{1}{4}$ pt [150 ml] meat or chicken stock
1 clove
3 black peppercorns
1 tsp flour

SHORT PASTRY
10 oz [285 g] flour
5 oz [140 g] butter
a pinch of salt
a little iced water
1 egg, beaten

196

Free the meat from skin and gristle and chop it fairly finely. Cut the mushrooms into small pieces and cook them with 1 oz [30 g] butter until they are tender. Heat the stock in a saucepan, add the clove and peppercorns, and simmer gently for a quarter of an hour. Melt the remaining half ounce [15 g] butter, and stir in the flour. Blend well, and then strain the stock into this, stirring all the time, and cook for 5 minutes. Add the mushrooms and the meat. Mix thoroughly, and let the mixture get cold. Make the pastry. Line the patty pans with it. Fill them with the lamb mixture; give them pastry tops decorated with tiny pastry leaves. Brush them over with the beaten egg. Make a hole in the centre of each one and bake in a moderate oven until the pastry is done. [*About 25 minutes at 350°F/180°C/gas 4. Makes 12 small pies. These may also be made with uncooked lamb, minced or finely chopped, first browned briefly, with a small chopped onion, in 1 Tbs each butter and oil.*]

When The Cook Is Away by Catherine Ives

Game Pie

IIII

Game pies were a staple winter food in the country houses, equally popular as a standby on the cold sideboard at lunchtime, or as part of a shooting lunch. They were made with a variety of game, either birds alone, or birds and animals mixed, depending on the season. They were always eaten cold.

FILLING
1 lb [450 g] stewing venison, in one piece
1 lb [450 g] rabbit, jointed
1 pheasant, or 2 grouse, or 2 partridges (old birds may be used)
1 onion, halved
1 carrot, halved
1 stalk celery, halved
1 bay leaf
3 stalks parsley
sea salt and black pepper
½ oz [15 g] gelatine

PASTRY
10 oz [285 g] flour, sifted
a pinch of salt
3 oz [85 g] butter

2 oz [55 g] lard
1 egg + 1 yolk
4–5 Tbs iced water

8 black peppercorns
8 juniper berries

Make a day or two in advance. Put the stewing venison in a casserole with the rabbit and the whole bird(s). Add the flavouring vegetables and herbs, sea salt and black pepper, and cover with hot water. Bring to the boil, cover, and simmer gently for 2 hours. Discard the vegetables and herbs and strain the stock.

While the meats are cooking, make the pastry. Put the sifted flour and salt in a food processor, and add the fats cut in pieces, then 1 egg. Process until blended, then add the iced water gradually through the lid while continuing to process, stopping when it all gathers into a ball. Turn out and knead briefly, then wrap in cling film and place in the bottom of the refrigerator for 2 hours. (If making by hand, sift the flour with the salt on to a board, make a well in the centre and put in the fats in small pieces, the egg and the water. Work together with the hands until blended, then knead well, until smooth.)

When the meat is cooked, lift it out of the pan with a slotted spoon and strain the stock. Cut the venison into small slices about ⅓ inch [7.5 mm] thick, pull the rabbit off the bone and divide into neat fillets, and cut the game off the bone, in neat pieces. Put 1 teaspoon sea salt into a mortar with the peppercorns and juniper berries and crush them all together roughly.

When the pastry is ready, roll out two-thirds of it to line a greased cake tin with removable bottom, holding about 2 pints [1.2 litres]. The pastry should be about ½ inch [1 cm] thick. Lay half the venison in the bottom, sprinkle with the crushed seasonings, then cover with half the rabbit, more seasonings, and half the game birds. Continue making alternate layers, seasoning each one, until all the meat is used up. Moisten with 4 tablespoons of the strained stock and cover with a lid of the remaining pastry. Overlap the edges by about ½ inch [1 cm], damp them to seal firmly, and roll to form a thick edge. Make a decorative device of some sort – rose, leaf, etc. – and stick it in the centre of the pie, then cut round it neatly and lift out. Replace, then brush all over with beaten egg yolk. Bake for 1 hour at 350°F/180°C/gas 4.

While it is baking, measure the remaining stock and add gelatine, allowing ½ oz [15 g] to each pint. (Dissolve it in a little of the heated stock, then mix it with the rest of the cool stock.) When the pie is cooked, lift out the centrepiece and pour in the cool stock gradually, a little at a time, through a funnel. Allow time for each lot to settle and be absorbed, before adding more. When the dish is full, replace the pastry centrepiece and leave to cool. Keep for at least 24 hours before eating; it can be kept for a week in the refrigerator. This makes a pie weighing about 3½ lb [1.7 kg], and will feed 6–8 people. Serve with pickled plums, fruit chutneys, or gherkins, and a mixed salad.

AB

Beef Sandwiches

||||

This is my favourite sandwich. In the past, it would have been served at picnic lunches or shooting parties. Nowadays, it makes a perfect supper for eating while watching television.

4 thin slices white bread, 1 day old
¾ oz [20 g] butter
2 Tbs horseradish cream (see page 59)
3 oz [85 g] rare roast beef, sliced
sea salt and black pepper
2 medium tomatoes, thinly sliced

Spread some thinly buttered bread with thick horseradish cream, lay a slice of beef on this [*sprinkle with sea salt*], and cover with thinly sliced and seasoned tomato and more bread and butter. [*Remove crusts. Makes 2 rounds: 4 sandwiches.*]

Lady Sysonby's Cook Book

Shooting Sandwiches

▌|||

Another good sandwich for winter picnics or expeditions, or for a simple Sunday night supper. This is an excellent way of making a toasted sandwich that I have not come across before. I like to use a whole-grain mustard, like Grey Poupon Old-Style, which would not have been available in the 1930s.

2 slices white bread, 1 day old, cut ¾ inch [1.5 cm] thick
½ oz [15 g] butter
2 Tbs sauce tartare (see page 182)
1 tsp whole-grain mustard
3 oz [85 g] cold roast meat, or game, sliced

Toast neatly trimmed slices of bread on both sides [*if they are too thick for the toaster they may be done under the grill*], then split and butter half of them with plain or savoury butter, and spread the rest with a stiff tartare sauce, to which you have added some French mustard. Cover the buttered pieces with the slices of meat or game, and press the rest of the toast on this. [*Remove crusts. Makes 2 rounds: 4 sandwiches.*]

Lady Sysonby's Cook Book

Norwegian Sandwiches

▌|||

This is a good example of the quite complex mixtures which were popular as sandwich fillings between the wars.

6 anchovies, boned and filleted
1 oz [30 g] unsalted butter
4 medium-thin slices white bread, 1 day old, toasted

4 oz [120 g] thinly sliced smoked salmon
1 small egg, hard-boiled and chopped
1 Tbs chopped parsley

Pound 6 anchovies to a smooth paste with 1 oz [30 g] butter, and spread the pieces of toast with this. Lay thin slices of smoked salmon, sprinkled with chopped hard-boiled egg and the parsley, between them. [*This is also good made with untoasted brown bread, or rye bread. Remove crusts. Makes 2 rounds: 4 sandwiches.*]

The Gentle Art of Cookery by Mrs C. F. Leyel and Miss Olga Hartley

Smoked Haddock Sandwiches

A substantial sandwich, good for a winter picnic, or a snack after the theatre.

IIII

1 oz [30 g] unsalted butter
3 Tbs chopped parsley
freshly ground black pepper
4 medium-thin slices brown bread, 1 day old *or* 2 slices white
  bread, ¾ inch [1.5 cm] thick, toasted
3–4 Tbs mayonnaise
4 oz [120 g] cooked smoked haddock, flaked free from skin and
  bone
1 hard-boiled egg, coarsely chopped (optional)

Mash the butter with half the chopped parsley and some freshly ground black pepper; no salt. Spread half the bread with this. If using toast, split the slices after toasting, so that you have 4 thin slices toasted on one side only. Spread half the untoasted sides with parsley butter. Spread the rest of the bread (or toast) generously with mayonnaise and sprinkle with the remaining chopped parsley. Lay the smoked haddock on the mayonnaise, cutting the larger flakes into pieces, and scatter the chopped egg (if used) over it. Cover with the buttered bread (or toast). If making in advance, for a picnic, or late supper, choose bread rather than toast. Remove crusts. Makes 4 rounds: 12 small sandwiches.

Adapted from *The Gentle Art of Cookery* by Mrs C. F. Leyel and Miss Olga Hartley

Jam Puffs

||||

At our home in Scotland, the jam puffs were somewhat more substantial than this, being made with short pastry and about 5 inches [13 cm] long. They only ever appeared for shooting lunches, as a pudding. This recipe makes lighter, more delicate puffs, just right for tea or picnic teas. If serving as a pudding, allow two per person. To make apple turnovers, simply use a fairly thick apple purée instead of the jam.

1 lb [450 g] puff pastry, home-made or bought
4–6 Tbs raspberry jam (or apple purée)
1 egg, beaten
icing sugar, sifted

Roll out the pastry to about ⅛ inch [3 mm] thick. Using a small patty tin as a guide, cut it out into circles about 3 inches [7.5 cm] wide. Roll each one out again lightly, just once or twice, until it is about 3½–4 inches [8.5–10 cm] across. Put a teaspoonful of jam (or apple purée) on one half of each, and brush the edges with beaten egg. Fold over and press the edges together to seal, then brush them all over with beaten egg. Use a fork to mark the sealed edges with parallel lines, and prick two or three times in the centre. Lay them on a greased baking sheet and chill until ready to bake.

Bake them for 15 minutes at 400°F/200°C/gas 6, until golden brown, then take out of the oven and sprinkle very lightly with sifted icing sugar. Serve warm whenever possible, or at least the same day as made. If to be eaten as a pudding, serve with cream. Makes 12; serves 6.

AB

Lady Moray's Fruit Cake

||||

This was my grandmother's recipe for a spiced fruit cake, which was served at our home in Scotland for shooting picnics, or for tea. It may be iced for Christmas. For a richer cake, use brandy – or whisky – instead of orange juice.

6 oz [180 g] unsalted butter
6 oz [180 g] dark brown sugar
1½ Tbs treacle, warmed

3 eggs
9 oz [250 g] flour, sifted
¾ tsp baking powder
1 tsp each ground cloves, cinnamon and nutmeg
3 oz [85 g] ground almonds
6 oz [180 g] each currants and sultanas
4 Tbs milk
4 Tbs orange juice

Cream the butter with the sugar. [*Or use a food processor.*] Stir in the treacle and mix well. Break 1 egg at a time into a cup and beat with a fork, then stir into the mixture; then fold in a spoonful of flour. Repeat with the remaining eggs, adding 2 more spoonfuls flour. Then mix the baking powder and spices into the remaining flour and fold in. [*If using a food processor, transfer to a bowl at this stage and continue mixing by hand.*] Stir in the ground almonds and dried fruit, then the milk and orange juice. Line a greased tin [*I use a loaf tin holding 2½ pt/1.5 litres*] with buttered greaseproof paper. Turn the mixture into the tin and bake for 2½ hours at 325°F/170°C/gas 3, loosely covered with a piece of foil. Remove the foil for the last 30–45 minutes to brown. Makes a 2½ lb [1.15 kg] cake. May be made well in advance; keeps well in an airtight tin.

Lady Moray

Ginger Cake

▌║

This was a very popular cake, both at the tea table and for the shooting lunch, where it was often served at the same time as an English cheese, the two being eaten together. At teatime, it was usually sliced and spread with butter. This recipe is based on one of Lady Portarlington's, who was renowned for her teas.

8 oz [225 g] flour, sifted
½ tsp bicarbonate of soda
1 tsp ground ginger
a pinch of salt
3 fl oz [75 ml] treacle
3 fl oz [75 ml] golden syrup
4 oz [120 g] unsalted butter, cut in bits

4 oz [120 g] dark brown sugar
2 eggs, lightly beaten
2 Tbs milk

Sift the flour into a large bowl with the bicarbonate of soda, ginger and salt. Make a well in the centre. Warm the treacle, golden syrup, butter and sugar until melted; do not let them get hot. Pour into the well and mix with a wooden spoon. Then stir in the lightly beaten eggs and the milk. Mix thoroughly, then tip into a 2 pint [1.2 litres] loaf tin which you have lined with buttered greaseproof paper. Smooth the surface and bake for 1 hour at 325°F/170°C/ gas 3. Remove from the oven, cool for a little, then tip out of its tin, remove the paper, and leave on a rack to finish cooling. When cold, wrap in a cloth and store in an airtight tin for 1 to 2 days, if possible, before eating. Serve sliced, with unsalted butter, for tea, or a picnic. If at a picnic, add a wedge of English Cheddar for an authentic pre-war touch.

Lady Portarlington

Mulled Wine

IIII

Hot mulled wine was often served at shooting lunches, or other winter festivities like Guy Fawkes, or carol singing.

the peel of 1 lemon
the peel of 1 orange
6 cloves
1 stick cinnamon
$\frac{1}{2}$ nutmeg
12 lumps sugar
$1\frac{1}{2}$ bottles red wine
4 Tbs brandy (optional)

Put the lemon and orange peel, the cloves, cinnamon, nutmeg and sugar in a saucepan with $\frac{1}{2}$ pt [275 ml] water. Bring to the boil and simmer till the sugar has melted. Add the wine and bring back to boiling point. Remove from the heat, add brandy if liked, and strain into a hot jug or bowl. Makes about 2 pt [1.2 litres].

AB

Sloe Gin

▌|||

Sloes are small bitter fruit, like tiny damsons, found growing wild in the woods in early October. Sloe gin is an excellent drink, very strong since it is made with neat gin. It is now made commercially by one or two firms, but used to be made at home. It was a winter drink, always drunk neat, usually as an aperitif, or as a quick nip to warm you up at a meet, or a point-to-point. It was also sometimes drunk after a sketchy meal, like a shooting lunch or winter picnic.

6 bottles dry gin
6 pt [3.6 litres] sloes
2½ lb [1.15 kg] sugar cubes

You really need an immense earthenware crock to make this in; a bread crock does well. Don't do like a friend of mine, who made her sloe gin in a glass container which broke when she was rolling it about on the cellar floor. Prick each sloe once or twice with a darning needle stuck in a cork, or a very fine pointed skewer. Then drop them into the crock which is half full of gin. (You can make it equally well in 2 smaller containers, or in half quantities.) Finally, add the sugar and close the jar tightly. Shake the crock, or roll it over if too heavy to shake, once a week. The sloe gin will be ready in 2½–3 months, just in time for Christmas. It makes an excellent present. Makes 8 pt [4.5 litres].

AB

Tea

||||
||||

'The ideal tea table should include some sort of hot buttered toast or scone, one or two sorts of sandwiches, a plate of small light cakes, and our friend the luncheon cake. Add a pot of jam or honey, and a plate of brown or white bread and butter – which I implore my readers not to cut too thin – and every eye will sparkle.' In *Lady Sysonby's Cook Book*, published in 1935, the author described the essence of the English tea: a relaxed, informal meal, lacking in any form of pretension.

Tea and breakfast had much in common, in that they were both informal meals, and very English. While breakfast in the English country house was served continuously from about nine till eleven thirty, with members of the family and guests alike coming down when they chose, tea was also very relaxed, with no obligation to be punctual, or even to put in an appearance. At neither meal were the guests waited on; once the tea had been laid out, the footmen left the room, and the guests waited on each other, or helped themselves. Even when there were fifty people staying, as at Eaton Hall, the hostess was still expected to pour out the tea herself, and the guests would pass it from hand to hand until everyone had been served.

Tea was never served in the dining-room. At Flete, when Helen Mildmay and her father were alone, they had tea in the library. When there was a house party, tea was served in the drawing-room. A folding table was carried in and spread with a white cloth by the footmen, who set it up at one end of the room. Small chairs were brought in, and others already in the room were rearranged around the table. There were two teapots, with a choice of China or Indian tea, a silver kettle over a spirit-lamp, and silver milk jug. To eat, there were usually scones with butter and Devonshire cream and home-made jam, a sticky ginger cake, an iced cake and little chocolate buns. After a day's shooting, the tea would be more substantial, with croissants baked by Mrs Woodman, who was an expert.

Various houses had their own customs, peculiar to them. In some, tea was served in the nursery, with Nanny presiding; in another, it was served in the billiard room, which was not usually frequented by ladies. Many had special dishes, like chocolate buns, orange jumbles, or ginger hats. The keynote was simplicity, and lack of ostentation, as Constance Spry explains in her classic cookbook: 'It was not considered good taste to have too many small things – one good plum cake, one light cake, perhaps of the sponge variety, or an orange cake, iced, might appear, and a hot dish of crumpets or buttered toast, anchovy toast or hot teacakes. Even on the most elegant of tea tables it was permissible to leave jam in its pot set on a plate unless you possessed a nice, plain glass jar. It was the fancy dish that was considered inelegant.'

While tea was served at five, or even five thirty, in country houses, in London it was earlier, at four thirty. This was a lighter, more elegant meal, served in the sitting-room, from a tray. A plate of cucumber sandwiches and a light sponge cake were all that most people would expect.

In some circles, bridge teas were very fashionable. The ladies would converge, all wearing hats, for an afternoon of cards and gossip combined. At some point in the proceedings the card tables were covered with white cloths, and an elaborate tea appeared. Bridge rolls were invariably served; these were usually filled with finely chopped egg and cress, the cress forming a delicate green fringe around the edges.

Lower down the social scale, tea meant high tea, which was a hybrid meal, not unlike breakfast, but with sweet things added. This was the main evening meal in working-class homes, and was served whenever the husband got home from work, some time between five and six.

The English high tea was a mixture of savoury and sweet foods, with tea to drink. The savoury element depended on the financial state of the household, and might run to sliced ham, sausages, or fish and chips when things were good. Otherwise it depended largely on bread, which could be spread with butter, margarine, jam, meat or fish paste, according to funds. This was followed by pastries, sweet biscuits or cakes. A light supper followed between nine and ten, but this was more in the nature of a snack before going to bed, and usually consisted of bread and cheese, with cocoa to drink.

It was in the country houses that tea reached its zenith. Although only a few were ever served at one time, the variety of dishes was impressive. The sandwiches alone were legion, and quite different in character from those of today. Apart from a very few, like cucumber or tomato, they were made with complex mixtures of different ingredients, all finely chopped and mixed together, similar to the sandwiches we find today in cities like Vienna and Turin. Hard-boiled eggs were never simply sliced, but chopped and mixed with mayonnaise, mango chutney, or watercress. Cream cheese was combined with chopped walnuts, dates, dried apricots or stem ginger, or with honey, or redcurrant jelly. There were many more savoury fillings than sweet, and brown or white bread was used, or a mixture of both, or soft finger rolls. For picnics or shooting lunches, substantial sandwiches were made with meat or fish: smoked salmon with anchovy butter, rare roast beef with horseradish sauce and sliced tomatoes, or cold game with sauce tartare. For the tea table, lighter versions were made on similar lines, using fillets of Dover sole, minced lobster, or potted shrimps. Vegetables were sometimes used in the form of asparagus spears, or a purée of green peas. Fruit, in the shape of sliced dessert apples, made an unusual filling, but the most exotic must be Mrs Leyel's rose petal sandwich.

In winter, a hot covered dish, in china or silver, was often to be seen on the tea table. This might hold any of the toasted breads or teacakes described by Constance Spry, or simple sandwiches of jam or marmalade that had been toasted, or even fried.

While a fairly substantial fruit cake, sometimes called a luncheon cake, was often made for picnics, those destined for the tea table were usually lighter. Plain cakes were very popular, and existed in many forms. Most were made on the pound cake principle – using equal weights of eggs, butter, sugar and flour. For a special occasion, they were flavoured with orange or lemon juice, and given a thin icing. More often, they were left very plain, like Madeira cake, seed cake, sand or rice cake. Then there were light sponge cakes, filled with butter cream, or fresh strawberries and whipped cream. For a tea party, an iced chocolate or walnut cake might put in an appearance, while a rich fruit cake was iced for Christmas. Sticky ginger cakes were always popular, often served sliced and spread with butter. All these cakes had something in common for they shared an essentially English simplicity, unlike the rich and creamy gateaux that were eaten on the Continent.

Savoury Sandwiches

||||

||||

Egg and Mango Chutney Sandwiches

||||

A subtle mixture of flavours, far removed from the simple egg sandwiches of today.

2 large eggs, hard-boiled
2 tsp mango chutney
2 Tbs chopped watercress
6 thin slices brown bread, 1 day old
¾ oz [20 g] butter

Hard boil the eggs; chop them finely with mango chutney and some watercress, and spread the [*buttered bread*] sandwiches with this mixture. [*Remove crusts. Makes 3 rounds: 12 small sandwiches.*]

The Gentle Art of Cookery by Mrs C. F. Leyel and Miss Olga Hartley

Egg and Prawn Sandwiches

||||

An excellent mixture of flavours, this sandwich is equally good for the tea table, a picnic, or a television snack.

2 hard-boiled eggs, chopped
6 oz [180 g] unshelled prawns, or 3 oz [85 g] shelled prawns
2 Tbs mayonnaise
sea salt and black pepper
6 thin slices brown bread, 1 day old
1½ oz [85 g] unsalted butter
1 basket cress

Mix the chopped eggs with the prawns cut in small chunks (3 to each prawn). Moisten with the mayonnaise and season with salt and pepper. Spread the bread thinly with butter, and lay the egg mixture on top. Scatter the cress over the top, then cover with the remaining slices of bread. Cut off the crusts before serving. Makes 3 rounds, or 12 small sandwiches.

AB

Lobster Sandwich

||||

A fabulous sandwich, the best ever. Ideal for a pre-theatre snack, with a green salad and a glass of white wine, or after the theatre, with some hot consommé. Not as extravagant as it sounds: a small lobster will feed two people.

1 x 1 lb [450 g] lobster, or 4 oz [120 g] lobster flesh, chopped
1 oz [30 g] finely chopped celery
2 Tbs mayonnaise
sea salt and black pepper
4 thin slices brown bread, 1 day old
1 oz [30 g] unsalted butter

You should have roughly 2 Tbs chopped celery to 8 Tbs chopped lobster. Mix the two together and moisten with the mayonnaise, adding salt and pepper to taste. Spread the bread thinly with butter, and fill the sandwiches with the chopped lobster. Cut off the crusts before serving. Makes 2 rounds, or 8 small sandwiches. White crabmeat can be used instead of lobster.

Adapted from *Vogue*

Potted Shrimp Sandwiches

||||

I remember eating these when I was just eighteen, at Goodwood Races. Potted shrimps are no longer so delicious as they used to be, thanks to modern technology. They are also extremely expensive, but fun on occasion. Potted shrimps can also be made at home (see overleaf); when made on holiday, with freshly caught shrimps, these are a revelation.

4 oz [120 g] potted shrimps
4 medium-thin slices brown bread, 1 day old
1 oz [30 g] butter
a few drops lemon juice
freshly ground black pepper

If using bought potted shrimps, turn them out of their cartons while still very cold and discard most of the butter. (Ignore the manufacturer's instructions about warming the cartons in the oven.) Spread the bread with fresh butter, lay the little shrimps on it and sprinkle with a few drops of lemon juice. Add a little freshly ground black pepper, and make into sandwiches, removing crusts. Makes 2 rounds: 8 small sandwiches.

AB

Potted Shrimps

IIII

These should really be made with clarified butter, otherwise you will get a watery deposit in the bottom of the dish. Small prawns can be used instead of shrimps; they are less fiddly to shell, although lacking in flavour.

1 lb [450 g] unshelled shrimps, or small prawns
3 oz [85 g] butter, preferably clarified (see below)
¼ bay leaf
freshly ground black pepper
a pinch of mace, or nutmeg

(To clarify butter: put 4 oz/120 g butter in a small pan and heat it slowly. When it boils, let it bubble for a few seconds, then pour it into a bowl through a small strainer lined with muslin. Leave to cool, then chill until it has set. Tip out of the bowl and scrape the sediment off the bottom.)

Shell the shrimps, put the (clarified) butter in a bowl standing over a pan of simmering water. When it has melted, add the shrimps and stir gently to mix with the flavourings. Leave over the heat for 10 minutes, stirring occasionally. Then discard the bay leaf, spoon the shrimps into a straight-sided dish (or 2 oeuf en cocotte dishes), and pour over enough of the butter to almost cover them. Leave to cool, then chill in the refrigerator. Serve in the dish, or dishes, as a first course, with warm brown toast, fresh butter and lemon wedges. Or tip out of the dishes, discard the butter, and use to make sandwiches. Serves 2 as a first course; makes 2–3 rounds of sandwiches.

Potted shrimps can be kept for 1–2 days in the fridge. If covered with a second layer of clarified butter, after the first has set, they may be kept for up to 2 weeks.

AB

Sole Sandwiches

▮|||

This unusual sandwich is perhaps best suited to a late-night supper or TV dinner, as it is too filling for tea, and rather fragile for transporting on a picnic. I use the minimum of butter, and add a little mayonnaise.

1 Dover or lemon sole (or plaice), skinned and filleted (approx.
   12 oz/340 g fillets)
2 oz [55 g] butter
2 Tbs milk
sea salt and black pepper
6 thin slices brown bread, 1 day old
3 Tbs mayonnaise (optional)
3 tsp finely chopped parsley

GARNISH
½ bunch watercress, cut in sprigs

Fillet a sole and cook it between two plates in the oven. [*Dot with ½ oz/15 g butter, add 2 Tbs milk, salt and pepper, and cook for 12 minutes in the oven at 350°F/180°C/gas 4, or laid over a large saucepan of boiling water.*] Let it get cold. Cut some thin slices of brown bread and butter, lay a thin fillet between [*dab with mayonnaise, if used, and salt and pepper*], sprinkle with powdered parsley, and serve the sandwiches piled up on a dish with cold watercress as a decoration. [*Remove crusts. Makes 3 rounds: 12 small sandwiches.*]

   The Gentle Art of Cookery by Mrs C. F. Leyel and Miss Olga Hartley

Watercress and
hrimp Sandwiches

▮|||

A very good combination for the tea table: sandwiches of white bread filled with fresh shrimps (or prawns), laid on a dish alternating with sandwiches of brown bread filled with watercress.

6 large slices brown bread, crusts removed
1½ oz [45 g] butter
½ bunch watercress
6 large slices white bread, crusts removed
1 lb [450 g] shrimps or prawns, in the shell
juice of ½ a lemon
freshly ground black pepper

Cut brown bread and butter it; pack sprigs of watercress closely all over half the slices; press the top slices firmly down upon the under slices. Do not trim off the characteristic little frill of green leaflets that escape beyond the brown edge of the sandwich; their stiff green border proves the freshness of the sandwich, and adds to its enjoyment. A delicious sandwich is fresh brown bread and cress alternated with white bread sandwiches of pink shrimps. [*Shell the shrimps, or prawns, and lay on slices of buttered white bread. Sprinkle with lemon juice and freshly ground black pepper, cover with more buttered bread, press down, then cut each one in half. Arrange both lots of sandwiches on a large flat plate. Makes 3 rounds, or 12 small sandwiches.*]

Food in England by Dorothy Hartley

Watercress and Walnut Sandwiches

▌|||

½ bunch watercress (4 Tbs leaves only, finely chopped)
2 Tbs chopped walnuts
1 Tbs mayonnaise
4 large thin slices bread, brown or white
1 oz [30 g] unsalted butter

Remove the watercress leaves and chop them quite finely, add the chopped walnuts, and bind with a tablespoon of mayonnaise. Butter the bread thinly, divide the watercress filling in half, and use to make sandwiches as usual. Remove the crusts and cut each round in 4. Makes 2 rounds: 8 small sandwiches.

Adapted from June Platt in *Vogue*

Sweet Sandwiches

▌‖‖

▌‖‖

Apple Sandwiches

An unusual sandwich, refreshing in hot weather.

▌‖‖

4 large thin slices brown bread
½ oz [15 g] unsalted butter
2–3 Tbs mayonnaise
1 Granny Smith, cored and cut in quarters

Spread half the bread thinly with butter, the other half with mayonnaise. Slice the unpeeled apple quarters fairly thinly and lay on the buttered bread. Cover with the rest of the bread and press together lightly. Remove the crusts and cut each sandwich in quarters. Makes 2 rounds: 8 small sandwiches.

Adapted from *Lady Sysonby's Cook Book*

Cream Cheese and Walnut Sandwiches

This was a very popular combination, often found on the tea table. It is capable of many variations, as you can see.

▌‖‖

Basic Sandwich

4 thin slices brown bread, 1 day old
½ oz [15 g] unsalted butter
2 Tbs cream cheese
2 Tbs chopped walnuts (8 halves)

Spread half the bread with butter, the other half with cream cheese. Scatter the chopped walnuts over half the slices, and make into sandwiches. Remove crusts, and cut each one into quarters. Makes 2 rounds: 8 sandwiches.

Variation I

Make as for Basic Sandwich, adding 2 Tbs chopped dates (4 dates, stoned).

Variation II

Make as for Basic Sandwich, spreading 1½ Tbs thick honey over the buttered slices of bread. Add chopped dates as well, if you like, for a very sweet sandwich.

Variation III

Make as for Basic Sandwich, adding 2 Tbs chopped stem ginger (2 pieces).

Adapted from contemporary sources

Honey and Oatmeal Sandwiches

A delicious and unusual combination.

▌▏▏▏

2 Tbs coarse oatmeal
4 thin slices brown bread, 1 day old
1 oz [30 g] unsalted butter
3 Tbs thick honey

Bake the oatmeal in the oven until pale brown. [*5–10 minutes at 350°F/180°C/gas 4.*] Spread buttered brown bread with honey, and sprinkle the browned oatmeal over it [*after it has cooled*]. Complete the sandwich with top slice in the usual way. [*Makes 2 rounds: 8 small sandwiches.*]

Lady Sysonby's Cook Book

Toasted Marmalade Sandwiches

||||

These are quite delicious: a welcome addition to any tea table. I cut them simply into 2 inch [5 cm] squares. Untoasted marmalade sandwiches are also very good.

4 thin slices white bread, 1 day old
1 oz [30 g] unsalted butter
3 Tbs orange marmalade

Make thin sandwiches well buttered and spread with orange marmalade. Remove the crusts and cut into pieces about 1 inch by 3 inches [2.5 cm by 7.5 cm. Or cut simply into quarters]. These may be made in advance. Cover with a damp cloth till wanted. Then toast quickly on both sides [under the grill], and serve piping hot.

June Platt in *Vogue*

Rose Petal Sandwiches

||||

When made with the whitest of white bread and bright-pink rose petals these are incredibly pretty. Damask roses have the strongest flavour, but even this is faint, though wonderful. The texture is also interesting.

1 oz [30 g] rose petals, preferably bright-pink Damask or old-fashioned roses
2 oz [55 g] unsalted butter
4 large thin slices white bread, 1 day old, crusts removed

[Start 1 day in advance.] Line a dish with rose petals, then place in it some butter [loosely] wrapped in its own paper. Cover the whole with more rose petals, pressing them closely together until the dish is full. Put it in a cool larder [or refrigerator] overnight. Then cut thin slices of [white] bread and spread them with the butter, make into sandwiches, and place [a single layer of overlapping] rose petals on the top of the butter so that the edges of the petals show outside the sandwich. [Makes 8 small sandwiches.]

The Gentle Art of Cookery by Mrs C. F. Leyel and Miss Olga Hartley

Large Cakes

IIII

IIII

Iced Lemon (or Orange) Cake

IIII

Simple iced cakes were very popular for teatime, both with grown-ups and children. This one is typical, based on the English pound cake, or French quatre-quarts system, whereby equal weights of eggs, butter, flour and sugar are used. It is quickly made in a food processor, and is also good without the icing.

4 oz [120 g] unsalted butter, at room temperature
4 oz [120 g] castor sugar
2 large eggs
4 oz [120 g] self-raising flour, sifted
1 Tbs lemon juice

ICING (OPTIONAL)
6 oz [180 g] icing sugar, sifted
approx. 3 Tbs lemon juice

Cut the butter in bits and put in the food processor. Add castor sugar and cream until blended, then drop in 1 whole egg. Process again, adding 1 Tbs flour, then drop in the second egg and process again. Now add the lemon juice, then the rest of the sifted flour and process once more. Turn into a 1½ pint [825 ml] tin – I use a small rectangular loaf tin – buttered and lined with buttered greaseproof paper. Bake for about 35 minutes at 375°F/190°C/gas 5, until the centre is fairly firm when pierced with a fine skewer. Take out of the oven and allow to cool in the tin for 15 minutes, then turn out on to a wire rack to finish cooling.

When it has completely cooled, lay on a flat surface for icing. Heat the lemon juice, then pour it gradually on to the sifted icing sugar, adding just enough to reach the right consistency, so that it will spread easily over the cake. Beat hard until it is totally smooth. Then pour it over the cake, smoothing the sides with a palette knife. (Or just ice the top if preferred.) Leave to set before lifting on to a plate.

TEA

This makes a delicious small cake without being too rich; golden brown on the outside and creamy white within, and with a lovely texture. An orange cake may be made by substituting orange juice for lemon juice, and adding the grated rind of 1 orange to the cake mixture, to reinforce the flavour. Makes a ¾ lb [340 g] cake.

AB

Chocolate Sponge Cake

||||

This is an unusually good chocolate cake: easy to make and very light, without being especially rich. One of the nicest things about it is the crust, so do not be tempted to ice it.

4 eggs, separated
6 oz [180 g] castor sugar
4 oz [120 g] chocolate
3 oz [85 g] flour, sifted
½ tsp baking powder, sifted

FILLING
4 oz [120 g] unsalted butter
3 oz [85 g] icing sugar, sifted

Separate yolks from whites, add sugar to yolks with 2 tablespoons of cold water, and beat over hot water till thick and creamy. Meanwhile have the chocolate melted in 4 tablespoons of water, add it to the yolks mixture, add flour and baking powder. Now beat the whites to a stiff froth, mix whites and mixture very lightly together, pour into two well greased [7–8 inch/18–20 cm] sandwich tins and bake in a moderate oven [350°F/180°C/gas 4] for ½ hour. Cream some butter and icing sugar, put between the sponges, dust with [sifted] icing sugar.

Food for the Greedy by Nancy Shaw

cky Ginger Cake

||||

An excellent ginger cake, moist and rich; best made a week in advance.

221

12 fl oz [340 ml] golden syrup
4 fl oz [120 ml] black treacle
3 oz [85 g] soft brown sugar
2 oz [55 g] unsalted butter
1 Tbs ground ginger
1 tsp mixed spice
10 oz [285 g] flour
½ tsp bicarbonate of soda
¼ pt [150 ml] milk
2 eggs, beaten

Put the syrup, treacle, sugar, butter and spices in a heatproof bowl and warm through for 30 minutes at 250°F/130°C/gas ½, or until the butter and sugar have melted. Then remove from the oven and turn up the heat to 375°F/190°C/gas 5. Stir in the flour, sifted with the bicarbonate of soda, then finally the milk and beaten eggs. Turn into a 2½ pt [1.5 litres] capacity loaf tin which you have lined with buttered greaseproof paper and bake for 1–1¼ hours. Take out of the oven and leave for about 20 minutes, then turn out on to a rack to cool. Then wrap in foil and store in an airtight tin or crock for a week or so before using. Cut in thick slices to serve, spread with unsalted butter. Makes a large cake, about 2½ lb [1.15 kg].

Mrs Arthur James

Madeira Cake

||||

In the eighteenth century, a plain cake of this kind was often served in the morning, with a glass of sherry or Madeira, hence its name. By the twentieth century it was to be found on the tea table, or served with a fruit fool as a pudding. It is one of the best of all plain cakes.

6 oz [180 g] unsalted butter
6 oz [180 g] castor sugar
3 eggs
1½ oz [45 g] ground almonds
grated rind or ½ lemon
6 oz [180 g] flour, sifted
1 tsp baking powder, sifted
1 Tbs water

This can be made by hand, or in a food processor. (I use a food processor.) Cream the butter and sugar, then add the eggs one at a time, beating (or processing) after each one. If the mixture shows signs of separating, add a spoonful of sifted flour. When all the eggs are incorporated, add the ground almonds and lemon rind. Then add the sifted flour and baking powder, and 1 Tbs water. Turn into a 1¼–1½ pt [720–825 ml] loaf tin lined with buttered greaseproof paper and bake for 65 minutes at 350°F/180°C/gas 4. On taking out of the oven, cool for about 15 minutes, then remove from the tin, leaving the paper intact, and lay on a rack to finish cooling. Once it is completely cool, wrap in foil and store in an airtight tin or crock. This excellent cake keeps well for several days, and is best eaten at least 1 day after making.

AB

Rice Cake

IIII

Another of these plain cakes which I find irresistible. They cannot be bought and are rarely made at home. I find them an excellent staple to fall back on over a holiday: for tea, or as accompaniment to an ice, or a fruit compote, or just as a snack.

4 oz [120 g] unsalted butter
4 oz [120 g] castor sugar
2 eggs
4 oz [120 g] self-raising flour
2 oz [55 g] ground rice
grated rind of ½ lemon

Beat the butter and sugar to a cream. [*Or blend in the food processor.*] Beat in the eggs one by one [*with 1 Tbs flour in between each egg*]. Mix the [*remaining*] flour with the ground rice and lemon rind and stir into the creamed mixture. [*All this can be done in the food processor.*] Bake in a moderate oven. [*45 minutes at 350°F/180°C/ gas 4, in a small loaf tin holding roughly 1¼ pt/720 ml, lined with buttered paper.*]

When The Cook Is Away by Catherine Ives

Seed Cake

IIII

Seed cake is an English phenomenon: enormously popular with some, but anathema to others. George Lassalle, author and cook, claims that, as a boy, he 'was once frightened by a seed cake in a cricket pavilion', but I find it delicious in a somewhat austere way. It was a regular feature on English tea tables between the wars, but is rarely seen nowadays.

6 oz [180 g] unsalted butter
4 oz [120 g] castor sugar
2 large eggs
8 oz [225 g] self-raising flour, sifted
½–1 Tbs caraway seeds
grated rind of ½ large orange

Beat the butter to a cream, sieve the sugar on to it and cream both together. [*Or blend in the food processor.*] Beat in one egg, and a little of the flour, then the second egg and more flour. When all the eggs and flour are in, add the caraway seeds and orange rind. [*If making for the first time, try ½ Tbs seeds, but if you are fond of seed cake use 1 Tbs.*] Beat altogether for about 10 minutes, lifting the mixture up to make it as light as possible. [*Or continue to blend in processor.*] Pour the mixture into the paper-lined tin [*I use a loaf tin holding 1½ pt/825 ml*] and bake in a moderate oven. [*1¼ hours at 325°F/ 170°C/gas 3.*]

When The Cook Is Away by Catherine Ives

Small Cakes

‖‖

‖‖

Brandy Snaps

‖‖

Brandy snaps were a favourite feature at children's parties, often filled with whipped cream. They are not hard to make, but rolling each individual one takes a little time.

4 oz [120 g] unsalted butter
4 oz 120 g] castor sugar
4 oz [120 g] golden syrup
4 oz [120 g] flour, sifted and warmed
1½ Tbs ground ginger
1–1½ Tbs lemon juice

GARNISH (OPTIONAL)
½ pt [275 ml] double cream, whipped
1 Tbs vanilla sugar, or, for grown-ups only, 1 Tbs castor sugar
and 1 tsp brandy

Melt butter, sugar, and syrup, add the warmed flour, ginger and lemon. Stir well and put out on a well-greased baking sheet in teaspoonfuls, 6 inches [15 cm] apart. Bake in a moderate oven until golden brown [*350°F/180°C/gas 4 for 10–12 minutes*], leave for a few moments to cool then roll up over the thick handle of a wooden spoon and fill with whipped cream [*after they have cooled. Makes about 3 dozen. If you find the rolling too lengthy, they can be left to cool flat, on a wire rack, and served as thin ginger biscuits*].

The *Constance Spry Cookery Book* by Constance Spry and Rosemary Hume

oconut Pyramids

‖‖

Coconut was much used as a flavouring in the inter-war years, mostly in sweet dishes like cakes and puddings, but also, to a lesser extent, in savoury dishes flavoured with curry. Rice paper can still be found in old-fashioned grocers, and is very easy to use.

ı egg whites
1 oz [30 g] potato flour
6 oz [180 g] dessicated coconut
3 oz [85 g] vanilla sugar, or castor sugar
¼ tsp vanilla essence, if using castor sugar
rice paper

Whisk the whites of egg to a very stiff froth. Sieve the flour, stir it in lightly, also the coconut, sugar, and vanilla essence [*if you have no vanilla sugar*]. Divide the mixture into small heaps, put them on the baking sheet lined with rice paper and bake in a slow oven until they are light brown. [*15–20 minutes at 300°F/150°C/gas 2. Once they have cooled, simply lift them off the baking sheet individually, breaking off the rice paper from around the edges. Makes about 12, using a heaped dessertspoon.*]

When The Cook Is Away by Catherine Ives

Devonshire Splits

▌|||

These small crisp scones are reminiscent of country teas in the south-west of England, where clotted cream often takes the place of butter. They are quick and easy to make, especially with a food processor.

6 oz [180 g] self-raising flour
a pinch of salt
¼ oz [7 g] castor sugar
2 oz [55 g] unsalted butter
3 fl oz [75 ml] milk
½ oz [15 g] butter, melted

Sift dry ingredients [*flour, salt and sugar*], rub in butter [*or blend in processor*], mix with milk to a soft dough. Knead lightly to free from cracks, and shape quickly into rounds the size of an egg. Place close together on a buttered tin [*baking sheet*], brush with melted butter, and bake in a quick oven [*25–30 minutes at 400°F/200°C/gas 6*].

When baked pull apart, and when cold split, spread with jam, and then with Devonshire cream [*or thickly whipped cream*] and put halves together. [*Makes 8–10.*]

Lady Sysonby's Cook Book

Fairy (or Melba) Toast

||||

My best friend's grandmother lived in the Ritz, in Paris. I was taken to lunch with her there, when I was sixteen, and we had fairy toast. It became for me the hallmark of a good restaurant, one that is rarely seen today. I am grateful to Prue Leith for allowing me to use her method.

Cut dry white or brown bread into very thin slices and toast them lightly on both sides. Then cut off the crusts and carefully split each slice in two, so that you have twice as many slices, even thinner than before. Lay them, toasted side down, on a baking sheet and bake for 1 hour at 250°F/130°C/gas ½. Serve after cooling, the same day as made.

Prue Leith

TEA

Carberry Ginger Hats

▮▮▮▮

These were a country house speciality: small ginger cakes usually served at tea. They also make a delicious pudding, served warm, with the creamy custard sauce (page 187), or the lemon and vanilla sauce (page 187), or with thick cream.

3 oz [85 g] plain flour
3 oz [85 g] self-raising flour
4 oz [120 g] soft brown sugar, dark or light
¼ oz [7 g] ground ginger
a pinch of mixed spice, or allspice
2 oz [55 g] treacle
2 oz [55 g] golden syrup
4 oz [120 g] unsalted butter
2 medium eggs, beaten

Put flours, sugar, ginger and spices through a sieve into a basin. Melt treacle and syrup with butter in a pan. When only just warm, mix it into the dry ingredients with the well-beaten eggs. [*Turn into small greased tins.*] Bake in a moderate oven [*about 25 minutes at 350°F/180°C/gas 4. Makes about 12 small cakes, or 6–8 individual puddings, depending on the size of the tins*].

Lady Elphinstone

Macaroons

▮▮▮▮

Ground almonds were the flavour of the month in the 1920s and macaroons were immensely popular, both for tea and for desserts, where they were used as the basis for soufflés and mousses. Most of these dishes are too sweet for modern tastes, but the macaroons themselves are very delicious. Rice paper may be bought at good grocers; but they can always be made without if need be.

4 oz [120 g] ground almonds
8 oz [225 g] vanilla sugar, or castor sugar
½ oz [15 g] rice flour, sifted
2 egg whites
rice paper
6–12 whole almonds, blanched and halved

Put the ground almonds, vanilla (or castor) sugar, rice flour and unbeaten egg whites into a food processor and blend for 2½ minutes. (If you don't have vanilla sugar, add a few drops vanilla essence.) Have sheets of rice paper laid on baking trays, and spoon the mixture on to them in round blobs. Bake for 15–20 minutes at 375°F/190°C/gas 5. Take out of the oven and press half a blanched almond into the centre of each macaroon. Lift the sheets of rice paper on to wire racks to cool. Later, after they have cooled, lift off each macaroon, breaking the rice paper. Serve the same day, or store in an airtight tin. Makes 12–24, depending on size.

Adapted from *Kitchen Essays* by Lady Jekyll

Orange Jumbles

IIII

These were a favourite teatime speciality in one or two country houses before the war. They are quickly made today, especially with the help of a food processor or mixer. I omit the cochineal.

3 oz [85 g] unsalted butter
4 oz [120 g] castor sugar
4 oz [120 g] coarsely ground almonds
2 oz [55 g] flour, sifted
grated rind and juice of 2 small oranges (about 5 Tbs juice)
a soupçon of cochineal (optional)

Mix [*either by hand or in a food processor or mixer, creaming the butter and sugar together first, then adding the other ingredients*], and put on a slightly greased baking tin in quantities of about 1 teaspoon to each jumble, allowing room to spread, and bake in a moderate oven. [*10–12 minutes at 350°F/180°C/gas 4.*] They will be the size of teacup rims, and should curl their crisp edges, faintly pink as the underneath of a young mushroom. [*Makes about 25. Good served with vanilla ice cream, at lunch or dinner.*]

Kitchen Essays by Lady Jekyll

Small Sponge Cakes or Fingers

||||

These were often served at lunch or dinner, as an accompaniment to a fruit fool or ice, as well as at tea. They are quick to make and freeze well. Fat sponge fingers – as opposed to langues de chat – should be made with a piping bag, but I find this too much trouble. I use a langues de chat tin, filling it half full for thin crusty langues de chat, and filled to the brim for big sponge fingers. I have slightly adapted the following recipe in that I prefer to separate the eggs and add the egg whites at the end, but the detailed instructions for preparing the tins are particularly good.

¼ oz [7 g] clarified butter, melted (see page 214)
2 oz [55 g] + 1 tsp vanilla sugar, or castor sugar
2 oz [55 g] + 1 tsp flour, sifted
2 eggs, separated
½ Tbs milk

Brush the inside of the tins carefully all over with just warm melted clarified butter. If the butter is too hot it will not coat the tins sufficiently thickly. Sift together 1 tsp castor sugar and 1 tsp flour; put these through a hair sieve and mix them well. Coat the whole of the inside of the tins with some of this mixture. It will adhere to the melted butter, and the whole should look evenly covered. Any flour and sugar should be shaken out of the tin. When the inside coating is set, the tins are ready for use.

Beat the egg yolks, add the sugar and beat again over hot water until thick. Then beat till cold. Fold in the slightly warmed flour [*alternately with the stiffly beaten egg whites*]. No further beating must be done. The mixture is just 'folded' together till evenly mixed. Half fill the tins with the mixture. Dust the tops with [*the remaining*] sifted sugar and flour, and bake in a moderate oven. [*350°F/180°C/gas 4. Langues de chat take 8–9 minutes, fat sponge fingers 12–14 minutes, and small sponge cakes 15–18 minutes. Makes 24 langues de chat, 12 fat sponge fingers, and 8 small cakes. Allow to cool for 3 minutes after taking out of the oven, then lift out of their tins carefully and lay on a wire rack to cool. Put in plastic bags for freezing, or in an airtight tin for 1–2 days, but best eaten the same day as made.*]

Good Cookery by W. G. R. Francillon

SAVOURIES

Savouries

IIII
IIII

Savouries were peculiar to England, having never existed in any other country. They took the form of a small, highly seasoned dish, often salty or smoky in flavour. In most cases they were made in individual servings, often laid on toast, or in a small pastry croûte. A few, like a cheese soufflé, were served in a large dish, but second helpings were not offered. They were almost always served very hot.

The Englishman has always had a preference for ending his meal on a savoury, as opposed to sweet, note. At luncheon, this was effected by the cheese, but this was never served at night, so the savoury course was devised. The explanation often given was that the men wanted something appropriate to accompany the remains of the wine, which was almost always red at this point in the meal, but this theory does not really hold water, since few savouries go well with wine, especially red. Foods like sardines, bacon, smoked haddock and anchovies are hardly conducive to an enjoyment of wine, even white, but what they did do was to clear the palate of sweet tastes before starting on the port.

The twenties and thirties saw the gradual decline of the savoury, as meals grew shorter and less formal. Although their place was still assured in old-fashioned houses, in more modern establishments the same dishes started to appear in another guise. As Ruth Lowinsky points out, in *Lovely Food*: 'their place is now very often taken at dinner by hors d'oeuvre served before the soup, or by a vegetable dish coming between the entrée and the sweet. It is amusing to vary this by arranging a tray with hors d'oeuvre to be served in the drawing-room with the cocktails.' Thus the old order began to crumble, as the former respect for tradition gave way to a longing for novelty.

Foreigners rarely understand the English love of savouries, although Escoffier does include a short chapter on the subject in his classic, *Ma Cuisine*. Savouries did not figure in the Italian cucina alto-borghese either, according to Lorenza de Medici in her book *The Renaissance of Italian Cooking*. In the 1920s and 30s the Italian upper classes ended their midday meal with cheese, followed by a fruit course; in the evening the cheese was replaced by a dessert, also followed by fruit.

In the days when meals consisted of four or five courses, it was considered perfectly acceptable to refuse one or two courses altogether. Thus, those without a sweet tooth might reject the pudding and merely eat the savoury, while others, usually the ladies, refused the savoury. From what I can remember – not much, since savouries were only ever served in the evening, when children were not present – savouries could be utterly delicious, or the most tedious things imaginable, depending on the skill with which they had been made, and the speed with which they were served.

The range of savoury dishes revolved around three or four themes, each with many small variations. The main ingredient was usually cheese, smoked or salted fish, bacon, or something 'devilled'. They were usually neatly contained, either in a pastry case, or on a canapé of toast, or within a wrapping of bacon. Oysters, prunes, chicken livers and grapes were all wrapped in thin rashers of streaky bacon and grilled, then served on squares of toast. Marrow bones were served wrapped in a napkin, with dry toast, and a silver scoop to extract the marrow. Toasted cheese was always popular, usually in the form of Welsh rarebit. Herring roes were served on toast, as was flaked smoked haddock and devilled kidneys. Eggs were sometimes used, since they would not have featured in the first course, as they often did at lunchtime. Scotch woodcock was made with scrambled eggs topped with anchovy fillets and capers. Cheese pastry cut into straws or small biscuits made a simple savoury, as did thin strips of streaky bacon, coated with grated Parmesan and grilled.

There were a few cold dishes, like a cheese or horseradish mousse. Savoury ices were not unknown, and recipes for a Camembert ice turn up in various books of the period, although I have never managed to make them work. Far more delicious, to my mind, is Nancy Shaw's glace pomme d'amour, a tomato cream ice made with a mixture of mayonnaise and cream. Other very simple savouries were made with pastes of pounded game, anchovies, smoked cod's roe or potted cheese, spread on little rounds of toast. These provided useful ways of using up the remains of other dishes. Unsweetened ice cream wafers could then be bought, and were used for making light savouries, spread with grated cheese and mustard and cayenne, then baked briefly in the oven.

Savouries at the end of a meal are just not practical today, since they demand help in the kitchen. The dishes themselves are still useful, however, served at another time. Almost without exception, they make good hot canapés or snacks to serve with drinks, before a meal. In this context, they are very similar to the small appetiser which many restaurants produce today, while you are studying the menu and choosing the wine. (But savouries were never served two or three at a time, as these little appetisers often are.) Made on a larger scale, many make good first courses. The French always serve croque monsieur as a first course, and this is merely a fried cheese and ham sandwich, very similar to many of our own hot savouries. Some of the simplest and best savouries, like cheese straws or bacon crisps, are very good indeed served with a hot consommé, as part of the first course. A few, like the cheese soufflé, or the tomato ice, could be served instead of a pudding.

I have been surprised to find some luxury foods like foie gras, black truffles, and smoked salmon quoted in this context, served as savouries at the end of a meal. And, in Siegfried Sassoon's diaries, while staying in Nuremberg in 1922, he recorded: 'We dined at the Bamberger Hof, which at first seemed disappointing. But the wine was excellent, and we concluded our meal with caviare.'

Potted Cheese

||||

Useful either as a savoury or as a snack, this is a good way of using up the remains of large cheeses. It can be made in any amount by simply doubling up the ingredients in the same proportions.

6 oz [180 g] Cheshire or Cheddar cheese
1 oz [30 g] butter
2 Tbs single cream, or rich milk, or an extra 1 oz [30 g] butter
2–3 Tbs beer, sherry, red or white wine
2 Tbs finely chopped chives

A good soft cheese can be made from ordinary Cheshire or Cheddar. Pound up in a mortar or put it through a sieve and add about one-sixth of its quantity in butter. A little cream or rich milk may also be used. When all is soft, add 2 or 3 tablespoonfuls of beer or wine and any chopped herbs you like. Chives are good and so is pennyroyal. Press into pots and keep in a cool place. [*Serve with hot toast, French bread, or water biscuits. Serves 4.*]

Come Into the Garden, Cook by Constance Spry

235

Water Biscuits

IIII

Home-made water biscuits are unusual, and good for serving with cheese, or with a clear soup.

1 oz [30 g] butter
4 oz [120 g] flour, sifted
½ tsp baking powder, sifted with the flour
a pinch of salt

Rub the butter well into the [*sifted*] flour with a pinch of salt and mix with a little [*4–5 Tbs*] cold water; roll them very thin [*cut in rounds*], prick, and bake in a good oven. [*20–25 minutes on a greased baking sheet, at 325°F/170°C/gas 3, until lightly coloured. Serve warm, soon after baking. Makes about 10 of 2½ inches/6 cm diameter.*]

A Medley of Recipes by Dorothy Allhusen

Bacon Crisps

IIII

These tasty little snacks are excellent for serving with drinks, or as part of an hors d'oeuvre, with the corn meal soufflé on page 87, for instance.

8 very thin (cut at No. 3) rashers green streaky bacon
¼ oz [7 g] butter or lard

Remove the rind and any small bones, and cut into very thin narrow strips [*about 4 inches x ¼ inch/10 cm x 5 mm*]. Put 1 teaspoonful either butter or lard [*in a frying pan*] and when very hot, put in the bacon. Fry on a quick fire till the bacon begins to curl, and is very brown and crisp, but not burnt. Drain on greaseproof paper [*or soft kitchen paper*]. When free of all grease, and quite dry, place in a glass dish and serve instead of salted almonds. A very attractive novelty at a cocktail party. [*Serves 4 as part of an hors d'oeuvre, or 8 with drinks.*]

Lightning Cookery by Countess Morphy

Parmesan Bacon

IIII

This is an unusually simple hors d'oeuvre, and can be easily made without help in the kitchen. The crisp bacon strips are also very good served with the corn meal soufflé (see page 87), or with a soup, or with drinks before dinner. They are easily eaten in the fingers.

12 very thin rashers unsmoked streaky bacon (cut at No. 3)
2 oz [55 g] freshly grated Parmesan
2 oz [55 g] fine, dry, white breadcrumbs

Cut the rind off the bacon. Mix the grated cheese and breadcrumbs. Heat the grill, laying the bacon rashers under it for a moment, just until the fat starts to melt. Then dip them in the mixed cheese and breadcrumbs, patting it on well. Set aside until ready to serve. Then put back under the grill and cook slowly, until crisp and golden, turning once. Drain briefly on soft paper, then lay on a flat dish to serve. Serves 4 as a savoury or light snack.

AB

Toasted Cheese Sandwiches

IIII

These make a delicious mid-morning snack, or late supper, or TV snack. Their only disadvantage as a savoury is that they have to be made at the very last minute.

quite thickly sliced white bread, 1 day old
butter
strong cheese, i.e. Cheddar
cayenne pepper

For each sandwich make two pieces of toast and butter them while still hot so that the butter sinks into them. Over one of them spread a good layer of strong cheese with a dash of cayenne. Place it under the broiler [*grill*] for a few moments and then put the other buttered slice on top of this and pop the sandwich under the broiler for two or three minutes, just long enough to warm the whole through.

Kitchenette Cookery by G. F. Scotson-Clark

Cheese Biscuits

IIII

These small cheese biscuits can be served equally well as a canapé, with drinks, with a clear soup, or at the end of the meal, with the last of the red wine, after, or instead of, a pudding. When made in the shape of small sticks, 2 inches x ¼ inch x ¼ inch [5 cm x 5 mm x 5 mm], these become cheese straws, for serving in the same way.

1 oz [30 g] butter
1 oz [30 g] flour
1 oz [30 g] freshly grated Parmesan
½ oz [15 g] grated Cheddar
1 small egg yolk
salt and cayenne

Rub the fat in the flour, add the rest of the ingredients, mix thoroughly, and bind with the egg. [*Roll out about ¼ inch/5 mm thick.*] Stamp the paste into small rounds [*about 2 inches/5 cm wide*], prick these, and bake in a cool oven till golden brown. [*8–10 minutes at 325°F/170°C/gas 3. Makes about 8 biscuits; can easily be made in double or treble quantities. The mixing is speedily done in a food processor.*]

Good Cookery by W. G. R. Francillon

Parmesan Fingers

‖‖

This was originally served as a savoury, but I find it useful to serve with drinks, or to accompany a hot consommé, like the one on page 51. It is best made with stale, rather than merely dry bread, and only prepared shortly before baking. Made in this way, the fingers stay crisp and delicious; otherwise they may be slightly limp.

3 large slices stale white bread approx. ½ inch [1 cm] thick, crusts removed
¼ pt [150 ml] double cream
2 oz [55 g] freshly grated Parmesan
freshly ground black pepper
¼ oz [7 g] butter

Cut stale white bread into fingers [*about 3½ inches x ½ inch/8.5 cm x 1 cm square*]. Soak [*or better still, dip briefly*] in cream then roll in grated parmesan and pepper and pat with knife so that cheese sticks well. Butter baking sheet and bake in a hot oven. Serve very hot. [*Bake for 6 minutes at 400°F/200°C/gas 6, turning them over halfway through. Makes about 15; serves 4–6.*]

A Medley of Recipes by Dorothy Allhusen

Fried Cheese Sandwiches

IIII

These are very good and quite unusual, like a savoury version of pain perdu. Like many old-fashioned savouries, they are not very practical today, since they must be eaten the moment they are made, which demands some help in the kitchen. They are more useful served as a first course, or a hot snack with drinks.

CHEESE FILLING
2 oz [55 g] grated sharp cheese, i.e. Cheddar and Parmesan mixed
3 fl oz [75 ml] milk
1 oz [30 g] butter
sea salt and black pepper
a pinch of cayenne
1 egg, beaten

12 large thin slices dry white bread
¼ pt [150 ml] milk
1 egg, beaten
salt and cayenne
a pinch of dry mustard
2½ oz [70 g] butter

Put the grated cheese, milk, butter, salt and pepper and cayenne in a double boiler and heat slowly until all has melted, stirring all the time. Then raise the heat slightly and stir hard, over boiling water, until it is smooth. Remove from the heat and stir in the beaten egg bit by bit, stirring constantly. Put back over low heat and stir until it has thickened slightly, like mustard, and is perfectly smooth. Tip into a bowl and leave to cool.

Later, use it to make sandwiches with thin slices of unbuttered white bread. Remove the crusts, and cut each round into two, or four, small sandwiches. Dip each one briefly in milk, then in egg beaten with a pinch each of sea salt, cayenne and mustard powder. Heat the butter in a broad frying pan and fry the sandwiches quickly on each side, until pale golden brown. Drain on soft paper and serve at once. Makes 6 rounds, or 12 sandwiches, or 24 small ones.

Adapted from contemporary sources

Mushrooms on Toast

▌|||

An elaborate version of this homely dish was considered suitable for a dinner party. Made on a larger scale, it can serve as a first course. This method for making croûtes comes from English Country House Cooking, *by Fortune Stanley.*

4 small slices dry white bread, ⅓ inch [7.5 mm] thick
2½ oz [70 g] butter
12 oz [340 g] mushrooms
1½ Tbs flour
¼ pt [150 ml] milk, heated
sea salt and black pepper

Cut the bread in circles, or squares, removing crusts, and spread both sides very thinly with butter. Lay on the oven rack and bake for 10–15 minutes at 400°F/200°C/gas 6, until golden and crisp. Remove and keep warm.

Reserve 4 small mushrooms and chop the rest roughly. Cook them in 1 oz [30 g] butter for about 8 minutes, until soft. Make a thick white sauce with 1 oz [30 g] butter, flour, and hot milk, sea salt and black pepper; mix with the chopped mushrooms. Dot the 4 whole mushrooms with tiny bits of butter and grill. To serve, divide the purée between the croûtes, piling it in mounds, then lay a grilled mushroom on top. Serves 4, or 2 as a first course.

AB

Canapés Fumés

▌|||

This popular savoury also makes a good snack, or light main dish, made in double quantities. It can be prepared a little in advance, then reheated at the last moment, while making the toast.

12 oz [340 g] smoked haddock
½ pt [275 ml] milk
½ oz [15 g] unsalted butter
½ Tbs flour
black pepper
1 egg, beaten
2 thick slices bread, brown or white
½ Tbs finely chopped parsley, or paprika

Put the haddock in a pan, add the milk and bring slowly to the boil. Cover the pan and remove from the heat; stand for 10 minutes, then drain off the milk through a strainer, reserving it. Flake the fish, discarding skin and bone, then chop the flakes roughly by hand. Melt half the butter and add the flour, stirring. Cook for 1 minute, then measure 4 fl oz [120 ml] of the milk the fish was cooked in and add to the pan. Stir till blended, adding some black pepper, and simmer gently for 3–4 minutes. Then remove from the fire and stir in the beaten egg, then the flaked fish. Put back over a low flame and cook gently, stirring, until the egg has cooked and thickened slightly. Remove from the fire. Make the toast, using white or brown bread as preferred. Spread the toast lightly with the remaining butter, cut each slice in half, removing crusts if serving as a savoury, and lay on hot plates. Pile the smoked haddock on top of the toast and sprinkle with very finely chopped parsley, or paprika. Serves 4 as a savoury, or 2 as a light main dish.

Adapted from *A Year's Dinners* by May Little

Smoked Cod's Roe Paste

IIII

This is the English version of taramasalata, now forgotten in favour of the Greek one. I like both, and make this often in the old way, using a pestle and mortar. (A food processor can well be used instead.) In pre-war days, this would have been served as a savoury, but it is more useful today as a first course, or snack, with spirits or beer – it does not go well with wine.

8 oz [225 g] smoked cod's roe, weighed after skinning
4 oz [120 g] unsalted butter, at room temperature
1 Tbs lemon juice
freshly ground black pepper

Put the skinned roe in a mortar and add the butter cut in bits. Pound until amalgamated, adding lemon juice and black pepper. (This can be done in a food processor.) Pile into a small dish, filling it to the brim. Chill for 2–3 hours before serving. Serves 4–6 as a savoury, piled on small squares of toast, or 2–3 as a first course, in its dish, with hot toast.

AB

Scotch Woodcock I

▌|||

8 anchovy fillets
4 Tbs milk
16 capers
4 thick slices dry white bread, crusts removed
1 oz [30 g] butter
6 eggs
sea salt and black pepper

Soak the anchovy fillets in the milk for 10 minutes, then rinse under the cold tap and pat dry. Rinse the capers in a small strainer, and pat dry. Toast the bread and cut into neat squares about 2 inches [5 cm] wide. Spread them with half the butter and keep warm. Beat the eggs, adding sea salt and black pepper, then scramble as usual in the remaining butter. Pile on to the squares of toast and lay the anchovy fillets crosswise over the top, laying a caper between each angle. Serve immediately. Serves 4 as a savoury, or 2 as a first course, on larger pieces of toast.

AB

Scotch Woodcock II

▌|||

This is a simplified version of the above. Instead of the anchovy fillets and capers, spread the buttered toast with Gentleman's Relish (Patum Peperium), or anchovy paste, then pile the scrambled eggs on top.

Herring Roes on Toast

▌|||

This was one of the best savouries. Made on a larger scale, it makes a very good first course, or even a light main dish.

4 large soft herring roes, or 8 medium ones
1–2 oz [30–55 g] flour
1 oz [30 g] butter
1 Tbs sunflower oil

2 thin rashers unsmoked streaky bacon
2 large slices fairly thick brown or white bread, toasted
1 tsp anchovy paste, or Gentleman's Relish (Patum Peperium)
salt and cayenne pepper
2 tsp chopped parsley
lemon wedges

Get fine, fresh, plump roes, about four per person. Wash under running hot water; this will remove the slime and stiffen them. Drain on paper kitchen towels. Put enough flour in a plastic bag, then gently shake the roes in it to coat all over. Remove from the bag, shake off surplus flour and lay on some greaseproof paper. Melt the butter with a slurp of oil in a good heavy frying pan; when it is just sizzling put in the roes and cook gently until golden brown on both sides. If you are dealing with more than one panful, keep the cooked roes warm in the oven having removed them from the pan and drained them on some kitchen towel. Grill the bacon until brittle. Have ready some hot toast spread with anchovy paste or Gentleman's Relish. Pile the roes on to the toasts, sprinkle with cayenne pepper and a pinch of salt, crumble the bacon over the top and strew with chopped parsley. Serve with wedges of lemon. [*Serves 4 as a savoury, or 2 as a first course.*]

    Feast Days by Jennifer Paterson

Glace Pomme d'Amour

IIII

Since savoury ices are almost unknown today, except in the form of sorbets between courses, this exquisite pale-pink ice cream is probably better suited for use as a first course. When made with fresh tomato juice and home-made mayonnaise it is truly delicious. The original version was filled with mayonnaise, surrounded by lettuce leaves and cheese made into balls. I prefer to add a cleaner, fresher taste: see below.

½ pt [275 ml] freshly made tomato juice
¼ pt [150 ml] mayonnaise (home-made)
¼ pt [150 ml] double cream
sea salt and white pepper
a dash Tabasco, or 2 tsp lemon juice

Fold the three main ingredients together, adding sea salt and white pepper, and Tabasco or lemon juice to taste. Pour into an ice cream machine (or freeze in icetrays) and run until it is about two-thirds frozen. Then spoon into a 1 pt [570 ml] ring mould and complete the freezing process.

This is easily turned out by dipping into warm water for about 30 seconds. Fill with one of the following: a) halved and seeded white grapes; b) the avocado filling on page 75; c) large prawns, cut in chunks, dressed with olive oil and lemon juice; d) a ceviche of sliced, raw scallops; e) chunks of lobster or white crabmeat, with oil and lemon. Serves 4.

Adapted from *Food for the Greedy* by Nancy Shaw

Salted Almonds

IIII

These were laid on the table in small dishes for people to nibble between courses in the evening. The service was often slow, since it was frequently some considerable distance from kitchen to dining-room. They are also very good served with drinks.

whole almonds
butter
sea salt

It is best to buy the almonds unskinned and blanch them yourself, if you have the time. Put them in a small bowl and pour some boiling water over them. Leave for a couple of minutes, then take out 3 or 4 and rub the skins off between your fingers. If it is hard to do, put them back in the hot water for a moment or two longer. They will get progressively harder as the water cools, so drain them once or twice and refill with more boiling water.

When all are blanched, dry them thoroughly by patting in a cloth. Heat some good butter in a frying pan and, when it is very hot, put in the almonds and fry them quickly, turning frequently, until they are a pale straw colour on both sides. Lift them out and drain on soft paper, then lay them on a plate and scatter some Maldon sea salt over them. (Some people add cayenne, but I prefer them simply salted.) Best eaten the same day as made, but they can be kept for a few days wrapped in foil and stored in a tin.

AB

DRINKS

Drinks

IIII
IIII

The variety of alcoholic drinks, and the manner of their serving, has not changed greatly since the 1920s. While the English still figured highly among the world's top buyers of French wines, their annual consumption was only one-sixth what it had been in 1900. This was largely due to heavy taxes levied on imported wines after the close of the First World War, making French wines very expensive. This did not deter the upper classes, however, for they had become dependent on claret and hock, champagne and brandy. Arnold Bennett, complaining of feeling unwell in 1922, blamed the 'four Cs – Cocktails, Caviare, Champagne and Cognac'. For over 250 years the English had been addicted to such luxuries. In 1688 they imported 20,000 barrels of French wine, and it was only when Queen Anne levied a tax of £55 per barrel (to favour the import of port from Portugal) that the figure dropped sharply, and levelled out at an average of 2,000 barrels a year for most of the eighteenth century.

In the large country houses between the wars, wine was drunk at dinner, at least when there were guests, but not at lunch. Then cider or beer was usual, with ginger beer as a Sunday treat for the children. (No one seemed aware that ginger beer has much the same alcoholic content as light ale; no wonder we all enjoyed it so much.) The wines were chosen with great care by the master of the household and laid down in the cellar for future use. The wine was left in total control of the butler; often his employer might have preferred to keep charge of the cellar key himself, for many butlers were secret drinkers.

The choice of what to drink with what was much the same as it is today, with a few exceptions. (The custom of drinking Sauternes with foie gras, at the beginning of a meal, only recently became fashionable.) In his book *What Shall We Have To Drink?*, published in 1933, Marcel Boulestin gives suggestions for fine wines to serve at a formal dinner. These could be followed today with advantage, could we afford it. It is interesting to note that, of the twenty-three wines mentioned, only two are unfamiliar today.

At the start of the meal, he suggests sherry with hors d'oeuvre or soup, or, with oysters, Chablis or champagne. With the fish, he offers a choice of white Burgundies – Pouilly, Montrachet or

Meursault – or a dry Loire wine like Muscadet; a Chablis, Moselle, or white Côtes-du-Rhône; or a dry white Bordeaux like Ch. Filhot, a white Haut-Brion, or the white Margaux called Pavillon-Blanc. With the entrée, usually a meat dish served in a sauce, M. Boulestin suggests a second growth, or light claret, thus keeping back the best wine for the second meat course. This was traditionally a roast bird, either game or poultry depending on the season, which showed off the great wines to their best advantage. He recommends a fine Burgundy – Chambertin, Corton or Romanée; one of the great Médocs – Latour, Lafite or Margaux; or a Saint-Emilion like Ausone or Cheval-Blanc.

With the pudding comes a sweet dessert wine. This would probably be a Sauternes – Yquem, Guiraud or Rieussec; or a wine from Saumur or Anjou, of which Boulestin was very fond, or of course champagne. To conclude, with the coffee, a glass of old brandy.

This account demonstrates how much better the formal dinner of the 1930s, with its two meat courses, suited the serving of fine wines. For in this case the second red wine, always the best, accompanied the simple roast bird. Whereas today, even in Bordeaux, the second red wine invariably accompanies the cheese, which makes for a less happy combination.

In the 1920s, drink began to prove a vast divide – larger by far than food – between the different socio-economic groups. Whereas the well-off upper-middle classes and the aristocracy liked to keep their cellars well-stocked, the impoverished and the lower classes never kept alcoholic drinks in the house. For one thing, it was expensive, and what housewife would pay for beer when food was her main priority? And social drinking in the home no longer figured below a certain level, where the man of the household preferred to go out and meet his friends in the pub. (The same is true today, but was not always so; before the First World War families often sent out to the pub for a jug of ale with their Sunday dinner.) Gradually drinking had become a separate activity, no longer connected with eating, but with smoking, playing darts and chatting.

At a higher social level, cocktails provided another chasm between the generations. While old-fashioned families like the Mildmays never drank before a meal, not even a glass of sherry, the young fashionable folk in London became addicted to cocktails almost overnight. Loelia Westminster felt obliged to offer her weekend guests cocktails, despite the fact that her husband abhorred them, and that the butler had never mastered the art of making them, so that a tray of lukewarm concoctions already poured into glasses was the best she could do.

This was one field where the Americans excelled, and none more so than Mrs Simpson, who introduced the Prince of Wales to old-fashioneds during a cruise on Lord Moyne's yacht, in 1934, and found him an enthusiastic convert. The number of different cocktails was legion; some had silly names, like Rosebud, Mimosa, the Doctor and Between the Sheets. The barmen in London clubs and bars vied with each other in inventing new combinations, and cocktail parties became the rage.

Wine cups were also very popular for parties; these were based on white wine, vin rosé and champagne, as well as non-alcoholic mixtures of fruit juices. Over and above its use in cocktails and cups, champagne continued to be hugely popular, just as it always had been, ever since its invention in the late-seventeenth century. All through the eighteenth and nineteenth centuries it was drunk by the English in great quantities; in 1887 imports reached a peak when nine and a half million bottles were drunk in the UK. In the 1860s, the English developed a taste for dry champagne. The French did not become converted till the First World War; until that time they made it expressly for the English, who were their biggest buyers. Until the 1930s, the French continued to export more champagne than they drank themselves.

Immediately after the end of the First World War, champagne sales in England rocketed, but soon fell again by half, thanks to a heavy duty imposed by none other than the then Chancellor of the Exchequer, Winston Churchill. By 1926, however, the tax had been lifted, and sales rose again. Champagne fitted perfectly with the mood of the late twenties: effervescent, irresponsible and hedonistic. It was drunk as an aperitif, throughout a meal, or just with the first course or pudding, or after dinner. The most popular after-dinner drinks for men were port or brandy, while the ladies might be offered a sweet liqueur like crème de menthe. At about ten thirty, in country houses, the butler would carry the 'grog tray' into the drawing-room. This held whisky and soda syphons for the men, and the inevitable barley water – or still lemonade – for the ladies.

Certain drinks were considered appropriate for outdoor activities, like sloe gin, cherry brandy and mulled wine. Sloe gin was made from wild sloes in early October and kept for two months before using. Thus it was ready in time for Christmas, but some would have been kept from the year before for drinking in November and early December. This was drunk before lunch, as an aperitif, and after shooting lunches, at meets or point-to-points. Cherry brandy was served on similar occasions, when a quick nip of something strong and warming was required: after a shooting lunch, or at a race meeting. Mulled red wine, drunk hot, was also popular at shooting lunches, or at any outdoor evening activity in wintertime, like firework parties, or carol singing.

Perhaps the greatest difference between the inter-war years and now lies in their fondness for mixtures of drinks, in the form of cocktails and cups. A few of these are popular today, like bloody Marys, kirs and Buck's fizz, but on the whole we prefer to drink our wines and spirits on their own, or in fairly austere combinations with tonic or mineral water.

Barley Water

IIII

This was often made, not just for invalids, but to serve after dinner parties for the ladies, who rarely drank spirits. When made for the sickroom, the lemon juice was usually omitted.

3 Tbs pearl barley
juice of 2 lemons
sugar to taste (about 2–3 Tbs)

Wash three tablespoonfuls of pearl barley in a quart [*2 pt/1.2 litres*] of water two or three times changed and thrown away. Put a fresh quart of water with the barley, bring to the boil, simmer slowly for 10 minutes. Strain into a jug, add juice of 2 lemons, sugar to taste, and set on ice till wanted. Enough for three or four.

Kitchen Essays by Lady Jekyll

Lemonade

IIII

Lemonade or barley water were usually on offer in the country houses, as many women preferred soft drinks. This is how it was made, and still is, at Sledmere, home of the Sykes family, in Yorkshire.

6 lemons
5 oz [140 g] sugar
1½ pt [825 ml] water

(Do put the lemons in a warm place before you squeeze them; this way you get the maximum juice from them.) Wash the lemons and dry. Grate the rind and put it in a pan with the sugar and water. Stir till the sugar has dissolved. Turn off the heat and let it stand till you squeeze the lemons. Strain the juice and when the syrup is cold, strain this also. Combine the juice and syrup and stir well. Serve in a glass jug with thinly sliced lemon, and ice in hot weather. The sugar can be adjusted to taste. For a less strong lemonade use 2 pt [1.2 litres] water.

Sir Tatton Sykes

Orangeade

IIII

Fresh orangeade was traditionally served at parties where young people were present; the grown-ups preferred lemonade, or the ubiquitous barley water. Orangeade is especially pretty when made with a proportion of blood oranges, perhaps half as many as the others, when they are in season.

3 oz [85 g] granulated sugar
pared rind of 2 oranges
pared rind of 1 lemon
juice of 6 oranges
juice of 1 lemon

GARNISH
3–4 thin slices orange, unpeeled
3–4 thin slices lemon, unpeeled

Put the sugar in a heatproof jug with the rinds. Pour on ½ pt [275 ml] boiling water and stir until the sugar has dissolved. Then leave to cool almost to room temperature. Strain out the rinds, add the juice of the oranges and lemon, and a further 1½ pt [825 ml] water. Pour into a glass jug and chill until ready to serve. Add the garnish shortly before serving. Makes about 2 pt [1.2 litres].

AB

Mrs Gibson's Iced Tea

▌▌▌▌

As American dishes started to infiltrate the social scene, iced tea began to supplant lemon barley water at tennis teas and garden parties. This is a particularly good recipe; I have reduced the sugar since our tastes have changed in this way, and I like to add some ginger ale at the last moment.

8 Tbs [1½ oz/45 g] Indian tea leaves
4 Tbs sugar
juice of 1 lemon

juice of 3 oranges
approx. 1½ pt [825 ml] ginger ale (optional)

GARNISH
lemon slices
sprigs of mint

Put ½ cup [8 Tbs] Lipton's tea [leaves] in a large pan. Pour over 2 pt
[1.2 litres] boiling water. Add sugar, stir well. Squeeze juice of 1
lemon and 3 oranges. Pour juices over a tray of ice [or through a
strainer filled with ice cubes]. Strain tea [also through ice], and add to
juices. Add 1 pt [570 ml] iced water and chill. [Makes 3½ pt/2 litres. I
pour it over ice cubes in tall glasses, adding half as much ginger ale just
before serving, and garnish with lemon slices and sprigs of mint.]

Mrs Nancy Lancaster

Raspberry Vinegar

▌|||

Flavoured vinegars are not a modern invention,
as might be supposed, but have been around for
many years. In France, as many as sixty-five
different flavoured vinegars were being manufactured by the great mustard firm of Maille, in
Dijon, in 1800. In England, a sweet fruit vinegar
was often used as a cordial, for diluting in water
or soda water. This makes an excellent and inexpensive drink in hot weather.

1 lb [450 g] raspberries
1 pt [570 ml] red or white wine vinegar
12 oz [340 g] sugar

Take 1 lb [450 g] raspberries to every pint [570 ml] best wine
vinegar. Let it stand for a fortnight in a covered jar in a cool larder.
Then strain without pressure, and to every pint [450 ml] put ¾ lb
[340 g] white sugar. Boil 10 minutes, let cool, and bottle in nice-
shaped medium-sized bottles. A teaspoonful stirred into a tumbler
of water with a lump of ice, or introduced to a very cold syphon [or
sparkling mineral water], will taste like the elixir of life on a hot day,
and is as pretty as it is pleasant. [Makes approximately ¾ pt/450 ml.]

Kitchen Essays by Lady Jekyll

Pussy Foot Cup

||||

This is pale green in colour, an utterly delicious non-alcoholic mixture to serve on a summer's day. Especially pretty served in a clear glass jug, with a mixture of pale- and dark-green fruit, with a few strawberries.

1¾ pt [1 litre] fizzy lemonade
¾ pt [450 ml] dry ginger ale
¾ pt [450 ml] tonic water
¾ pt [450 ml] soda water, or sparkling mineral water
6 fl oz [175 ml] orange juice
6 fl oz [175 ml] lemon juice
1 green apple, unpeeled, quartered, cored and sliced
peel of ¼ cucumber
3 large sprigs mint
a few strawberries

Serve in a large jug with ice. [*Makes about 5 pt/2.75 litres.*]

The Complete Hostess by Quaglino

The Doctor

||||

This is the classic rum punch formula, which someone must have brought back from the West Indies: one of sour, two of sweet, three of strong, four of weak. It makes a delicious long (alcoholic) drink for a hot summer day, with lots of ice. For a shorter, stronger version, reduce the 'weak' content, i.e. the water, by as much as half. I use white Bacardi rum.

1 part fresh lime juice
2 parts sugar syrup (see page 257)
3 parts rum
4 parts water

Shake up with frappé [*crushed*] ice.

The Perfect Hostess by Rose Henniker Heaton

Champagne Cocktail

||||

Nothing conjures up the spirit of the twenties better than a champagne cocktail, redolent of Noël Coward's lyrics, and the Café de Paris.

In each champagne glass put:

1 small lump of sugar
2 or 3 drops of Angostura bitters (on the sugar)
1 tsp brandy

Fill the glass with champagne. Place a slice of lemon or orange on top.

Mrs Nancy Lancaster

Cup Quaglino

||||

This is a good cup for serving at parties, like a cross between a champagne cocktail and a Buck's fizz, only less alcoholic.

1 bottle non-vintage champagne, chilled
½ pt [275 ml] fresh orange juice
3 fl oz [75 ml] brandy
3 fl oz [75 ml] orange curaçao
8 fl oz [250 ml] soda water, or sparkling mineral water
sliced fruit in season: oranges, apples, peaches, lemons, etc.

Put a large piece of ice in a big jug and add the liquid ingredients. Decorate with different kinds of fruit in season.

The Complete Hostess by Quaglino

White Wine Cup

||||

An unusually delicious cup, easily made by anyone who makes their own elder flower syrup. Otherwise, use Belvoir Elder Flower Cordial.

2 bottles dry white wine (Alsace wine is good for this)
1 bottle [¾ pt/450 ml] soda water
1 wine-glassful brandy
1 wine-glassful elder flower syrup, or cordial
sliced lemon
strawberries
cucumber rind
borage
ice

Mix all together one to two hours before serving.

Party Food and Drink by Rosemary Hume

Wine Cup

||||

This recipe came from Justerini & Brooks, one of the leading wine merchants in the inter-war years, by appointment to King George VI. Justerini & Brooks were established in the 1750s, and are still going strong. This is a most delicious cup, pale pink in colour. It is slightly too sweet for drinking at a meal, but perfect for a pre-lunch drink, or at a party, on a summer day. The original recipe called for maraschino as well as brandy, but this is very hard to find nowadays, so I leave it out.

1 bottle good vin rosé
3 fl oz [75 ml] brandy
¾ pt [450 ml] fizzy lemonade
¾ pt [450 ml] soda water, or sparkling mineral water
a few slices (unpeeled) green apple, oranges and lemons
a few strips cucumber peel

Serve very cold.

The late Edward Tatham, former Managing Director of Justerini & Brooks

Sugar Syrup

IIII

Sugar syrup is a necessary adjunct for making cocktails, since sugar alone does not dissolve properly. The exception is the champagne cocktail where a lump of sugar is the traditional sweetener. It can be prepared in larger amounts, as needed, and stored in the refrigerator in a covered jar.

4 oz [120 g] granulated sugar
¼ pt [150 ml] water

Put sugar and water into a small pan and bring slowly to the boil. Simmer for about 3 minutes, until the sugar has completely melted, then pour into a small jug and leave to cool. Once it has cooled, store in the refrigerator and use as needed. It can be kept for a week under refrigeration. If making in larger quantities, and keeping for longer, it is best kept in an airtight container. Makes ¼ pt [150 ml].

AB

Bibliography

||||

||||

Cookery Books

||||

Acton, Eliza: *Modern Cookery*, London 1845
Allhusen, Dorothy: *A Book of Scents and Dishes*, London 1926
Allhusen, Dorothy: *A Medley of Recipes*, London 1936
Beeton, Mrs: *All About Cookery*, London 1961
Boulestin, X. Marcel: *Simple French Cooking for English Homes*, London 1923
Boulestin, X. Marcel: *The Conduct of the Kitchen*, London 1925
Boulestin, X. Marcel: *What Shall We Have Today?*, London 1931
Boulestin, X. Marcel: *What Shall We Have To Drink?*, London 1933
David, Elizabeth: *Spices, Salt and Aromatics in the English Kitchen*, London 1970
David, Elizabeth: *English Bread and Yeast Cookery*, London 1977
Escoffier: *Ma Cuisine*, Paris 1934
Fisher, M. F. K.: *With Bold Knife and Fork*, New York 1968
Floyd, Keith: *Floyd on Britain & Ireland*, London 1988
Francillon, W. G. R.: *Good Cookery*, London 1920
Grigson, Jane: *The Observer Guide to British Cookery*, London 1984
Harben, Philip: *Philip Harben's Cookery Encyclopedia*, London 1955
Hartley, Dorothy: *Food in England*, London 1954
Hastings, Macdonald and Carole Walsh: *Wheeler's Cookery Book*, London 1974
Heath, Ambrose: *The Queen Cookery Book*, London 1960
Heath, Ambrose: *Personal Choice*, London 1970
Heaton, Rose Henniker: *The Perfect Hostess*, London 1931
Heptinstall, William: *Hors d'Oeuvre and Cold Table*, London 1959
Hindlip, Minnie: *Minnie Lady Hindlip's Cookery Book*, London 1925

Hume, Rosemary: *Party Food and Drink*, London 1950
Irwin, Florence: *Irish Cookery Recipes*, Belfast 1937
Ives, Catherine: *When The Cook Is Away*, London 1928
Jekyll, Lady: *Kitchen Essays*, London 1922
Leyel, Mrs C. F. and Miss Olga Hartley: *The Gentle Art of Cookery*, London 1947
Little, May: *A Year's Dinners*, London 1930 (approx.)
Lowinsky, Ruth: *Lovely Food*, London 1931
Lowinsky, Ruth: *More Lovely Food*, London 1935
Lowinsky, Ruth: *Food for Pleasure*, London 1951
Lucas, Elizabeth: *Vegetable Cookery*, London 1931
Luke, Sir Harry: *The Tenth Muse*, London 1954
McDouall, Robin: *Robin McDouall's Cookery Book for the Greedy*, London 1963
McDouall, Robin: *Clubland Cooking*, London 1974
McNeill, F. Marian: *The Scots Kitchen, Its Lore and Recipes*, Glasgow 1929
Marion, Lucie: *Be Your Own Chef*, London 1948
Martineau, Mrs Philip: *Caviare to Candy*, London 1927
Martineau, Mrs Philip: *Cantaloup to Cabbage*, London 1929
Martineau, Alice (Mrs Philip): *More Caviare and More Candy*, London 1938
de Medici, Lorenza: *The Renaissance of Italian Cooking*, London 1990
Molyneux, Joyce: *The Carved Angel Cookery Book*, London 1990
Morphy, Countess: *Lightning Cookery*, London 1931
Paterson, Jennifer: *Feast Days*, London 1990
Platt, June: *June Platt's Party Cook Book*, Boston 1936
Platt, June: *June Platt's Plain and Fancy Cookbook*, Boston 1941
Powell, Hilda: *Vogue's Cookery Book*, Edited by Hilda Powell, London 1939
Quaglino: *The Complete Hostess*, Edited by Charles Graves, London 1935
Rohde, Eleanour Sinclair: *A Garden of Herbs*, London 1936
Rohde, Eleanour Sinclair: *Vegetable Cultivation and Cookery*, London 1938
de Salis, Mrs: *Tempting Dishes for Small Incomes*, London 1892
Scotson-Clark, G. F.: *Kitchenette Cookery*, London 1925
Shaw, Nancy: *Food for the Greedy*, London 1936
Spry, Constance: *Come Into the Garden, Cook*, London 1942
Spry, Constance and Rosemary Hume: *The Constance Spry Cookery Book*, London 1956

Stanley, Fortune: *English Country House Cooking*, London 1972
Sysonby, Lady: *Lady Sysonby's Cook Book*, London 1935
Toklas, Alice B.: *The Alice B. Toklas Cook Book*, London 1954
Toklas, Alice B. and Poppy Cannon: *Aromas and Flavors*, New York 1958
White, Florence: *Good Things in England*, London 1932
Wijk, Olof: *Eat At Pleasure Drink By Measure*, London 1970
de Wolfe, Elsie: *Elsie de Wolfe's Recipes for Successful Dining*, New York 1934

General Books

IIII

Asquith, Lady Cynthia: *Haply I May Remember*, London 1950
Beaton, Cecil: *Self Portrait with Friends, Selected Diaries of Cecil Beaton*, Edited by Richard Buckle, London 1979
Beauman, Nicola: *Cynthia Asquith*, London 1987
Campbell, Susan: *Cottesbrooke, An English Kitchen Garden*, London 1989
Carrington, Letters and Extracts from her Diary, Chosen by David Garnett, London 1970
Cecil, Hugh and Mirabel: *Clever Hearts, Desmond and Molly MacCarthy – A Biography*, London 1990
Channon, Sir Henry: *Chips, The Diaries of Sir Henry Channon*, Edited by Richard Buckle, London 1967
Cooper, Artemis: *A Durable Fire, The Letters of Duff and Diana Cooper 1913–1950*, Edited by Artemis Cooper, London 1983
Coward, Noël: *The Noël Coward Diaries*, Edited by Graham Payn and Sheridan Morley, London 1982
Crawford, Sir William and H. Broadley: *The People's Food*, London 1938
Davidson, Caroline: *A Woman's Work Is Never Done*, London 1982
Devonshire, The Duchess of: *The House, A Portrait of Chatsworth*, London 1982
Donaldson, Frances: *Edward VIII*, London 1974
Driver, Christopher: *The British at Table, 1940–1980*, London 1983

Drummond, J. C. and Anne Wilbraham: *The Englishman's Food*, London 1958
Field, Rachael: *Irons In The Fire, A History of Cooking Equipment*, London 1984
Fitzgibbon, Theodora: *The Food of the Western World*, London 1976
Fleming, Anne: *The Letters of Anne Fleming*, Edited by Mark Amory, London 1985
Forbes, Patrick: *Champagne, the wine, the land and the people*, London 1977
Jones, Chester: *Colefax & Fowler, The Best in British Interior Decoration*, London 1989
Lindsay, Loelia: *Grace and Favour*, London 1961
Lutyens, Mary: *Edwin Lutyens by his daughter Mary Lutyens*, London 1980
McKendry, Maxine: *Seven Centuries of English Cooking*, London 1973
Meynell, Francis and Vera Mendel: *The Week-End Book, a new edition*, Edited by Francis Meynell and Vera Mendel, London 1928
Mitford, Jessica: *Hons and Rebels*, London 1977
Murphy, Sophia: *The Duchess of Devonshire's Ball*, London 1984
Nicolson, Harold: *Harold Nicolson Diaries and Letters*, Vol. I, Edited by Nigel Nicolson, London 1966
Olivier, Edith: *Edith Olivier's Journals*, Edited by Penelope Middleboe, London 1989
Orwell, George: *The Road to Wigan Pier*, London 1937
Palmer, Arnold: *Moveable Feasts*, Oxford 1952
Partridge, Frances: *A Pacifist's War*, London 1978
Partridge, Frances: *Memories*, London 1982
Ritchie, Charles: *The Siren Years, Undiplomatic Diaries 1937–45*, London 1974
Saintsbury, George: *A Scrap Book*, London 1922
Saintsbury, George: *A Last Scrap Book*, London 1924
Sassoon, Siegfried: *Siegfried Sassoon Diaries 1920–1922*, Edited by Rupert Hart-Davis, London 1981
Sebba, Anne: *Enid Bagnold*, London 1986
Shand, P. Morton: *A Book of Food*, London 1927
Soyer, Alexis: *The Modern Housewife*, London 1872
Stobart, Tom: *The Cook's Encyclopedia*, London 1980
Sykes, Christopher Simon: *Country House Camera*, London 1980
Sykes, Christopher Simon: *Private Palaces*, London 1985

Tannahill, Reay: *Food in History*, London 1973

Tims, Barbara: *Food in Vogue*, Edited by Barbara Tims, London 1976

Tims, Barbara: *Food in Vogue*, Edited by Barbara Tims, London 1988

Toynbee, Philip: *Friends Apart, A Memoir of Esmond Romilly and Jasper Ridley in the Thirties*, London 1954

Visser, Margaret: *Much Depends On Dinner*, London 1989

Warren, Geoffrey: *The Foods We Eat*, London 1958

Waterson, Merlin: *The Country House Remembered*, Edited by Merlin Waterson, London 1985

Wilson, C. Anne: *Food and Drink in Britain*, London 1973

Wilson, C. Anne: *The Book of Marmalade: Its Antecedents*, London 1985

Woolf, Virginia: *The Letters of Virginia Woolf*, Vols. 3–6. Edited by Nigel Nicolson, London 1977–80

Wyndham, Ursula: *Astride the Wall*, London 1988

Main Index

IIII

Page numbers in **bold** denote recipes.

A

almonds 228
  salted 34, **244**
anchovies 242
anchovy butter **200**, 211
  essence xi, 170
  paste 242
apple puddings 138
apples, baked 23
  Charlotte **140**
  hat **140**
  sandwiches **217**
  sauce with horseradish **183**
  sauce with sage **172**
  tart, Lady Portarlington's **141**
  turnovers **202**
apricot jam sauce **186**
artichoke bottoms, with broad beans **119**
asparagus ice 3, **22**
aspic jelly **172**
avocados, sliced, in oil and lemon **75**

B

bacon crisps **236**
  Parmesan **236**
baked egg with shrimps, cold **65**
Bakewell tart 137, **144**, 149
barley water 249, **250**, 251–2
Bath Club 138, **154**
beans, broad, with artichoke bottoms **119**
beef
  broth with cabbage toasts **51**

cottage pie **100**
  olives **99**
  oxtail, braised **104**
  roast ribs **98**
  sandwiches **199**
  sea pie **101**
  silverside, boiled **101**
  spiced **102**
  stew **103**
Beestings 24
Benedict, eggs **66**, 180
Bird's Custard 138, 170–1
Bismarck herrings 64–5
Blancmange 138
Boiled leg of mutton with caper sauce **111**
Bombe favorite **162**
Borscht 54
Bottled sauces xi, 170
Bouillon de poisson **56**
Braised oxtail **104**
Bramley apples 138
Brandy 5, 248
  butter **186**
  cherry 249–50
  snaps **225**
Bread
  and butter pudding 13, 138, **143**
  crumbs, browned 94, 169, **185**
  puddings 138
  sauce 94, 169, **174**
  stuffing **185**
Breakfast 33–5
  cereals 33
  dish, a **43**
Bridge rolls 210
  teas 210

Broth, beef, with cabbage toasts **51**
  Scotch 194
Brown Betty 138
Brown bread ice cream **165**
Browned breadcrumbs 94, **185**
Buck's fizz 250, 255
Butter, anchovy **200**, 211
  clarified **214**, 230
  maître d'hôtel **85**
  parsley **201**

C

Cabbage toasts, with beef broth **51**
Cakes 209–11
  Carberry ginger hats **228**
  chocolate sponge **221**
  fruit cake, Lady Moray's **202**
  ginger cake, Lady Portarlington's **203**
  ginger cake, sticky 192, **221**
  lemon cake, iced **220**
  luncheon cake 209, 211
  Madeira **222**
  pound 220
  rice **223**
  sand 211
  seed **224**
  small sponge cakes, or fingers **230**
Canapés fumés **240**
Canary pudding **145**
Caper sauce **111**
Caramel ice cream **164**
Carberry ginger hats **228**

263

Index of Sources

||||

269

READ MORE IN PENGUIN

In every corner of the world, on every subject under the sun, Penguin represents quality and variety – the very best in publishing today.

For complete information about books available from Penguin – including Puffins, Penguin Classics and Arkana – and how to order them, write to us at the appropriate address below. Please note that for copyright reasons the selection of books varies from country to country.

In the United Kingdom: Please write to *Dept. JC, Penguin Books Ltd, FREEPOST, West Drayton, Middlesex UB7 0BR*

If you have any difficulty in obtaining a title, please send your order with the correct money, plus ten per cent for postage and packaging, to *PO Box No. 11, West Drayton, Middlesex UB7 0BR*

In the United States: Please write to *Penguin USA Inc., 375 Hudson Street, New York, NY 10014*

In Canada: Please write to *Penguin Books Canada Ltd, 10 Alcorn Avenue, Suite 300, Toronto, Ontario M4V 3B2*

In Australia: Please write to *Penguin Books Australia Ltd, 487 Maroondah Highway, Ringwood, Victoria 3134*

In New Zealand: Please write to *Penguin Books (NZ) Ltd, 182–190 Wairau Road, Private Bag, Takapuna, Auckland 9*

In India: Please write to *Penguin Books India Pvt Ltd, 706 Eros Apartments, 56 Nehru Place, New Delhi 110 019*

In the Netherlands: Please write to *Penguin Books Netherlands B.V., Keizersgracht 231 NL–1016 DV Amsterdam*

In Germany: Please write to *Penguin Books Deutschland GmbH, Friedrichstrasse 10–12, W–6000 Frankfurt/Main 1*

In Spain: Please write to *Penguin Books S. A., C. San Bernardo 117–6° E–28015 Madrid*

In Italy: Please write to *Penguin Italia s.r.l., Via Felice Casati 20, I–20124 Milano*

In France: Please write to *Penguin France S. A., 17 rue Lejeune, F–31000 Toulouse*

In Japan: Please write to *Penguin Books Japan, Ishikiribashi Building, 2–5–4, Suido, Tokyo 112*

In Greece: Please write to *Penguin Hellas Ltd, Dimocritou 3, GR–106 71 Athens*

In South Africa: Please write to *Longman Penguin Southern Africa (Pty) Ltd, Private Bag X08, Bertsham 2013*

BY THE SAME AUTHOR

Mediterranean Cookbook

At one time the hub of the known universe, a colourful, sun-drenched medley of trade and culture celebrated in myth and history by poet and tourist alike, the Mediterranean has exerted its influence on the Western world for centuries.

Politically and linguistically diverse as they may be, the countries of the Mediterranean have many culinary features in common. Arabella Boxer's meticulously researched and beautifully organized book constitutes a gastronomic grand tour of a region where spices, olives, tomatoes, yogurt, salads, fruit and the clever use of fish and meat combine so satisfyingly and memorably.

'Arabella Boxer has managed to conjure up the rich and colourful atmosphere of Mediterranean food . . . a great resource for cooks and a solid piece of work on the real conditions in which these recipes first took root and flourished' – *Sunday Times*